WORK AND PAY IN JAPAN

Provides a comprehensive overview of Japanese labour market institutions and practices with respect to employment issues and labour payments. It contains extensive discussion of the effects of industrial relations, small business activity, business cycles and schooling on work and pay. An early chapter is devoted to presenting, in an accessible manner, essential labour market ideas and concepts that recur throughout the text.

Important topics covered include unions and wage determination, the breakdown of total labour costs, the Japanese bonus system, the employment life-cycle, small businesses and subcontracting, and pay and productivity over the business cycle.

A key feature is that subject areas and themes are examined within a comparative United States/European framework. This allows assessments of whether or not the structure and performance of the Japanese labour market have differed from experience elsewhere.

Robert A. Hart is Professor of Economics at the University of Stirling. He is Editor of the *Scottish Journal of Political Economy*. He has published widely in journals including *Economica*, *European Economic Review*, *Economic Journal* and *Oxford Economic Papers*. His previous books include *Human Capital, Employment and Bargaining* (1995), co-authored with Thomas Moutos.

Seiichi Kawasaki is Professor of Economics at the School of Informatics and Sciences, Nagoya University. He has published widely in journals including *American Economic Review*, *Econometrica*, *Demography*, *Applied Economics* and *Journal of the Japanese and International Economies*.

WORK AND PAY IN JAPAN

Robert A. Hart
and Seiichi Kawasaki

CAMBRIDGE
UNIVERSITY PRESS

PUBLISHED BY THE PRESS SYNDICATE OF THE UNIVERSITY OF CAMBRIDGE
The Pitt Building, Trumpington Street, Cambridge, United Kingdom

CAMBRIDGE UNIVERSITY PRESS
The Edinburgh Building, Cambridge CB2 2RU, UK http://www.cup.cam.ac.uk
40 West 20th Street, New York NY 10011-4211, USA http://www.cup.org
10 Stamford Road, Oakleigh, Melbourne 3166, Australia

First published 1999

Printed in the United Kingdom at the University Press, Cambridge

Typeset in 9.5/13 Times New Roman in QuarkXPress™ [SE]

A catalogue record for this book is available from the British Library

Library of Congress cataloguing in publication data

Hart, Robert A.
Work and pay in Japan / Robert A. Hart and Seiichi Kawasaki.
      p.   cm.
Includes bibliographical references and index.
ISBN 0 521 57137 5 (hb) – ISBN 0 521 57772 1 (pb)
1. Wages–Japan. 2. Employee fringe benefits–Japan.
3. Compensation management–Japan. 4. Labor economics–Japan.
5. Labor economics–United States. 6. Labor economics–Europe.
I. Kawasaki, Seiichi. II. Title.
HD5077.H36   1999
331.2′1′0952–dc21   98-53588   CIP

ISBN 0 521 57137 5 hardback
ISBN 0 521 57772 1 paperback

To our children Jennifer, Linsey, Nobuya, Rosalind and Tetsuya

Contents

Figures

Tables

Preface

Work and pay in Japan have been subjects of considerable interest among students of comparative international labour markets. There are two main interrelated explanations of this. First, important aspects of the Japanese labour market appear to differ significantly from experience elsewhere. Examples include the structure of the union system, the size and coverage of bonus payments, lengths of wage and employment contracts, the age of official retirement and the importance of subcontracting. Secondly, the Japanese labour market has appeared to perform somewhat differently from those of its main competitor economies during the post-war period. Among other features, it has generally experienced more employment stability, lower unemployment and greater wage flexibility.

We have attempted in this book to provide a more comprehensive coverage of these and related issues than has hitherto been available under a single cover. Further, for most topics, we provide considerably more depth of empirical and analytical coverage than can be found in existing texts. Not only do we examine the main features of employment and payment systems in Japan but, throughout the book, we also provide background details of related European and United States evidence and experience. Moreover, we extend the definition of 'pay' to include non-wage labour costs that do not constitute direct remuneration but, nevertheless, are necessarily incurred by the employment of labour.

We have purposely written the book in a non-technical way so as to appeal to a readership whose interests stretch well beyond the confines of labour market economics. Inevitably, some of the issues and problems we discuss have been examined by researchers who have adopted labour market models and concepts that are not immediately familiar to non-specialists. Rather than ignore a vital body of work, we go to some lengths to explain conceptual details in an accessible way.

In chapter 1, we set the scene by introducing the key areas of interest. Issues directly relating to work and pay are merely highlighted at this stage before being dealt with in far greater depth at later stages. However, less direct topics – involving job tenure, worker participation and unemployment – are covered in more detail. Chapter 2 is also introductory in nature in that it is designed to explain, in a non-technical way, a number of important labour market theoretical and empirical models that are referred to at various later stages. Particularly strong emphasis is given to human capital models and the use of wage–experience profiles.

The industrial relations context of work and pay decisions forms the subject area of chapter 3. Inevitably, the enterprise union system and its relationships to wage determination and human capital formation make up the main thrust of analysis in this chapter. Comparisons are also made with industrial relations structures in Europe and the United States. Special attention is given to union density, the 'spring offensive', industrial wage equalisation, joint consultation, quality control circles and comparative international assessment.

Wage and non-wage labour costs are concentrated on in chapters 4 and 5. In chapter 4, we provide a complete breakdown of direct and indirect labour costs not only in Japan but also in a comparative international setting. Important differences in cost structures between Japan and elsewhere are established. Chief among the latter is the unique importance of bonuses in Japan, and chapter 5 is completely devoted to a discussion of such payments. We provide a full analysis of the main competing hypotheses advanced to explain the relative importance of bonus payments in Japan and a critical appraisal of the available empirical evidence.

Chapter 6 deals with the main phases of employment over the working life-cycle – that is from recruitment to retirement via training and promotion. Our evidence on recruitment expenditures by firms is based on detailed data that are uniquely available in Japan. In an international comparative setting, we provide empirical evidence on promotion systems and on the changing age structure of retirement. Only in the case of training expenditures do we find that, as in all other countries, a complete evaluation is prevented by the very partial coverage of related cost statistics.

The issues of human capital formation in particular and employment and wage systems in general, have strong implications for the expected reactions of employment, labour productivity and labour costs over the business cycle. Such concerns are analysed in chapter 7. Most of the empirical studies discussed present international comparative evidence and so provide very useful yardsticks on which to base judgements of differences and similarities in Japanese cyclical labour market performance.

Chapters 8 and 9 deal with two special topics of work and pay in Japan that have been given particular Japan-related attention in the labour market and industrial literature. After establishing the quantitative importance of its subject matter, chapter 8 deals with small business aspects of work and pay. Inevitably, the chapter devotes considerable attention to the role and quantitative importance of the Japanese subcontracting system. The link between pre-work education and the subsequent path of wage growth forms the basis of chapter 9.

Finally, in chapter 10, we attempt succinctly to summarise the importance of work and pay in Japan within a broader international setting.

1 **Setting the scene**

We begin by highlighting a number of key Japanese work and pay issues. Several topics – such as wage and bonus payments, employment and working time – are dealt with in some depth in later chapters and so we merely draw attention to a number of salient features at this stage. Other areas – such as the length of jobs, unemployment and labour force participation – are discussed in detail here in order to serve as a useful backdrop to related points of interest at later stages. In common with most of the ensuing text, we discuss topics in a comparative international setting.

From an international perspective, interest in Japanese employment, remuneration and labour costs has stemmed, primarily, from perceived differences in organisation and performance compared to other major industrial economies. One theme of the book is to question the extent to which Japanese differences are real or apparent. Four examples are as follows. First, in chapter 3, we question the degree to which the Japanese enterprise union system is unique. Second, in chapter 5, we examine the cases for and against the claim that the bonus system constitutes a unique form of remuneration. Third, we consider in the present chapter whether Japanese post-war unemployment experience has been significantly different from elsewhere. Fourth, in the present chapter and elsewhere, we investigate whether job tenure and labour turnover and their relationships to wage growth have played a distinct role in Japan.

1.1 Economic growth and labour productivity

By OECD standards, Japan's economic growth performance taken over the whole of the post-war era has been remarkable. While the pattern of growth has not been even, the economy has experienced significantly longer periods of above-OECD-average compared to below-OECD-average real growth. The 'miracle' years occurred during the period from the early 1950s to 1973 when annual real GNP growth often exceeded 10 per cent and averaged about 9 per cent, well in excess of other OECD member countries.

1

Recovery from the first OPEC supply shock in 1973/4 marked the beginning of a more modest era of real growth up to the late 1980s, yet it remained above the OECD average. More recently, the 1990s have witnessed a significant worsening of relative growth performance. The bubble of asset price inflation, that built from 1986, burst in 1989 with accompanying problems of dampened consumer spending, low investment in a high-risk environment, falling land prices and lack of confidence in financial markets. Argy and Stein (1997) present a useful discussion of these phases of economic activity.

During the 1950s and 1960s Japan's average growth rate of around 9 per cent compared to a rate of around 4 per cent in the United States. One way of determining the absolute and relative contributions of different productive factors to overall growth is the supply-side approach of decomposing production functions into each of the separate inputs.[1] At the aggregate level, the three important factor inputs are labour, capital and technological progress. These can each be further subdivided into: (i) *labour*: employment, hours, sex/age composition, education; (ii) *capital*: inventories, non-residential structures and equipment, dwellings, international assets; (iii) *technological progress*: knowledge, improved resource allocation, scale economies.

Compared to the United States in the 1950s and 1960s, Japan experienced a higher absolute contribution to its growth rate from each of the three aggregated factors as well as from most of their component parts (Denison and Chung, 1976). In relative terms, about 55 per cent of growth performance within Japan was attributable to technological progress, about 24 per cent to capital and about 21 per cent to labour. Respective relative contributions to growth in the United States were 48 per cent, 20 per cent and 32 per cent. Interestingly, the *absolute* contribution of employment within the labour factor was the same in each country although, given differences in national economic growth, it accounted for 13 per cent of Japan's and 29 per cent of the United States' growth. A key labour difference was hours of work which contributed to around 2 per cent of Japanese growth but had a *negative* 5 per cent effect on growth in the United States.

During the 1970s, Japan's average growth fell substantially, to around an average of about 4.8 per cent. Shinohara (1986) analyses factor contributions for this later period. The contribution of technological progress to growth fell substantially in absolute terms, though it was still over 50 per cent in relative terms. Labour's absolute contribution also fell but it also held up in relative terms. However, while the hours component of labour made a modest contribution in the earlier period, it had a slightly negative impact in the second period. Both the absolute and relative contributions of capital diminished in the later period.

The contribution of employment and hours, especially up to the early 1970s, would suggest that Japan's post-war hourly labour productivity has grown relatively strongly. This is certainly the case in relation to Europe, for example. Figure 1.1 compares the quarterly measure of hourly productivity in Japan with those of the Federal Republic of Germany (FRG) and the UK between 1960 and 1989 (FRG) and 1996 (UK). The period of rapid growth up until the early 1970s witnessed Japan's rate of productivity rise from roughly half those of the two European countries in 1960 to virtual parity by the late

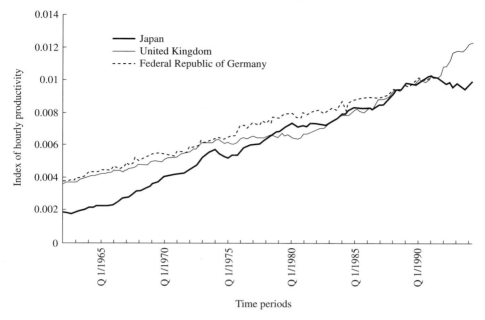

Fig. 1.1. Hourly labour productivity in Japan, the Federal Republic of Germany and the United Kingdom, 1960–96. Data for Germany on a comparable basis are not available after 1989. (*Source:* OECD labour force statistics.)

1980s. Noticeably, however, Japan's productive performance has fallen back somewhat during its 1990s economic crisis.

At least with respect to major economic shocks, it would appear from figure 1.1 that Japanese labour productivity varies directly with the business cycle. For example, it dips quite noticeably after the 1973/4 OPEC supply shock and again after the burst bubble in the early 1990s. What accounts for this direction of reaction? This question is associated with two important and interrelated areas of comparative international labour market research involving Japan. The first of these involves an explanation of the observed productivity cycle. This concerns the view that Japan is *less* likely than other major economies to buffer against recessionary events by allowing its employment stock to vary in size. In this event, pro-cyclical hourly productivity may be associated with the fact that, during economic downturns and upturns, employment fluctuates less than proportionately to output because firms show high propensities respectively to hoard and dis-hoard labour. The second area of research is closely linked to cyclical productivity and is central to neoclassical labour and macro-economics. A central tenet of neoclassicists is that the optimising firm equates the ratios of marginal productivities of labour and capital to their respective marginal costs. In a short-run context, a propensity to hoard labour, for example, may prevent the realisation of such a goal on the employment front. This and other short-run influences may in turn induce systematic cyclical patterns in price–cost mark-ups. Both these avenues of interest are investigated in some detail in chapter 7.

1.2 Wages, bonuses and non-wage costs

Most Japanese workers receive the major part of their direct remuneration via two channels. First, and familiar to many workers in other countries, they are paid in the form of regular (usually monthly) wages. Secondly, they receive bonus payments which, typically, are paid twice a year. The bonus constitutes around one-fifth to one-quarter of total cash earnings. As we show in chapter 4, bonus payments in most other countries are very small by comparison. A few countries do have significant per-worker bonuses and other premiums. However, such payments (even the highest of these, such as in France and Germany) are less than half of Japanese bonuses when expressed as proportions of total labour costs.

Interest in the Japanese bonus system stems not merely from its uniqueness but also from the possibility that it may somehow be linked to the relatively strong Japanese economic performance in the post-war era. Bonuses in Japan have been variously argued to serve a number of economic roles. They may simply be regarded by the firm and its workforce as a component of total compensation that behaves in a largely indistinguishable manner from regular wages. Thus, the market forces of demand and supply for labour services may largely determine both forms of compensation. Bonuses alternatively may represent a form of efficiency wage by providing a reward for greater effort. By contrast, and at a general level, wages may reflect more systematic and structural elements of remuneration, such as seniority-based pay scales (the Nenko system), while bonuses are used to adjust total compensation to fluctuations in firms' economic experiences. In this event, we might expect that the bonus should display more flexibility than the wage. One school of thought in this respect regards bonuses as a form of profit-sharing between the firm and its workforce. Another holds that bonuses reflect shared returns to investments in firm-specific skills and know-how.

Beyond direct remuneration in the form of wages and bonuses, firms incur labour costs associated with statutory and private welfare provision, recruitment and training, severance compensation, and other forms of non-wage labour costs. There are a number of interesting differences between Japan and elsewhere in several items of these costs and these are highlighted and discussed in chapter 4.

1.3 Enterprise tenure and labour turnover[2]

The length of stay by workers in given jobs is a crucial labour market subject area. Theoretical and empirical developments centred on this variable have important Japanese links. Relative to most major economies, higher proportions of Japanese male workers, at least up to the age of 55, enjoy long-tenure jobs. The contrast is particularly stark when length of tenure is compared with that in the United States, as in the following comparison of the period 1979–89 in Japan with 1983–91 in the United States.

[A]lmost 40 per cent of American men in the 37–40 age range had 0–4 years of tenure in 1983 and only about one in three of them is estimated to last another eight years with the firm. By contrast, only 17 per cent of Japanese men aged 35–39 had under 5 years of tenure in 1979, and almost half will go on with the firm for at least another ten years.

[A]lmost regardless of age or tenure, Japanese men are significantly more likely to be with the same employer ten years later. For example, among American men in their mid twenties just starting work in 1983, fewer than 25 per cent were still employed with the same firm eight years later. In contrast, over 50 per cent of Japanese men in their mid-twenties were still with their original employer ten years later. (*OECD Employment Outlook*, 1993)

A possible, although partial, explanation of the above differences, especially among younger workers, is that Japanese employers devote more effort and expenditure towards finding appropriate new recruits directly from schools and universities. This may result in good job matches being established at an early, formative, stage. In contrast, the United States may rely more on workers themselves sampling jobs in the early work years before finding good job matches through a process of trial and error (Topel and Ward, 1992). We deal with links between schooling, tenure and wage growth in chapter 9.

Another line of reasoning focuses on investments in firm-specific human capital skills and organisational know-how. Where significant investments take place, premature separations – due to quits or layoffs – may result in large turnover costs. Accordingly, bargaining parties may expend considerable effort in attempting to preserve the returns accruing to specific investments by minimising costly separations. Job tenure and specific investments would be expected, therefore, to be positively associated. Ideas in this area are developed in some detail in chapter 2 and examined empirically in several later chapters.

While hard facts on comparative international levels of per-worker human capital investment are lacking, circumstantial evidence would appear to support the case that Japan is high in the league table. Most comparative work has featured Japan and the United States. One type of supporting evidence is based on the incidence of formal enterprise training and tenure. Table 1.1 reveals that, for a range of enterprise sizes, the Japanese labour force enjoys (i) longer tenure, (ii) higher incidences of formal training, and (iii) lower percentages of workers with less than one year of tenure.[3] As we will see in chapters 2 and 5 and elsewhere, length of tenure is associated in the human capital literature with firm-specific investments in worker skills and know-how and, in turn, such investments impact on wage growth. Therefore, the comparative longevity of job tenure in Japan has much wider ramifications than purely employment-related questions.

The general picture portrayed in table 1.1 is confirmed in a wider context in table 1.2 which presents comparative European and United States data. These data reveal that, relative to the other countries, (i) a lower proportion of Japanese workers have tenure of one year or less, (ii) median tenure for Japanese men is relatively long, and (iii) average tenure for men and women is relatively long (the OECD unweighted average is 8.7 years).

At least from a human capital perspective, we might expect specific investments – and, therefore, length of tenure – to be greater in large than in small firms. At given pay levels,

Table 1.1. *Incidence of formal enterprise training and tenure by establishment size*

Establishment size	25–99 employees	100–499 employees	500–999 employees	1000 + employees
		Japan 1989[a]		
Percentage of employees who received formal company training	59.5	75.5	83.6	89.5
Average tenure (years)	8.9	← 10.2 →		13.7
Percentage of employees with less than one year tenure	11.2	← 8.4 →		5.1
		United States 1991[b]		
Percentage of employees who received:				
Formal company training	10.6	13.2	18.4	26.2
Any kind of training	34.5	41.9	47.7	52.2
Average tenure (years)	5.4	6.8	7.0	8.4
Percentage of employees with less than one year tenure	23.2	18.4	16.4	15.5

Notes:
[a] Enterprise size for training is 30–99, 100–499, 500–999 and 1000 + regular employees. Enterprise size for tenure is 10–99, 100–999 and 1000 + regular employees. Training incidence for establishments with 100–499 regular employees is an unweighted average of the incidence across the size groups 100–299 and 300–499.
[b] 'Any kind of training' refers to skill improvement through schooling, formal company training, informal on-the-job training and 'other'. Data refer to all wage and salary workers.
Source: OECD Employment Outlook, 1993.

workers will be less likely to separate, and so investments will be better protected, if longer promotion ladders and a wider range of new employment opportunities exist. This might mean, from the firm's viewpoint, that investment risks are reduced because longer investment amortisation periods are secured. Table 1.3 presents, for the years 1979 and 1989, tenure lengths by firm size, age and sex in Japan and the United States. Almost without exception, tenure is longer in large firms than in small ones for all age groups and for both sexes in the two countries. In line with the previous table, the figures reveal that, given firm size, tenure is longer for males and females in Japan than in the United States. Over the 1980s, female and male tenures in Japan appear generally to have grown, although confined to ages 35 and over in the case of large firms. By contrast, there is a dominant downward trend in male tenure in the United States at this time, while the female evidence is somewhat mixed.

Table 1.2 *Distribution of employment by enterprise tenure, 1991*

	France[a]	Germany[b]	Japan[a]	United Kingdom	United States
Current tenure (percentages)					
Total	100.0	100.0	100.0	100.0	100.0
Under 1 year	15.7	12.8	9.8	18.6	28.8
1 and under 2 years	10.7	10.3	16.1[b]	12.4	11.6
2 and under 5 years	15.6	17.9	11.5[b]	23.9	21.3
Under 5 years	42.0	41.0	37.4	54.8	61.7
5 and under 10 years	16.2	17.8	19.7	16.1	11.7
10 and under 20 years	25.6	24.5	23.6	19.3	17.8
20 years and over	15.8	16.7	19.3	9.6	8.8
Unknown	0.4	—	—	0.1	—
Average tenure (years)					
All persons	10.1	10.4	10.9	7.9	6.7
Men	10.6	12.1	12.5	9.2	7.5
Women	9.6	8.0	7.3	6.3	5.9
Median tenure (years)					
All persons	7.5	7.5	8.2	4.4	3.0
Men	7.9	9.5	10.1	5.3	3.5
Women	7.0	5.0	4.8	3.7	2.7

Notes:
[a] 1990
[b] 1 and under 3 years, and 3 and under 5 years.
Source: OECD Employment Outlook, 1993.

1.4 Unemployment, labour force participation and labour hoarding

A major stylised fact in the realm of international comparative labour markets is that post-war Japanese recorded unemployment has been consistently well below that of its major OECD competitors. This is illustrated in figure 1.2 which shows female and male Japanese unemployment rates between 1970 and 1995 together with comparable rates in the United States, France and Sweden. Unemployment rates at between 1 and 3 per cent in Japan compare with rates that are twice as large in the United States and, since the early 1980s, three to four times higher in France. Even Sweden, with one of the lowest post-war European unemployment records, has experienced rates during the 1990s that are three times higher than in Japan.

In fact the very poor unemployment performances of European countries compared with Japan are even more pronounced when the recent problem of long-term unemployment is taken into account. The *OECD Jobs Study* (Organisation for

Table 1.3. *Average tenure profiles by age and establishment size*
Private non-agricultural wage and salary employment, years

	1979		1989	
	Small firm	Large firm	Small firm	Large firm
	Japan[a,b]			
Age groups				
Men				
20–24	2.5	3.8	2.5	2.8
25–34	5.8	9.0	5.9	8.2
35–44	10.2	16.3	10.6	18.2
45–54	11.7	23.2	14.5	25.3
55–64	10.3	18.7	13.2	25.3
Women				
20–24	2.4	3.4	2.4	2.9
25–34	4.6	7.2	5.1	7.5
35–44	6.4	8.7	7.6	11.7
45–54	8.4	12.9	10.3	14.9
55–64	10.1	12.6	12.3	17.2
	United States[a,c]			
Age groups				
Men				
20–24	2.1	2.0	2.0	2.0
25–34	3.5	5.1	4.0	4.8
35–44	6.4	10.8	6.1	9.8
45–54	10.5	17.7	8.4	16.7
55–64	12.0	21.1	11.3	20.2
Women				
20–24	1.4	1.8	1.7	1.8
25–34	2.2	4.6	3.1	4.3
35–44	4.8	7.4	4.5	8.1
45–54	6.1	12.1	6.9	10.3
55–64	9.9	14.8	8.6	12.3

Notes:
[a] For Japan, a small firm has 10 to 99 and a large firm has 1000 or more employees. For the United States, a small firm has less than 100 and a large firm has 1000 or more employees.
[b] Data for both 1979 and 1989 are weighted averages of tenure by five-year age groups.
[c] Data for 1979 are unweighted averages of tenure by five-year age groups.
Source: OECD Employment Outlook, 1993.

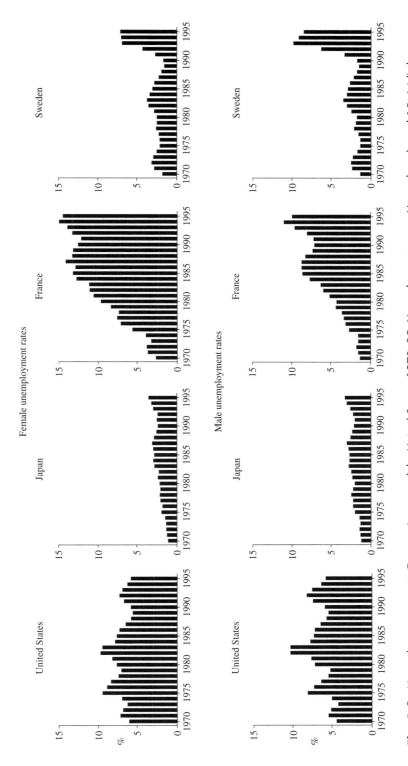

Fig. 1.2. Unemployment rates in Europe, Japan and the United States, 1970–95. Unemployment rate = Unemployed aged 15–64/Labour force aged 15–64 × 100. (*Source: Darby et al.*, 1999.)

Economic Co-operation and Development, 1994) shows that, in 1992, more than 40 per cent of the unemployed in the European Community had been out of work for twelve months or more compared with a figure of only 15 per cent in Japan. Actually, North America shows even more resilience than Japan in this respect, with 11 per cent long-term unemployed in the same year.

Note further that, compared with the other countries, Japan displays less cyclical unemployment variation. Japan's relative low unemployment rates combined with their lack of cyclical variation appear to reflect an economy that has experienced reasonably sustained growth and employment stability. We have seen in the previous section, however, that Japan's growth after the early 1970s was neither even nor sustained. Further, while employment stability amongst males, especially in large firms, has been a post-war feature, it certainly does not represent the picture for the entire labour force. Prima facie, it would appear that recorded unemployment rates in Japan do not capture the complete picture of underutilised labour resources in the Japanese labour market. What is missing?

Let D and S stand for, respectively, the demand for and supply of labour. If N is employment and U is the recorded number of unemployed, then a conventional measure of excess labour supply may be written

$$\frac{D-S}{S}=f\left(\frac{N-(N+U)}{N+U}\right)=f\left(\frac{-U}{N+U}\right) \tag{1.1}$$

As emphasised by Taylor (1970), equation (1.1) is an inadequate measure of excess supply for two reasons.

In the first place, as discussed in chapter 7, it ignores the possibility that firms may hold underutilised units of labour among their *existing* workers. As product demand fluctuates, some firms may reveal a risk-averse propensity to hold on to existing labour stocks if turn-over is costly owing to recruitment, training and redundancy costs. In this event, unemployed labour resources may be manifested through fluctuations in labour utilisation rates on firms' intensive margins rather than through changes in unemployment rates on extensive margins. This intensive margin phenomenon is referred to as labour hoarding. Let us assume that such hoarding does take place and let it be denoted by R.

In the second place, on the extensive margin, some workers may be effectively unemployed but not *recorded* as such. Under the so-called 'discouraged worker effect' some workers without a job may be reluctant to register as officially unemployed and seeking work because of extremely low expectations of employment opportunities. In effect, they cease to participate in the labour market and become 'hidden' unemployed because of their lack of registration. Such hidden unemployment is denoted by H.

Combining the notions of hoarded labour and hidden unemployment with conventional recorded unemployment produces a more general measure of excess labour supply, given by

$$\frac{D-S}{S}=g\left(\frac{(N-R)-(N+U+H)}{N+U+H}\right)=g\left(\frac{-(U+R+H)}{N+U+H}\right) \tag{1.2}$$

The two key questions in relation to (1.1) and (1.2) are whether we would expect the two additional measures of excess supply – hoarded labour and hidden unemployment – (i) to be quantitatively important on the Japanese labour market and (ii) to behave differently in Japan than in other major economies. Interestingly, the answer to the first of these questions is yes. Hoarding in Japan is relatively large in comparison with other major economies. Evidence of Japan's relatively high propensity to hoard labour is provided by several studies (e.g. Odagiri, 1992; Hart and Malley, 1996). One approach to explaining this behaviour is based on human capital considerations. Some evidence is presented later in this section. We leave deeper developments and discussion of relevant ideas to chapter 2 and return to more extensive empirical details on hoarding in chapter 7.

Hidden unemployment is linked to labour force participation. Figure 1.3 displays the level and trends in male and female labour force participation between 1970 and 1995 for the same four countries as in figure 1.2. In general, sustained rises in female participation over the period contrast with systematic falls in the male rates. Female participation rates in Japan are both lower and flatter than in the other three countries while the Japanese male rates are largely unexceptional compared with the European rates and lower than in the United States.

For present purposes, however, the major consideration is the degree to which falls in participation represent permanent downturns due to the discouraged worker effect.

Note in figure 1.3 that an exceptional reduction in female participation occurred after the first OPEC supply shock while a somewhat shallower fall took place in the more recent early 1990s recession. Aoki (1988) claims that in the earlier period, a fall in demand tended to discourage a large proportion of Japanese females from job search and so they retired early from the labour market. Estimates quoted by Aoki for 1978 show that the proportion of discouraged workers who were not in the labour force was 8.9 per cent in Japan and 1.4 per cent in the United States. These percentages compare with respective unemployment rates in the same year of 2.2 and 6.0 per cent.[4]

Darby *et al.* (1998) investigate the extent of 'hidden' unemployment for the four countries and over the period shown in figure 1.3, distinguishing between males and females as well as among age groups. In particular, they investigate the responses of participation rates to shocks in business sector GDP. In order to separate the discouraged worker effect from other reasons for not participating, their estimation approach attempts to distinguish two aspects of the participation decision. First, in line with several studies in this area (e.g. Pencavel, 1986), they distinguish between temporary and more sluggish participation responses to deviations from trend growth. Secondly, they test whether participation responses to upward fluctuations in the cycle are symmetric with those to downward fluctuations. Sluggish and asymmetric responsiveness would be expected to be closely linked to worker discouragement. In the latter respect, it might be anticipated that patterns of downward participation response will not correspond with upward movements. For example, workers near to retirement might regard decisions not to participate as irreversible. It may be difficult to persuade employers to reinvest in the human capital of older workers owing both to the erosion

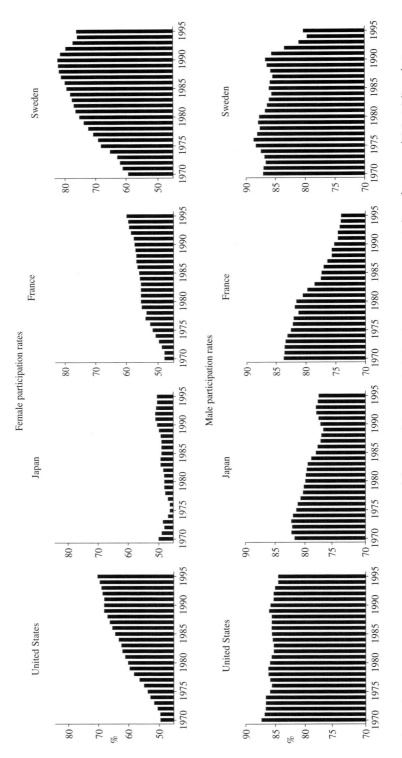

Fig. 1.3. Participation rates in Europe, Japan and the United States, 1970–95. Participation rate = Labour force aged 15–64/Population aged 15–64 × 100. (*Source: Darby et al.,* 1998.)

of skills during non-participation and to short expected job 'lifetimes' over which to earn an investment return.

The study found that in Japan, France and the United States there is strong evidence of the discouraged worker effect. Such discouragement is predominantly a female phenomenon, especially among 45–54 year olds. Moreover, the Japanese evidence is more marked than in the other countries. The two oldest female groups – aged 45–54 and 55 + – exhibit significant asymmetric responses; participation adjustments to negative shocks are much larger than the adjustments to positive shocks. In the case of the 45–54 group, an estimated fall in participation given a downward shock contrasts with *no* adjustment for the upward direction. This work corroborates earlier findings of Tachibanaki and Sakurai (1991) that the discouraged worker effect is essentially a female phenomenon in Japan, with the added refinement that the brunt of such discouragement is borne by older females.

The foregoing evidence suggests that representing Japanese excess labour supply purely in terms of recorded unemployment, as in equation (1.1), may not only serve significantly to understate Japan's unemployment position but also to misrepresent its comparative international standing with respect to excess labour supply. At a first approximation, it would seem to be more appropriate to describe excess supply in terms of equation (1.2) which incorporates the hoarded labour and hidden unemployment aspects of the problem. The following simple exercise is based on Taylor (1970) and borrows from the study of Darby *et al.* (1999). Thus, we adopt the so-called 'trends-through-peaks' methodology to obtain values of R (hoarding) and H (hidden unemployment) in equation (1.2).

In the case of hoarded labour, estimation proceeds as follows.

- Examine the time series of output per hour of employed workers and determine the peaks. These peaks are taken to represent maximum labour utilisation, with no labour hoarding taking place.
- Join the peaks by fitting linear segments. The fitted lines are taken to represent the full-employment output to labour ratio at time periods between the peaks.
- Hoarded labour at time t (R_t) is taken as the ratio of actual output per hour to the estimated full-employment output per hour. It is expressed:

$$R_t = \left[1 - \frac{(Q/N)_t}{(Q/N)_t^*} \right] N_t \tag{1.3}$$

where $Q = $ GNP and $(Q/N)^*$ is the full employment/output ratio.

For estimates of hidden unemployment, the procedure is quite similar.

- Examine the time series to find the full-employment levels of participation. At the peaks, the labour force is assumed to have reached its full (short-term) level of participation.
- Obtain full participation non-peak estimates by, again, fitting linear segments to the peaks.
- Hidden unemployment at time t (H_t) is given by the difference between actual participation and full employment participation, or

$$H_t = P\left[\left(\frac{L}{P}\right)^*_t - \left(\frac{L}{P}\right)_t\right] \tag{1.4}$$

where P is all persons over the age of 16, L is the recorded labour force and $(L/P)^*$ is the full-employment participation rate.[5]

Figure 1.4 shows the decomposition of unemployment rates into recorded, hoarded and hidden unemployment for Japan, the United States and the United Kingdom between 1960 and 1996. Hoarded and hidden unemployment estimates are based, respectively, on equations (1.3) and (1.4). In the first place, they emphasise the stylised fact that recorded unemployment in Japan is significantly lower than elsewhere. Secondly, hidden unemployment is shown to be of a reasonably similar magnitude in all three countries. Thirdly, hoarded unemployment in Japan is higher than in the United Kingdom and considerably higher than in the United States.[6] Adding these components together, transforms the relative unemployment positions. While Japan continues to enjoy the lowest unemployment rates, the differentials with the other countries – and especially the United States – narrow appreciably.

Notes

1 Ito (1992) presents a simple introduction to the methodology involved as well as a review of the empirical findings.
2 Most of the empirical material contained in section 1.3 is obtained from a very interesting article in *OECD Employment Outlook* (Organisation for Economic Co-operation and Development, 1993).
3 The information in table 1.1 may be somewhat misleading in that it omits the length of labour market experience before entering the current firm or the extent to which the training required by firms involves firm-specific or general skills. Thus, if required training has large general elements, then US workers may have acquired much of the training in previous employment. In this event, table 1.1 would give a distorted picture.
4 Aoki (1988, pp. 172–3) goes on to state that 'recent studies suggest that the effect of "discouragement" is becoming weaker and the phenomenon of "involuntary" part-time workers has become more common'. The extent to which part-time workers would prefer a full-time job or a longer part-time job also has a bearing on the measurement of excess labour supply. However, we do not consider this issue here except to note that Japan was not exceptional in experiencing in the 1980s a rise in part-time employment as a share of total employment. Canada, France, Germany and the United Kingdom were among countries that experienced larger rises (see Organisation for Economic Co-operation and Development, 1994).
5 We note that the measure of hidden unemployment here is only a first approximation. It does not distinguish carefully between workers who want to work but are discouraged from participation in the labour market and those who may choose not to participate for other reasons. For example, during tight labour market

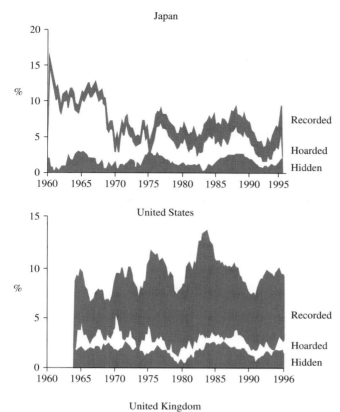

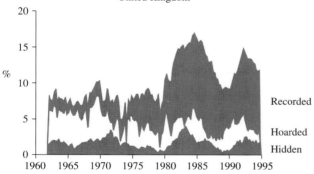

Fig. 1.4. Composition of unemployment rates in Japan, the United States and the United Kingdom, 1960–96. To facilitate comparisons, the three measures of unemployment are expressed in straight-time hours equivalents. (*Source:* Darby *et al.*, 1998b.)

employment conditions at cyclical peaks, high wages and other non-wage benefits may induce higher participation. In troughs, by contrast, workers may voluntarily choose not to participate because they value non-work activities higher than available paid work. The adopted measure, therefore, probably overestimates the degree of hidden unemployment.

6 Japanese hoarded unemployment is especially pronounced in the 1960s and early 1970s. Tentatively, the OPEC shocks of the middle and late 1970s may have served to promote a more efficient utilisation of the labour stock compared with the earlier periods.

2 Labour market concepts

At various stages throughout the book, the discussion of work and pay in Japan is set against the background of several established theoretical concepts of the labour market. In many of the studies we consider, human capital theory is the dominant tool of analysis. It lies behind developments of such topics as the expected length of employment tenure, the shape of wage–tenure profiles, wage flexibility, the returns to schooling, and the business cycle behaviour of employment and working time. In order for the reader to achieve a firmer grasp of subsequent labour market discussion and empirical outcomes – as well as to progress further by referring to the labour market literature cited in the text – it is useful to become familiar with a few key theoretical developments. Fortunately, it is possible to cover a significant part of the field with recourse to a few, relatively simple human capital concepts. Beyond this, it is also worthwhile becoming aware of the importance of incentive-compatible wage contracts that do not, necessarily, incorporate human capital arguments. This chapter is designed to provide an introduction to this material in an accessible manner.

2.1 General and firm-specific human capital

Let us begin in the world of a textbook profit-maximising firm operating in competitive product and factor markets. We are interested in a short-run period for which the stock of capital is fixed. The firm employs homogeneous labour which can be represented simply by the number of workers; we assume that every worker works the same number of per-period hours with no variation in hourly effort across workers. Workers receive a given wage rate and no other labour costs are incurred. In the absence of further assumptions, workers' abilities and skills are pre-endowed; they are acquired by workers prior to employment in the firm.

Profit maximisation is achieved at the point where the value of marginal product (V) – i.e. product price times the marginal physical product of labour – is equal to the wage rate (w). Suppose that the wage rate is fixed in the short run. Assuming diminishing marginal productivity, an unanticipated fall in product demand leading to a fall in product price would induce the firm to lay off workers to the extent that profit-maximising equilibrium is restored.

Becker (1964) and Oi (1962) elaborated this standard model by allowing for the fact that firms often incur human capital expenditures. Hiring and screening costs attach to new workers, and training costs may be incurred with respect to both new and existing workers. Without omitting any essential aspects, we concentrate purely on training investment with respect to new workers. In particular, suppose the firm's previously installed technology is such that it is found to be profitable to train workers – in a fully prescribed training programme – in order to achieve the most efficient operation. Essentially, we are assuming that (i) the type and extent of training are pre-conditioned, (ii) the associated per-worker costs of training are pre-determined and (iii) training enhances worker productivity. There are two periods.[1] During period 1, workers have a lower value of marginal product (V_1) and undertake training. During period 2, they have a higher value of marginal product (V_2) due to training. The returns to training are not realised until the commencement of the second period. In essence, training provides an increment to the pre-endowed marginal product.

Total training cost in the first period has two elements: expenditures on general training and those on specific training. Thus

$$C = C_g + C_s \tag{2.1}$$

where C_g is general training cost and C_s is specific training cost.

What is the equivalent here to the wage-equals-marginal-product condition for profit maximisation in the simple profit-maximising firm that introduced this section? There are now two costs to be taken into account. At the point of hiring, *variable* labour cost consists of the first period wage plus the discounted value of the second period wage. Additionally, *fixed* labour cost, or cost that is independent of output, comprises the expenditure on training in the first period. Return is the value of marginal product in the first period and the discounted value of marginal product in the second period. As in the simple case, the firm will hire labour up to the point where cost is equal to return for the marginal worker. Algebraically, we have

$$C = V_1 + \frac{V_2}{1+r} - w_1 - \frac{w_2}{1+r} \tag{2.2}$$

where r is the discount rate.

In the first place, suppose that the training programme consists solely of general training (i.e. $C_s = 0$ in (2.1)). This means that the returns to training are of value not only to the firm in question but also to competing firms. What are the consequences for first and second period marginal products and wages such that (2.2) is satisfied? The key features are illustrated in figure 2.1. In period 1, the firm will pay a wage w_1 which lies below V_1, with the difference representing the cost of the training. Following the logic of Becker (1964), the firm would not pay for general training since, by definition, it enhances the

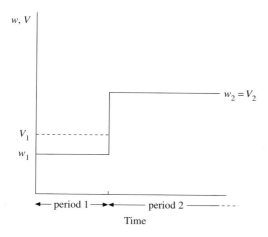

Fig. 2.1. Workers' returns to general training.

opportunity wage, or the best alternative wage that can be achieved in alternative employment. In period 2, the worker receives a higher wage, w_2, equal to the full value of the marginal product, V_2. The firm cannot pay less than V_2 if it wishes to retain the worker, because this is the worker's worth in alternative employment.

It is quite simple to think of examples of training that produces skills of use to many different firms. Workers may be required to familiarise themselves with standard computer software or to learn the efficient use of machine tools that are commonly adopted throughout industry or to acquire knowledge of statutorily imposed operational requirements in the workplace. By contrast, other forms of training may involve skills that are specific to the requirements of the individual firm; that is, which carry zero value elsewhere. Especially in a competitive environment, it is difficult to suggest examples in this respect. For the present, we investigate a few implications of introducing the assumption of specific training and we will attempt to motivate the concept of specificity in section 2.3.

Again, assume that the firm's technology is such that the degree and cost of training are pre-conditioned; this time, however, the skills acquired on the training programme are purely firm-specific. The returns to such investments cannot be realised in alternative employment. Adopting an equivalent two-period analysis, with training undertaken in period 1 and its fruits not realised until period 2, figure 2.2 represents the new w-V configurations. In period 1, the firm would pay, at least, the value of the worker's pre-endowed product, i.e. $w_1 \geq V_1$. Why would the worker refuse to contribute to the cost of the training in period 1? If the worker paid for a significant part of the training, an unscrupulous employer may pay a wage in the second period that was higher than the opportunity wage, w_1, but not sufficient to recoup the worker's share of the training cost. In figure 2.2, $V_2{}^*$ is the second period value of marginal product while V_2 is $V_2{}^*$ net of the discounted value of training expenditure. So-called quasi-rent from specific investment is $V_2 - V_1$. The firm's share of rent is $V_2 - w_2$ while the worker's share is $w_2 - w_1$. Essentially, the firm and the worker share the costs and returns to firm-specific training.

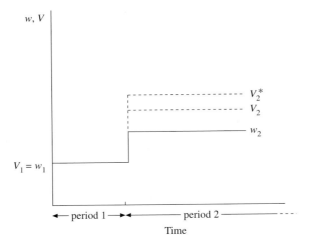

Fig. 2.2. Workers' returns to specific training.

The firm and the worker set w_2 so as to achieve agreed shares of the quasi-rents resulting from the specific training. The gains to the worker are (i) receiving a wage that lies above the opportunity wage and (ii) more job security, since the surplus stemming from training investment will discourage the firm from laying off workers. The firm gains through (i) its own rent share and (ii) a reduced propensity to quit by workers, since they are receiving a wage above their outside 'market worth', w_1.

Significant rent shares are likely to achieve relative employment stability. In a short-term context, an unanticipated fall in product price may not lead the firm to attempt to lay off workers so as to restore the equilibrium given by (2.2). Investment in human capital constitutes a sunk cost and the firm would be better off in the short run retaining a worker as long as marginal product covers the wage and a part of the training expenditures. It follows that firms with relatively high human capital investments in relation to total labour costs are likely to display relatively sluggish labour force adjustments in the face of fluctuations in product demand. In a business cycle context, firms with significant fixed human capital investments would be more prone to exhibit pro-cyclical productivity. During downturns of the cycle, productivity will fall as such firms retain, or 'hoard', labour in order to protect investment outlays. In effect, effort levels per unit of time will be allowed to fall. During upturns, productivity will rise as increased output per worker is achieved through 'dishoarding', that is through the restoration of 'normal' work rate requirements. In the present context, for example, we might expect that relatively capital-intensive firms, requiring more training investments, will be more prone to display such productivity trends.

Rent shares and employment stability may well serve to protect significant specific investment outlays as well as fostering a climate conducive to continued investments in new skills and organisational know-how. We would expect the length of employment tenure within firms to be positively related to specific human capital, especially if new specific investments are undertaken on a recurring basis. In fact, for many workers, tenure will be encouraged through increasing investment outlays, resulting in greater rent opportunities. As workers gain in seniority and undertake tasks that require more individual decision-making and initiative as well as more interactive skills, on-the-job and for-the-job training would be expected to increase in importance. As mentioned in section 1.3 in relation to job tenure and firm size, such a process may be particularly apparent in larger firms where more opportunities of promotion into senior-level jobs are available (Hashimoto and Raisian, 1989).

Skill creation and efficiency gains through human capital investments bring potential benefits to shareholders and workers as well as to the wider macro-economy. Significant investments may not be conducive, however, to the attainment of efficient rates of job mobility whereby a competitive environment ensures that workers are matched to jobs that realise their most productive capabilities. The subjects of worker–job attachments and efficient separation have been of central importance in the literature on Japanese work and pay and we now examine this research area.

2.2 Job attachment and feasible wage contracts

The foregoing discussion is undertaken within a somewhat artificial setting because it does not directly embrace the fact that investment in human capital involves risk and uncertainty. Also, for simplicity, the models in section 2.1 treat training investments as exogenously determined by the firm's given technology. In the models to be discussed here, human capital is a choice variable for the firm. Returns to investments within the firm may be lower (or higher) than expected. New process innovations in other firms may serve to reduce or eliminate comparative technological advantage at a faster than anticipated rate. Unanticipated variations in product demand may warrant revised calculations of estimated returns. Expected lengths of employee tenure – which form the planned amortisation period of specific investments – may be shorter (or longer) than expected owing to unforeseen changes in outside employment opportunities. A number of path-breaking studies have attempted to extend the human capital theory of the firm to embrace explicitly such uncertainty considerations. We confine attention here to a general discussion of the central issues involved. Given that these ideas lie behind a number of developments that appear later in the book, we also provide a somewhat more formal, though accessible, discussion of the underlying theory in an Appendix to this chapter.[2]

Imagine a two-period construct, as in figure 2.2, in which firm-specific training is undertaken in period 1 and, under the assumption that the training is productive, the return is realised in period 2. As before, we assume that the rent emanating from such investment will be shared by the firm's shareholders and workers. Now, however, rather than assuming simply that the cost of training is pre-determined by (for example) technological constraints, we now introduce the notion that these two parties bargain over their respective shares of returns and costs. In much of the relevant literature, a critical assumption is made over the nature of the bargaining process: *the bargaining parties agree on the first and second period wages before training commences in period 1.* Essentially, therefore, it is assumed that the parties avoid exchanging and updating relevant bargaining information as it becomes available in the second period. Why might they do this? The reason hinges on the concept of the transaction costs of communicating and verifying information (Williamson, 1975; Hashimoto, 1979). Agreements over second period wages at the beginning of the second period require the parties, after investment costs are sunk, to agree on the worker's post-training productivity and alternative wage. Such agreement might be very costly to reach, involving time and effort. Failure to agree will result in investment losses as costly separations occur. Potential bargaining problems will be particularly acute if information is asymmetric between the parties. By this is meant that the quality of information obtained by one party as to the value of the investment and alternative wages differs from that obtained by the other. Information exchange under these circumstances raises problems of moral hazard as one party attempts to obtain a larger rent share by presenting information in the best supporting light. Setting the second period wage at the start of the first period allows the parties to avoid these transaction costs in a future bargaining round. As we will see, however, they incur a penalty since only a second-best rate of worker–firm separation is achieved.

At the point of bargaining, the return to specific training is clearly uncertain. For example, unanticipated fluctuations in product demand could produce differences between *ex ante* expectations and *ex post* outcomes. To capture this, it is useful to divide the expected returns from training into 'fixed' and 'random' components. Both parties are able to agree costlessly on the fixed element; some aspects of future demand – perhaps based on information from existing order-books – may be confidently anticipated and agreed by both sides. We may think of the fixed parameter as the most likely outcome while the random component represents fluctuations in the returns above or below the fixed element. The *ex post* outside wage also might differ from its *ex ante* expected value. This wage can also be divided into fixed and random components. Some aspects of the labour market may be costlessly agreed between the parties while others may involve much greater uncertainty. Given anticipated positive returns from specific investment, the fixed element of the investment return exceeds the fixed element of the outside wage.[3]

Suppose that a bargain is struck at the beginning of the first period over the first and second period wages. What would induce the parties to separate at the point of realisation of second period returns? If the realised value of the second period marginal product turned out to be less than the outside wage then it would be in the mutual interest of the parties to separate. This would be a first-best solution.[4] It would require full agreement not only on the fixed but also on the random components of returns to training, and the level of the opportunity wage would be required. In effect, the parties are required to agree on a flexible wage contract in which they would fine-tune their respective wage and profit shares in line with realised outcomes of the random elements. But, owing to transaction costs, our *ex ante* wage contract rules out this possibility.

Hashimoto (1979) adopts this two-period formulation, incorporating the situation in which information on random components is asymmetrically held by the parties.

He assumes that the firm is better informed about the returns to specific investment while workers are better informed about the outside wage. Bargaining over wages in both periods takes place at the beginning of period 1. Given no observations of the random components, the parties agree on a fixed wage, rent-sharing contract. The wage agreed at the outset (i.e. before training begins) consists of the fixed component of the outside wage and a rent share consisting of a part of the difference between the fixed components of the investment return and the outside wage. The advantage of such a contract is that it serves to avoid costly negotiations over productivity and outside wage outcomes in the second period. The disadvantage is that it leads to a higher frequency of inefficient separations. These are separations that occur despite positive joint rent. In other words, the parties could have been better off if they had been able to agree on observed outcomes in the random components and to adjust wage and profit margins. Sometimes separations will occur when the value of the second period marginal product is higher than the outside wage and sometimes separations will not occur when this inequality is reversed. Indeed, the distinction between quits and layoffs now becomes meaningful. Occasions will arise when a worker quits because a random shock causes the outside wage to rise above the (fixed) rent share. Under a completely flexible contract, with zero transaction costs, information on the effects of the shock – as understood by the parties – would have been communicated accurately and, if it remained in their mutual interest to remain together, incorporated into a revised rent-sharing agreement that avoided the unnecessary separation. Occasions will also arise when the firm experiences an adverse productivity shock which means that it makes a loss on its investment. This may result in a layoff when it might have been mutually beneficial for the parties to adjust rent shares and to remain together.

Promotion ladders based on years of service, with prescribed minimum and maximum periods of time between job grades, feature prominently in the Japanese firm (e.g. Aoki, 1988). While not directed specifically towards the Japanese system, Carmichael (1983) integrates the idea of (pure) seniority-based pay within the Hashimoto framework. Again, within a two-period formulation, period 1 and 2 wages are negotiated at the outset of period 1. Specific investment is undertaken in period 1 and the returns realised in period 2. As before, information on random components of investment returns and outside wages – which are realised in period 2 – is asymmetrically distributed.[5] Once the bargain is struck, information cannot be subsequently exchanged. Again, a fixed wage, rent-sharing contract specifies a higher period 2 wage. For simplicity, Carmichael assumes the firm employs a fixed number of workers; that is, new hires exactly match quits or layoffs. Carmichael's innovation is to introduce a seniority rule under which a fixed number of workers who 'survive' to period 2 receive a seniority bonus in addition to their period 2 wage. Both of these latter variables are negotiated at the outset. The wage and the seniority bonus provide the bargainers with two choice variables in period 2, as opposed to the wage alone in Hashimoto's version. Carmichael shows that the addition of the bonus rule renders the contract more efficient than if only period 2 wages are bargained over.[6] However, the contract is less efficient than a completely flexible wage contract with zero transaction costs that allows the parties to react to the realisation of returns and job satisfaction.

An interesting outcome in Carmichael's work is that the workers who receive the bonus in period 2 earn more than the value of their marginal product in the second period. As we will discuss in section 2.5 in relation to a different approach to modelling wage contracts, this result relates to retirement and early retirement decisions.

While the random components of investment returns and the alternative wage are not easily observable and involve costs of communication, it may still be in the parties' interests to agree to flexible wage contracts that are contingent on observed and simple variables that correlate with the random components (Hashimoto and Yu, 1980). Among other possible indicators, vacancy data and job advertisements may be used to gauge the prospects for outside wage opportunities. Sales data and current negotiations with potential customers may be included in the assessment of internal returns.

It is the contention of Hashimoto (1979, 1990) and others that the Japanese labour market enjoys relatively low transaction costs, experiences relatively flexible payment systems and thus minimises the sort of costly separations that are linked to fixed wage contracts. As we will see in later chapters, this area has interesting implications for the interpretation of the Japanese bonus system, as well as for employment relative to wage adjustments over the business cycle.

2.3 The nature of firm-specific human capital

The preceding discussion has been in terms of the employment of a marginal worker. This has the advantage of providing great analytical simplicity without loss of essential detail. While it is easy to define what is meant by firm-specific human capital in the context of economic modelling, it is difficult at the level of the individual to argue other than somewhat generally (and perhaps vaguely) about what constitutes such investment. Obviously firms can and do develop techniques of manufacture, modes of organisational structure, and product and process innovations that require firm-specific knowledge on the part of their workers. In many instances it may well not be possible to gauge the degree of specificity, since this requires detailed information about the activities of competitors. It is especially difficult to judge the length of time for which the specificity of a given investment will endure – and therefore the appropriate amortisation period – in the face of technological advances and economic fluctuations, as well as changing conditions within capital and labour markets. Factor mobility is also a relevant consideration. For example, if specific human capital investment is geared towards individual workers, and if returns on such investment prove favourable, it may be profitable for competitors to 'buy' the specific know-how by paying a premium and recruiting a few key workers.

Uncertainty regarding the returns to investments at the level of the individual – from both within and outside the firm – are captured in Hashimoto's model of rent-sharing discussed in the previous section. In important respects, however, investment specificity may derive from an organisational structure that is not captured by these modelling approaches. Training schedules may be designed for groups, or teams, of individuals who are required to acquire proficiency over a range of interrelated work and organisational activities within the firm. Emphasis is not so much on skill requirements that attach to single job tasks but more on an acquired understanding of how to function efficiently over a number of interactive tasks within a broader organisational context. Moreover, depending on the aspirations and personalities of group members, the group as a whole is likely to evolve its own unique identity. Specificity derives from the fact that it is not particularly meaningful or viable to transfer from one firm to another the role of one, or several, individuals from within an 'alien' group structure. The argument is well summarised by Doeringer and Piore, who state:

[P]erformance in some production or managerial jobs involves a team element, and a critical skill is the ability to operate effectively with the given members of the team. This ability is dependent on the interaction skills of the personalities of the members, and the individual's work 'skills' are specific in the sense that skills necessary to work on one team are never quite the same as those required on another.   (Doeringer and Piore, 1971, p. 16)

One potential disadvantage of group-oriented work practices is that monitoring the performance of individual group members may be rendered particularly costly. It is more difficult to isolate and to evaluate the productive contribution of an individual worker when job descriptions entail interdependent and mutually supportive team effort. This leads Oi (1983) to suggest that the advantages of collective team organisation are more effectively realised within the contexts of product specialisation and standardised volume production. For example, where relatively large firms are engaged in line or large-batch production, they can standardise job task specifications, as well as job schedules and rotations, within work routines designed to enhance the returns to group interaction. Where inherently complex production systems can be broken down and programmed systematically, the monitoring of group activity becomes a more transparent and less costly activity.

Interaction skills among group members are 'essentially collective goods, as they are not individually appropriable' (Aoki, 1984, p. 26). Are such goods likely to be more prevalent, and associated labour productivity more specific, within the Japanese firm than elsewhere? The reason why group-related work practices have been particularly emphasised among Japanese labour market analysts stems from the observations that quality circles, job rotations and flexible working arrangements are all relatively strong features on the Japanese industrial scene. One problem with group-related work is that associated monitoring costs would be expected to be relatively high. However, in the case of the typical Japanese firm, Hashimoto's argument of low transaction costs of communication between the firm and its workers would suggest that this type of cost could be offset. The goal of achieving a low transaction cost environment may well be enhanced by Japan's unique enterprise-based union system. We look in some detail at this system in the following chapter. If firm–union bargaining is focused on the single enterprise, and is independent of other outside interest groups, the enterprise union would seem to be ideally suited not only to act as the representative agent for group members within the enterprise but also to monitor group effort.

The enterprise union controls members' shirking and malfeasance as well as guards against employer actions that are harmful to workers. The union has the incentive to monitor its members within the enterprise, to uphold the reputation of its members as well as to protect their interests from being deflected by the employer. The monitoring function may be served more effectively by a union organized within firms rather than across firms.   (Hashimoto, 1990, p. 54)

The notion that a union may be concerned to monitor workers' performance in order to maintain the reputation of its members suggests that the bargaining relationship between the firm and its workforce within the typical Japanese company may be far removed from that of players engaged in an adversarial game. Indeed, the leading paradigm is that of a coalitional firm where the bargaining parties seek to find co-operative game solutions (Aoki, 1984, 1988). The coalition comprises shareholders and workers and 'decisions within the firm are reckoned as outcomes implicitly or explicitly agreed upon by the members of the firm and characterized by balancing the powers of the members as well as internal efficiency from the viewpoint of the members' (Aoki, 1984, pp. 7–8). Workers and shareholders contribute informational and financial assets and bargain, explicitly or implicitly, over all variables that affect the payoff of the firm. This broadly based bargaining agenda embraces decisions over the share of so-called organisational rent which arises from cost reductions – compared to using the outside market – stemming from co-operative interaction within and between the groups of shareholders and workers.[7] Again, firm-specificity is not embodied in single agents but, rather, spread throughout shareholders and workers: 'resources are firm specific in the sense that they are value-less in isolation and productive only in their steady association with the corporate firm as the nexus of association' (Aoki, 1984, p. 30).

Decisions over human capital investments in such a setting are more likely to be made with regard to the total workforce, through bargaining between the firm and its enterprise union. Hart and Moutos (1995) develop models of firm–union bargaining over the costs and returns to human capital investments that move away from the individual-based 'marginal worker' approaches. One question these authors attempt to answer relates to the existence and role of the enterprise union itself. Why would a firm – for strictly economic reasons and in the absence of outside political and social pressures – choose voluntarily to bargain with a union? Their explanation involves the accumulation of specific human capital. Such accumulation bestows future strength on workers since unplanned separations lead to potential rent losses. In fact, *ex post* bargaining cannot be avoided as workers will attempt to exercise their acquired bargaining power. Bargaining with a union at the outset of specific investment decisions will result in higher profits if the firm feels that the power of the union at that stage is not greater than that acquired at a later stage once the investment gains are realised.

2.4 Wage–tenure profiles

The general human capital story attached to figure 2.1, its specific human capital equivalent in figure 2.2, and the more elaborate transaction costs models of Hashimoto and

Carmichael suggest that wages rise with seniority within the firm. In the case of general human capital investment, workers pay for the cost of training and receive the full benefit of the returns. The associated wage rise reflects (i) the re-establishment of wage levels after payment for the training is complete and (ii) the incremental productivity increase due to the training. The mutual benefits of rent-sharing for the firm and its workers – which involves sharing both costs and returns – also establish a positive wage–productivity correlation in the case of specific training. In reality, many workers would be expected to incur such investments throughout their career with the firm, through specially designed training programmes and/or through the accumulation of skills on the job. For given workers, we might reasonably expect that a series of discrete steps in the wage–tenure profiles is generated by a continual process of training pro- grammes, new work experiences and learning-by-doing.

Since general skills are readily transferred from job to job, and assuming that workers typically continue to acquire new general skills throughout their economically active years, we would expect that wages rise with labour market experience. Suppose that a 'typical' worker commences working in a firm immediately after leaving school and remains in employment, without experiencing any spell of unemployment, until the age of retirement. Then, at any given time, 'experience' is taken to mean the age of the worker minus the length of time spent in formal education minus the number of pre- school years. Providing we take account of firm-specific human capital, this latter measure by itself can be taken to proxy the influence of general human capital accumu- lation on wage growth during years of employment. In each job undertaken by the worker between leaving school and retirement,[8] specific investments additionally serve to increase productivity. But specific investment, by definition, is not transferable to alternative employment. Therefore, at any given stage during the worker's career, the influence of specific capital on wage growth can be proxied by length of tenure of the *current* job. Finally, a complete coverage of human capital influences on wage growth must account for returns to education prior to the commencement of work. Schooling may directly affect productivity on the job or it may act to signal to employers the poten- tial of applicants to perform well in the firm's own training programmes. The topic of schooling is examined in chapter 9.

This discussion suggests that, from a human capital perspective, wage growth is func- tionally related to the lengths of (i) general labour market experience (including time in current employment) (X), (ii) tenure of the current job (T) and (iii) schooling (S).[9] A rig- orous derivation of such an equation is provided by Mincer (1974);[10] this may be expressed

$$\log W = B_0 + B_1 X + B_2 T + B_3 S + \text{higher order and interaction terms in}$$
$$X \text{ and } T + \text{control variables} \tag{2.3}$$

where $\log W$ is the logarithm of the real hourly wage rate. Mincer and Jovanovic (1981) provide one of numerous empirical applications of this equation. From theoretical, applied econometric and empirical perspectives, it has proved to be one of the most seminal developments in the study of labour markets. Using cross-sectional establishment-level data, Hashimoto and Raisian (1985) find that, for all sizes of firm, growth rates in compensation attributable to firm-specific tenure between the peak years and the initial years with the firm are greater in Japan than in the United States. Steeper wage trajectories due to firm-specific tenure are also found by Mincer and Higuchi (1988) using micro data. Turnover rates are also lower in Japan and these latter authors attribute two-thirds of the turnover differential to the relative steepness in the wage profiles.

2.5 Incentive-compatible contracts

One of the best known uses of equation (2.3) in a Japanese context is the comparative Japan/US study on wage–tenure profiles by Hashimoto and Raisian (1985). They find that Japanese workers have steeper profiles than their US counterparts. While they argue that this and other related findings are compatible with lower transaction costs and higher per capita fixed investments in Japan, they also point out that other interpretations of rising wage–tenure profiles do not require, necessarily, an accompanying story of human capital investment. The best-known alternative theory that predicts a rising profile stems from the so-called agency approach of Lazear (1979, 1981, 1986). This emphasises delayed payment contracts that are designed to produce greater work effort.[11]

From the foregoing, it is clear that significant human capital investment will be undertaken in a climate where there are relatively high probabilities that worker–firm attachments will ensure that investment outlays are recovered over given amortisation periods. As workers' tenure extends, their existing stock of capital will depreciate and the rate of depreciation will be either less than or greater than the rate of new specific investment. The productivity of older workers will vary. For the more productive, the rate of new investment will exceed stock depreciation, while less productive workers will eventually experience net decreases in investment. It seems somewhat strange, therefore, that many workers in Japan and elsewhere face an official, or mandatory, age of retirement. A pre-specified termination date may serve to deter significant new investments in older workers who are highly productive, with a resulting loss in rent opportunities. Premature separation may also be encouraged by private pension schemes. As discussed by Lazear (1983) in the case of early retirement in the United States, some pension schemes yield a higher present value of benefit if early retirement is taken. It might be argued that mandatory retirement at least serves the purpose of curtailing the employment of workers of lower productivity, thereby allowing firms to replace them with more productive new recruits. However, if the value of the marginal product is falling in later years of tenure and if the value of leisure is constant – or, perhaps more realistically, increasing – then it is quite likely that the same result, or better, could be achieved through voluntary retirement decisions.

As in human capital theory, we can assume that employment of the marginal worker is predicated on the profit-maximising rule that wage equals marginal product over the worker's expected length of tenure with the firm. For simplicity, there is no human capital investment undertaken by the firm. Based on past experience, the firm believes that a subset of its workers is likely to shirk. If the wage is set to equal marginal product at each and every time period for the duration of tenure and if the cost of monitoring workers' performance is high, then there may be little discouragement to shirking activity. In the first place, shirkers have a high probability of not being caught. Second, even if they are caught and dismissed, they might find it easy to receive the same wage in another firm. What if the wage-equals-marginal-product dictum were achieved by an alternative configuration of wages and productivity over the period of tenure? Lazear posits a wage–tenure profile based on an implicit contract whereby the worker receives less than the value of marginal product in the early years with the firm and more than marginal product in later years. Such a contract is productivity-enhancing since it reduces the propensity to shirk compared with a contract where, in each time period, the worker receives the value of marginal product. Shirking is discouraged because workers realise that, if caught and dismissed, they will be forgoing periods when wage premiums are earned. For all workers, long tenure is also encouraged by the availability of premiums in later periods of tenure.

This theory produces upward-sloping wage–tenure profiles without the necessary recourse to human capital investment. Moreover, such a profile provides a gain compared to other wage–tenure configurations; the lifetime value of the worker's marginal product is enhanced because the profile provides an incentive to a higher level of effort.

Mandatory retirement and/or pension benefits designed to encourage early retirement are necessary requirements of such incentive-compatible contracts. Growing wage premiums by length of tenure encourage workers to remain with the firm and mandatory retirement is needed to 'close' the contract in order to achieve outcomes in which expected lifetime cost equals marginal product. The previously cited work of Carmichael (1983) on promotion ladders also suggests such a requirement because, as in Lazear, workers with the longest tenure receive wage payments in excess of marginal product. Lazear's agency approach is arguably more powerful, however, because its predictions do not depend on the outlay of significant human capital investment.

Appendix: Theoretical background to section 2.2

Following the work of Mortensen (1978), Hashimoto (1979), Hashimoto and Yu (1980), let us assume that, after specific investment has been undertaken, the value of a worker's marginal product both within and outside the firm is subject to random shocks. This is expressed

$$V_i = \mu_i + \theta_i, \quad i = f, a \tag{2A.1}$$

where μ_i is a fixed parameter, θ_i is a random productivity element and $i = f$ refers to the firm in question and $i = a$ refers to all other (alternative) firms. Let $m \equiv \mu_f - \mu_a$. Then m can be regarded as a 'permanent' productivity differential between the firm in question and other firms if we assume $E(\theta_i)=0$. An efficient separation will occur if and only if $V_f<V_a$ or, using expression (2A.1), if and only if

$$m<\theta_u-\theta_f. \tag{2A.2}$$

Expression (2A.2) is intuitively appealing. Efficient separation depends on (i) the size of the difference between the permanent elements of productivity (m), (ii) the relative sizes of the random shocks (θ_f and θ_a), and (iii) the correlation between the shocks. For given m, efficient separation is most likely to occur if the firm experiences a negative shock that induces an especially low marginal product (i.e. θ_f is significantly less than zero) or if there is an opportunity elsewhere that offers a substantial productive gain (i.e. θ_a is significantly greater than zero). *Ceteris paribus*, significant changes in the values of θ_f and θ_a are most likely to induce efficient separation if their movements are only weakly correlated.[12]

The size of m in (2A.2) is a choice variable for the firm and its workers. If human capital investment is productive, then a larger expenditure on a worker's productive performance will increase the size of m and so reduce the probability of separation. But, of course, this does not mean that the two parties will not seek to effect a separation that is mutually advantageous. This necessarily requires them to communicate and to agree on the nature of the internal and external productivity shocks. In reality, such a process is not likely to be a simple one since the informational requirements could be extensive and complex.

For the moment, however, assume that an unrelated third party observes and fully communicates the permanent components (i.e. μ_f and μ_a) and random components (i.e. θ_f and θ_a) of the internal and external productivities to the firm and its workers. Without loss of generality, human capital investment is purely specific. Further, in line with the developments referred to in figure 2.2, we assume that the contractual arrangement between the firm and its workers involves rent-sharing, or sharing the productivity difference V_f-V_a. Again, we assume that the marginal worker receives specific training in the first period and works without further training in the second period. At the beginning of the first period, agreement is reached over the first and second period wage. Neither the worker's value of the second period marginal product nor the alternative wage is revealed until the start of the second period.

The worker's wage (w) is given by

$$w=Va+\alpha(V_f-V_a)=V_a+\alpha m+\alpha(\theta_f-\theta_a), \tag{2A.3}$$

while the firm's profit (π) is given by

$$\pi=V_f-w=(1-\alpha)(V_f-V_a)=(1-\alpha)m+(1-\alpha)(\theta_f-\theta_a), \tag{2A.4}$$

where α is a pre-determined sharing rule with $0<\alpha<1$. As expressed in (2A.2), the parties would choose to separate if and only if $m+(\theta_f-\theta_a)<0$ since this implies that $w-V_a<0$ and $\pi<0$.

Under these conditions, a separation between a worker and the firm would be by mutual agreement. But the conditions are unlikely to prevail. Hashimoto (1979) and Carmichael (1983) examine the likely event that information on random shocks is asymmetrical between the two parties. In particular, it is assumed that only the employer observes θ_f while only the worker observes θ_a. In the event that communication of this information from one party to the other is fraught with difficulty – perhaps due to suspicion about one another's motives – the parties agree to bargain at the beginning of period 1 over wages in both periods. The second period wage is the one determined by the expected values of the internal and external productivities. Taking expected values of (2A.3) we have,

$$\overline{w} = \mu a + \alpha m. \tag{2A.5}$$

The distinction between quits and layoffs is now meaningful. The worker will quit if $\overline{w} - V_a < 0$ or, using (2A.1) and (2A.5), if

$$\theta_a > \alpha m. \tag{2A.6}$$

With a fixed wage, the firm's profit is given by $\hat{\pi} = V_f - \overline{w}$. The firm will lay off the worker if $\hat{\pi} < 0$ or, using (2A.1) and (2A.5), if

$$\theta_f < -(1 - \alpha)m. \tag{2A.7}$$

Examination of the quit and layoff rules under a fixed wage – i.e. (2A.6) and (2A.7), respectively – and the optimal separation rule in (2A.2) where the wage is purely flexible, reveals that they do not correspond. Only on the average, that is where expected outcomes concerning productivity shocks hold, will quit and layoff decisions coincide to give optimal separation. Some separations will occur when, if the parties had been able to recontract under a flexible wage agreement, it would have been in their mutual interest to remain together (i.e. $V_a < V_f$). Some decisions to remain together will occur despite an advantage in separating (i.e. $V_a > V_f$). The objective of the parties is to find values of α that minimise such inefficient outcomes. This solution is presented in Hashimoto (1979) and Carmichael (1983).

A low transaction cost environment in which there is reliable information concerning the estimated values of θ_f and θ_a, encourages the formulation of a flexible wage contract as in (2A.3). In turn, this serves to minimise the risk of costly separations due to losses of specific human capital investments. This does not necessarily mean that the parties can directly observe realisations of θ_f and θ_a. Hashimoto and Yu (1980) demonstrate that if estimates of random components are based on observed proxy variables that are likely to correlate with the shocks, then flexible wage contracts may still be more desirable than fixed wage equivalents. The better the proxies, the greater the chance of achieving efficient separation behaviour.[13] In contrast, poor communication between the firm and its workers and low information reliability are likely to promote fixed wage contracts, under which misjudged layoffs and quits have a higher probability of occurrence.

Notes

1 See also the expositions by Hutchens (1989) and Hart and Moutos (1995).
2 Parsons (1986) provides an excellent review of the relevant literature, and this forms the basis of the developments in the Appendix. A number of the most important

considerations are also very clearly elaborated and discussed by Hashimoto (1975).

3 As we show in the Appendix, the random components of investment returns and the outside wage have distributions with mean zero so that the difference between the fixed components can be regarded as 'permanent' productivity differences. The covariance of the distributions of the random components is assumed to be zero. Suppose that the firm is better informed about workers' productivity while workers hold superior information about outside job opportunities. Then the covariance assumption is tantamount to imposing the restriction that the employer's view of the worker's productive contribution is independent of the worker's assessment of outside opportunities.

4 It is not meaningful to distinguish between quits and layoffs if such a first-best separation rule were to be applied. If marginal product is less than the outside wage in the second period, the firm has just as much incentive to lay off the worker as the worker has to quit.

5 Actually, Carmichael's equivalent to the outside wage is worker job satisfaction. This is a more convincing vehicle of asymmetric information. The worker is almost bound to form a different view from the firm on the satisfaction provided by the job (relative to perceived outside possibilities) as well as on the qualities of work and social environments.

6 As shown by Carmichael, the efficiency gain stems from the fact that changes in the second period wages and bonuses operate differently on separation decisions. A rise in the wage reduces quits and increases layoffs. A rise in the bonus reduces quits but leaves layoffs unchanged. This latter outcome is predicated on the assumed seniority rule. If the bonus rises, layoff only saves the firm the second period wage since there is a fixed number of senior jobs.

7 Firm-specific resources can be generated through co-operative behaviour that serves to stimulate a greater willingness to take risk by shareholders, better worker co-operation in management-led initiatives to monitor performance, greater accumulation of on-the-job skills, fewer restrictions on management decisions on how best to allocate internal financial resources, and stronger commitment to the formation of group skills.

8 For example, Hashimoto and Raisian (1985) calculate that by the time the typical male worker reaches 65, he would have had five jobs in Japan and eleven in the United States.

9 Alternatively, specific qualification attainments, where available, may provide a more sensitive indicator of the role of pre-work education.

10 However, the rigour depends on several heroic assumptions; see Blinder (1976).

11 See the review article by Hutchens (1989) for a brief discussion of competing models.

12 If random fluctuations influence the firm in question and other firms in the same direction, then the opportunities for efficient separations will not be so clearly demarcated and, for given θ_i fluctuations, such separations are likely to be reduced in number.

13 In the absence of costly search, workers may find it difficult to locate specific instances of potentially higher outside wage offers. However, they may use less direct labour market signals to judge the chances of success. Word-of-mouth from

acquaintances in other firms, job advertisements, and employment agency information may all serve to give reasonable estimates of θ_a. For its part, the firm may use data from its order-books, and general indications from customer enquiries and current sales negotiations, as well as the sales trends and prospects of trading partners, as indicators of changes in θ_f.

3 **Industrial relations**

3.1 **Enterprise unionism**

3.1.1 Institutional characteristics

The normal unit of an enterprise union is either the company or the establishment (a single site of a company). Union members directly register and pay their membership fees within that unit. The enterprise union has been by far the most prominent union structure in post-war Japan: by 1994, it included about 92 per cent of total union membership. It is an independent decision-making body with financial autonomy in relation both to the firm and to union federations at industry and national levels. A major characteristic is that only those workers who are employed on a regular basis by a firm can be members. Anyone who loses her/his job also loses union membership automatically. Part-timers and temporary workers are usually not part of the membership. Small firms are less unionised than large ones. Where firms are unionised, a potentially wide range of employees belongs to the union. Many firms adopt a union shop system whereby regular employees who are not in supervisory or management positions must become union members. Both blue-collar and white-collar workers within a given company or establishment belong to the same union.

Only union members can be elected as union officers. Therefore, a firm's union officers must be employees of a unionised firm, and typically its own employees. Union officers are usually on temporary leave from their own firm and eventually return to posts within the firm. Their salaries are paid from union membership fees.

Enterprise unions typically form multi-layered federations. Within a large firm, a union unit is organised at each establishment or factory, and these units form a federation for the whole firm. Unions whose base firms belong to the same business group form a federation for the group.[1] Many enterprise unions join industry federations of unions.[2] In some industries, unions from large firms and small firms form separate federations because of, for example, differences in their working conditions. Further industry federations form national federations. In 1995, the Japan Trade Union Confederation had 61.2% of total membership, the National Confederation of Trade Unions 6.8%, the National Trade Union Council 2.2% and other national federations 22.2%, while 9.3% of firms did not belong to any national federation.[3]

3.1.2 Are Japanese unions unique?

Koike (1988) has criticised the somewhat stereotyped view that Japanese unions are different because they exist only at the level of the enterprise, in contrast to European and US unions which are typically industry- or craft-based with less firm-level representation. According to his study, most of the large US establishments in manufacturing or tertiary industries have local unions that negotiate various working conditions – such as promotion, redundancy and transfers – at establishment level. On the other hand, industry unions deal with wage increases at national level. Local unions have a strong voice on such matters as promotion, which are often based on rigid rules of seniority and largely preclude managerial discretion. In the case of Germany, Koike found that works councils play a role very similar to Japanese enterprise unions. The formation of a works council is a legal requirement for an establishment with more than five employees. Councils are formally distinct from trade unions in that they cannot institute strike action, nor form a federation extending outside the firm. Nevertheless, they co-determine employees' welfare issues with employers, they have to be consulted on personnel matters and they can ask for information on the firm's financial position. Thus, Koike concludes that the German works council should be viewed as a *de facto* plant-based union.

In general, it seems to be a reasonably persuasive argument that both Japanese and Western unions perform similar functions at local and industrial levels. Both systems have developed various institutional arrangements to deal with multi-layered negotiations. The stereotyped concept that Japanese unions function only at the enterprise level while Western unions concentrate more on industry issues is misleading. We cannot ignore, nonetheless, that important differences between Japanese and Western unions do exist. For instance, there are differences in organisational functionality. Since the basic decision-making unit is at the enterprise level in Japan, Japanese unions are more effective at considering and dealing with enterprise-specific conditions. They tend to share more in policy-making with other stakeholders in their enterprise. In contrast, local unions in the United States are basically administrative units of national unions, and financially and administratively dependent on national unions. Therefore, unions in the United States or countries with similar systems are more effective at confronting industry- or nationwide labour market issues. In the case of Germany, separate organisations – works councils and national-level unions – are designed to tackle local and industry-level problems respectively. However, this involves potential problems of co-ordination, especially where local and national issues are closely related.

3.1.3 Why are enterprise unions so prevalent in Japan?

There is a fairly widely accepted rationalisation of the existence of enterprise unions that concerns the development of internal labour markets in industrialised countries. In the traditional labour markets of early industrialisation, workers acquired their own skills and sold their labour service in the open market. In order to bargain more effectively for better terms, workers formed craft or industrial unions. The emergence of huge corporations as the major industrial entities changed the nature of labour markets drastically. Modern technological and managerial structures in large firms increasingly required a multitude of hierarchically ordered job groups. Since such jobs are specialised and firm-specific, the firm became unable to hire appropriate persons from existing labour markets. Therefore, large firms employed relatively unskilled workers in the first instance, trained them to their appropriate job levels, and filled vacant job slots primarily from these internally trained resources. In this arrangement, an optimal strategy for the workforce is to control labour service from inside the firm, namely to form an enterprise union. Not only for employees but also for management, the enterprise union became the basic platform for exchanging information, negotiating firm-specific working conditions and striking mutually acceptable bargains.

This, of course, begs the question of why enterprise unions have developed fully only in Japan when the internalisation of labour markets has produced similar developments of industrial structures and organisations in all industrialised countries. Comparing employment systems in Japan and Britain, Dore (1973) offered a hypothesis based on the late development theory of Gerschenkron (1966). The Japanese, it is argued, have been able to adopt a more advanced union system matching the new stage of industrialisation because of their far later industrial development. Large corporations were set up at the outset of Japanese industrialisation.[4]

In Britain, by contrast, the giant corporation emerged as the culmination of a century of slow industrialization, long after a labour-market-oriented employment system adapted to a fluid small-firm pattern of industry had become highly, indeed rigidly, institutionalized in the existence of national trade union organizations beyond the power of any individual employer to reconstruct. (Dore, 1973, p. 339)

However, Dore produces some evidence of convergence to Japanese-type employment systems in Britain.

Historically, the origin of Japanese enterprise unions can be traced to the early twenties (Komatsu, 1971). During this period, Japan experienced a new stage of industrial expansion with heavy manufacturing replacing traditional textile industries. Many large corporations emerged. Against the backgrounds of economic boom and spreading democratic ideas, workers claimed the right to organise unions. They demanded better working conditions and basic rights. Collective bargaining and labour disputes became more common phenomena. These early unions consisted of craft or industrial unions as well as enterprise unions. Enterprise unions represented 38 per cent of total union membership in the period between 1926 and 1930 (Sakurabayashi, 1985, pp. 72–3).

As the labour movement expanded, the national government tried to contain labour disputes given its priority of a nationwide resource mobilisation system for domestic control and expansionist foreign policies. One of the mobilisation tools for industrial relations was the 'Industrial Association for Serving the Nation' (Sangyo-Hokoku-Kai) (Magota, 1965; Sakurabayashi, 1985). Eventually, all trade unions were dissolved and absorbed into this organisation. It operated not only as a national control mechanism but also as a *de facto* bargaining platform between employees and employers, as well as a welfare administration system for employees. Although it was formally a national organisation, it enhanced internal integration within the firm. It was during this regime that blue-collar workers obtained union status almost equal to their white-collar counterparts. This government-led intervention is regarded as an important antecedent of the post-war enterprise union structure (Magota, 1965).

3.1.4 Union effects

Traditionally, US and Western European labour market analysts have expended considerable theoretical and empirical effort in examining the ability of unions – through quasi-monopoly control of labour supply – to achieve compensation gains for their members greater than in equivalent non-unionised sectors. Typically in the United States, it is found that unionised workers enjoy wages about 10 to 15 per cent higher than non-unionised workers (Lewis,1963, 1986; Pencavel, 1991).[5] By contrast, in work based on 689 companies in 1991, Tachibanaki and Noda (1993) found no significant differences between union and non-union wages in Japan. It does not necessarily follow that Japanese unions have no bargaining power to raise wages. Rather, as discussed later in this chapter, it may reflect strong spillover effects. Alternatively, Japanese unions may act to moderate wage increases in exchange for job security as well as mutual gains from company prosperity (Morishima, 1991a, 1991b).

Freeman and Medoff (1979, p. 71) emphasised another aspect of the union's role, applying Hirschman's (1970) theory to union behaviour. According to them, 'a trade union is the vehicle for collective voice – that is, for providing workers as a group with a means of communicating with management' (Freeman and Medoff, 1979, p. 71). Their empirical results are consistent with the view that US unions reduce quit rates and, moreover, these 'voice' effects appear to be significantly larger than the monopoly effects of unions. Muramatsu (1984b) estimated the union effects on quit rates for 1978 Japanese data and found, after controlling for monopoly effects, that union voice is also relatively strong. An average quit rate of 9.6 per cent for the total sample is reduced to 4.9 per cent in the unionised sectors. Tomita (1993) confirmed the existence of significant voice effects using a set of micro-data for 1991. The quit rate of firms with unions was 5.63 per cent which was 2.27 per cent points lower than in non-unionised firms. Muramatsu (1984b) also found positive union effects on productivity, and Brown and Medoff (1978) found similar positive effects in the United States.

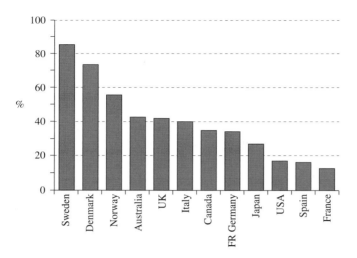

Fig. 3.1. Union density by country, 1988. (*Source:* Visser, 1991.)

3.1.5 Union density

An international perspective

Figure 3.1 shows three broad groups of countries in terms of union density, i.e. union membership as a percentage of total employees. The Nordic countries exhibit very high density. Most European countries tend to cluster in the medium density range. The low density group includes the USA, Spain and France. Japanese density hovers between medium and low: its 26.8 per cent density in 1988 is slightly lower than the OECD weighted average rate of 28 per cent, but higher than the US rate of 16.4 per cent.[6]

As shown in table 3.1, there is a wide spread of Japanese union densities across industries. Sectors such as government, electricity/gas/water, finance and mining have high densities, while wholesale/retail and services have low densities. Figure 3.2 compares union densities by different firm sizes in Japan and the UK. The larger the firm, the greater is the density in both countries. In part this reflects the relatively high per capita costs of organising and maintaining union services in smaller firms. We note also that the size differential is far larger in Japan.[7] This contrast reveals one of the basic characteristics of Japanese enterprise unions: it is very difficult to organise a union in a small firm.

Figure 3.3 shows Japanese union density averaged over all industries for the period 1953 to 1994. The density remained around 34 per cent in the fifties, sixties and early seventies, and then declined continuously thereafter. As illustrated in figure 3.4, this latter trend has also been experienced in the United States and France, while union density has increased in Sweden. Union density in the UK has declined, albeit quite slowly, since the mid-1970s. German density showed a slight increase until the mid-1980s before starting to decline.

Table 3.1. *Union density by industry (percentages)*

	1955	1965	1975	1985	1995
Agriculture, forestry & fisheries	17.1	23.6	24.3	17.2	8.9
Mining	80.6	57.9	41.3	48.7	25.7
Construction	25.5	24.2	18.1	19.7	18.9
Manufacturing	36.6	38.3	39.7	33.7	30.8
Wholesale & retail	15.9	18.1	11.1	9.3	9.1
Finance & insurance	n.a.	n.a.	62.1	49.3	44.0
Transportation & communication	83.3	70.5	65.0	57.9	43.9
Electricity, gas & water	n.a.	n.a.	71.3	67.9	44.1
Services	33.8	27.7	26.0	18.2	12.9
Government	55.0	66.6	66.9	76.4	67.5

Source: Ministry of Labour, Basic Survey on Labour Unions.

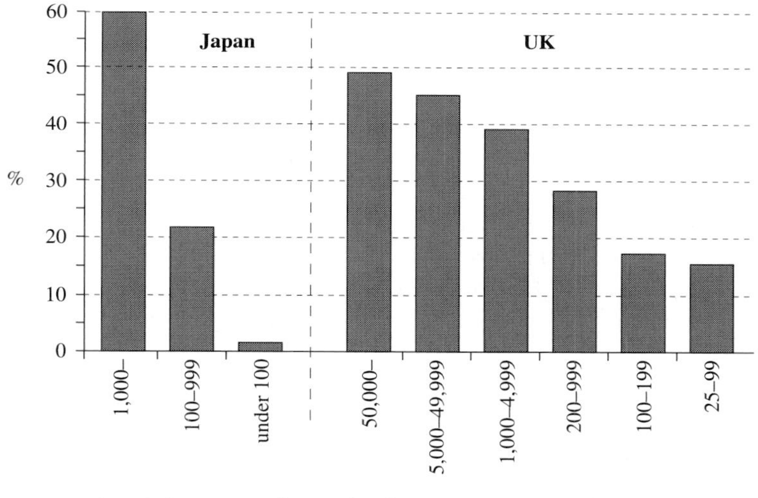

Fig. 3.2. Union density by firm size: Japan and the United Kingdom. (*Source:* Sato, 1996, p. 1090.)

Why has Japanese union density declined?

Why has Japanese union density declined since the late seventies? The most popular set of explanations centres on structural shifts in employment:

(1) the proportion of employees working in retail and service industries, which traditionally have lower union densities, has been increasing steadily;
(2) large firms with high union densities have been restructuring and reducing employment;
(3) the number of part-timers and temporary workers has been increasing;
(4) the number of employees who are in supervisory or managing positions has been

Fig. 3.3. Union density, Japan, 1953–94. (*Sources:* Ishihata, 1990; Ministry of Labour, Basic Survey on Labour Unions; Management and Coordination Agency, Labour Force Survey.)

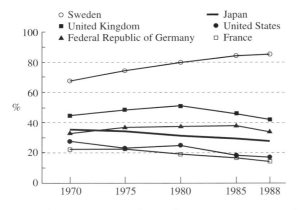

Fig. 3.4. Union density by country, 1970–88. (*Source:* Visser, 1991, p. 101.)

increasing owing to a general aging of the population as well as rising educational levels. (Sato, 1996)

Freeman and Rebick (1989) criticise an excessive emphasis on these structural arguments, pointing out that these same factors have been observed throughout the world, even in the countries which experienced rising union density in the same period. They evaluated the contributions of these structural factors to the decline of Japanese union density during the period from 1975 to 1986. According to their results, industrial shifts explained 23.0 per cent of the density decline, ageing and management posts 9.9 per cent, and part-timers and temporary workers 9.8 per cent. Altogether structural factors, including other items such as gender and firm size, explained only 44 per cent of the density decline.

In order to explore further the reason for the decline, Freeman and Rebick decomposed density change in terms of a flow–stock relation[8], and found that about 65 per cent of the union decline could be explained by the fall in the rate at which unions organise new establishments. In short, Japanese union density declined mainly because unions failed to organise new unions during this period. But what accounts for the decline in the organisation rate of new unions?

In the United States, there exists a substantial wage differential between unionised and non-unionised firms, as discussed previously. According to Freeman (1988), enhanced management resistance to unionisation contributed significantly to the decline of US union density. Freeman and Rebick (1989) tried to apply the same explanation to Japan, and argued that the economic hardship following the oil crises gave rise to a strong management offensive to suppress union activities in Japan. However, they offered no substantial evidence to support this claim. Further, the number of unfair labour practices appealed to the Central Labour Committee[9] in relation to the number of total employees has been declining since the late seventies according to Tsuru (1995). Economic hardship would also raise workers' resistance, and this was one of the main reasons why Japanese union density jumped to near 60 per cent from almost zero immediately after the war. Therefore, a more plausible explanation may be that workers' interests in unions have dwindled (Japan Institute of Labour, 1993; Tsuru, 1995). Based on a survey on workers living in the Tokyo metropolitan area, Tsuru (1995) identified two reasons why workers turned away from unions:

(i) unions have not been able to adapt to the diversifying needs and views of workers; and, more importantly,
(ii) workers have a low confidence in the ability of unions to improve wages and working conditions.

3.2 The spring offensive

3.2.1 The origin and institutional framework

Immediately after the Second World War, union legislation introduced by the Allied forces, combined with extremely low living standards, brought about a surge in collective labour organisation and action. Union density rose sharply to 60 per cent from almost zero and union movements became radicalised. The process resulted in large wage increases and high inflation rates.

The economic recession following the Korean war led to overt attempts to limit wage increases and management started to introduce job-related wage systems. Labour launched counter-offensives to overcome diminishing union power by unionising its collective bargaining. At first, five federations of industrial unions (synthetic chemistry, coal, private railways, electric power, and paper and pulp) set up the core organisational structure for the offensive in 1954. In 1955, unions in electrical machinery, metals and general chemistry joined and started simultaneous wage demands and negotiations in the spring of 1955. Other unions followed this lead, including public services, steel, shipbuilding and national railways. In 1955, about 730,000 workers participated in the spring

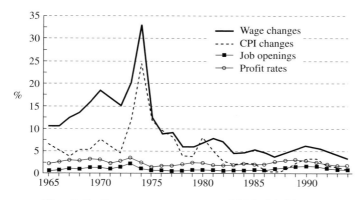

Fig. 3.5. Spring wage increases, 1965–94. (*Sources:* See table 3.2.)

offensive. The number increased rapidly to 4,390,000 in 1961, 9,680,000 in 1975 and 10,000,000 in 1984 (Shirai *et al.*, 1986, p. 180).

During the spring-time collective bargaining, individual enterprise unions negotiate with their employers. Japanese labour law guarantees that anyone with a union mandate can negotiate with employers. In reality, however, unions and employers both avoid involving outsiders. Nonetheless, during the bargaining process, unions often consult intensively with other unions and co-ordinate wage demands through their business connections[10] as well as through regional, industrial and national federations. Employers network in similar fashion. From time to time, unions set up a unified negotiating body and this negotiates with the federation of their employers.

3.2.2 What determines the size of spring wage increases?

Previous studies have identified the following three major factors that strongly influence the magnitudes of spring wage increases: (i) demand and supply conditions in the labour market, (ii) consumer price levels, and (iii) business conditions (Ministry of Labour, 1975; Sano, 1989). During the rapid growth period of the 1960s, a strong demand for labour helped unions to achieve significant wage increases. Consumer price levels were a particular focus of arguments supporting the need for increased wage levels during the oil crises. As for business conditions, Sano (1970, 1981) found that spring wage increases are explained more successfully by the average profits of all industries than by each individual industry's profits. This implies that there exists a strong tendency for wages to converge to a uniform national level. Only in depressions has the variance of wage changes tended to increase slightly.

Figure 3.5 shows the relationship between, on the one hand, the rates of spring wage increases and, on the other hand, the rate of change in the consumer price index (CPI), the active job openings ratio (= active job openings divided by active job applications), and the ratio of recurring profits to sales. We carried out a simple regression analysis to examine the impact on spring wage increases of the three variables shown in figure 3.5. Table 3.2 presents the results of this analysis. Consumer prices are the most significant

Table 3.2. *Explaining spring wage increases, 1965–95: OLS regression results*

	Coefficients	*t*-ratios
Constant	−3.76	−1.85
Consumer price index (rate of change)	1.07	10.41
Active job openings ratio (active job openings divided by active applications)	2.13	1.06
Ratio of recurring profits to sales	2.48	1.84

Notes:

Dependent variable: Spring wage increases (rates of change) in major listed firms; $R^2 = 0.85$; number of observations = 31. Data Sources: Labour Relations Bureau, Ministry of Labour (for spring wage increases); Management and Co-ordination Agency (for consumer price index); Ministry of Finance, financial statements of corporations by Industry (for profit rates); Employment Security Bureau, Ministry of Labour (for job openings).

determinant of wage increases, as figure 3.5 clearly suggests. Although nominal wage increases dominate price increases on the whole, maintaining the real wage level has been a strong stimulus behind wage increases. That is, maintaining and improving real wage levels has been the major motivation behind nominal wage increases. Profit rates are also a significant factor, but the active job openings ratio – representing demand and supply factors – does not appear to be influential. This may be because the job openings ratio is highly correlated with profit rates (the correlation coefficient is 0.795), or because the job openings ratio is a poor indicator of labour market conditions.

3.2.3 Effects of spring wage increases

Japanese real wages have increased considerably from near starvation level at the end of the Second World War to one of the world's top levels. Spring labour offensives have no doubt contributed to this as well as to improvements in other working conditions. However, it is very difficult to quantify the role of union power *per se* in the post-war wage increases.

When viewed in relation to productivity, Japanese wage increases have been rather moderate. As illustrated in figure 3.6, productivity growth rates have usually exceeded real wage growth rates throughout the post-war period. Only in the years of the first oil crisis and around several deep recessions have real wage changes exceeded productivity growth. The average annual productivity growth and real wage growth rates were 8.56 per cent and 4.07 per cent respectively during the period 1955–65, 9.31 per cent and 7.09 per cent for 1965–75, 6.36 per cent and 1.40 per cent for 1975–85, and 3.15 per cent and 1.39 per cent for 1985–95.[11] Dividend payments to shareholders have been rather meagre throughout the post-war period. Surpluses, created by productivity growth in excess of real wage growth, have been directed mainly towards further investments.

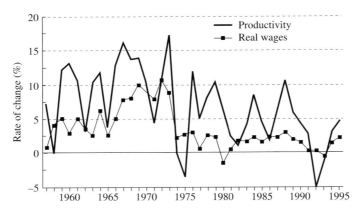

Fig. 3.6. Productivity and wages, 1957–95. (*Sources:* Productivity index from Japan Productivity Centre; nominal wages from Ministry of Labour, Monthly Labour Survey. Additionally, real wages use consumer price index from Management and Coordination Agency.)

The institution of spring wage increases provides a focus that generally helps workers, employers and shareholders to achieve sharing arrangements within a climate of mutual co-operation and moderation of self-interest. From six months in advance of the bargaining period, the parties prepare background data, advance their own demands and criticise one another's positions through the mass media. In this way, a nationwide consensus is achieved and the whole process reflects considerable flexibility in Japanese industrial relations. A prime example of the merits of the system occurred at the time of the serious economic crises following the sudden OPEC oil embargo in 1974. Wages skyrocketed owing to high inflation and general economic confusion. However, in the course of their deliberations in the spring negotiation processes, both employers and employees quickly came to realise the foolishness of wage–price spirals. As a result, Japan was able to overcome the shock of the oil crises relatively successfully. Another positive effect of the spring offensive is scale economy of negotiation. Both employers and employees reduce the costs of information-gathering and negotiation by concentrating on one interval of time. Deliberation, argument and possible industrial disputes are dealt with in a relatively short period.

3.2.4 Equalisation of wage increases throughout industries

The pattern-setters of wage increases have been labour and management in the leading industries of the time: chemistry, coal, private railways, public services in the fifties; iron and steel in the sixties; steel, shipbuilding, electronics and cars in the seventies and eighties; and, more recently, cars and electronics. Spring wage increases spread throughout domestic labour markets, first influencing wage negotiations within private enterprises in all industries. They also impact on the recommendations of the National Personnel

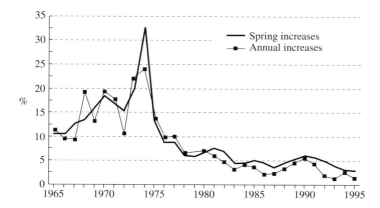

Fig. 3.7. Annual wage increases and spring wage increases, 1965–95. Annual wages are monthly contractural earnings including overtime payments but excluding annual bonuses in establishments with over ten employees. Spring wage increases are for unionised companies with more than 1,000 employees listed in the first section of the Tokyo or Osaka Stock Exchanges. (*Sources:* Annual wage increases from Ministry of Labour, Basic Survey on Wage Structure; spring wage increases from Survey of Labour Relations Bureau, Ministry of Labour.)

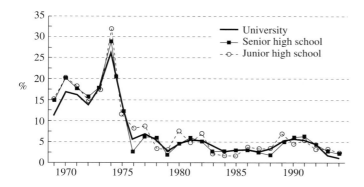

Fig. 3.8. Changes in annual wages (starting levels) by education, 1969–94. Males starting salaries for newly graduated employees, all industries. (*Source:* Ministry of Labour, Basic Survey on Wage Structure.)

Authority which advises on public sector pay awards. Even the level of rice prices, set by government, is strongly influenced by the spring wage agreements.

Therefore, spring offensives have become the major determinant of nationwide wage increases in Japan. Figure 3.7 shows that, averaged over all Japanese industries, annual wage increases closely follow the movement of spring wage increases. Average annual wage increases from 1965 to 1995 were 8.14 per cent overall and 7.89 per cent for spring offensives.

Figures 3.8, 3.9 and 3.10 show, respectively, wage increases by education level of newly

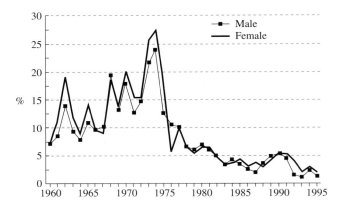

Fig. 3.9. Wage changes by sex, 1960–95. Monthly contractual earnings including overtime payments but excluding bonuses in establishments with over ten employees. (*Source:* Ministry of Labour, Basic Survey on Wage Structure.)

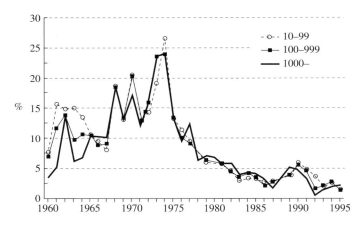

Fig. 3.10. Wage changes by firm size, 1960–95. Monthly contractual earnings including overtime payments but excluding bonuses in establishments with over ten employees. (*Source:* Ministry of Labour, Basic Survey on Wage Structure.)

hired employees, by sex, and by size of firms. They reveal that wage increases move very similarly across these different variables. Table 3.3 shows the average annual rate of wage increases for various categories of employees. Again, it is noticeable that rates are rather similar;[12] moreover, there is a slight but clear tendency in the long run for the rates of lower wage groups (small firms and female workers) to converge towards those of the higher wage groups (large firms and male workers).

Table 3.4 shows both the amount in yen and the rate of wage increases of major automobile companies from 1987 to 1997. Both sets of figures display wide variations in line with fluctuations in business conditions in the automobile industry. The most interest-

Table 3.3. *Average annual percentage wage increases by firm size and sex, 1954–95*

Total	Small firm (10–99 employees)	Medium firm (100–999 employees)	Large firm (1000 or more employees)	Male workers	Female workers
7.73	8.40	7.87	7.67	7.61	8.05

Note:
Monthly contractual earnings including overtime payments but excluding annual bonuses in establishments with over ten employees.
Source: Ministry of Labour, Basic Survey on Wage Structure.

ing feature of the table, however, is that wage increases are quite similar across companies, although Toyota, as the most successful company, has given slightly larger increases than the other companies.

Koike (1962) studied in detail industrial wage bargaining in cotton mills, steel and private railway industries. One important finding was that the level and rates of wage increases tended to be equalised among firms of similar sizes in the same industry even if their pay structures and career paths were quite different. For instance, the ten largest cotton mill companies had rather similar pay increases with, at most, 10 per cent differences. Yet these similarities occurred despite the workforces having different mixes of job descriptions and different forms of compensation systems, such as piece rates and time rates. In private railways, the amount and rate of wage increases were quite similar, both within the union demands and in the subsequent negotiated results. On the other hand, there were considerable differences in the career paths of workers among the railway companies. For example, there were two distinct career paths for drivers. In the specialist type of company, drivers started as assistant drivers and became fully licensed drivers of local trains, then drivers of express trains, then supervisors of train drivers. In the generalist type, workers started as station clerks, then became conductors, then drivers, then managers, and finally station masters. Nevertheless, despite these diverse career progressions, workers with the same length of tenure had remarkably similar wage levels and pay increases across firms of similar size (see Koike, 1962, fig. 10, p. 237).

3.2.5 Why is there a tendency towards wage equalisation?

Japanese firms have developed elaborate training systems and internal labour markets. As a result, Japanese employees are supposed to have accumulated a considerable amount of firm-specific human capital. This being so, and in the light of the theoretical discussion of chapter 2, we might expect that the wages of two workers with the same tenure but in different firms could be quite different. In general, the evidence tends to run counter to this expectation. Why is there a tendency towards wage equalisation in a market that is characterised by firm-specific human capital investments? This is an

Table 3.4. *Spring wage increases in major car companies, 1987–97*

	Amount of increases (yen)				Percentage of increase from base wage				
	Toyota	Nissan	Honda	Mitsubishi	11 makers (average)	Toyota	Nissan	Honda	Mitsubishi	11 makers (average)
1987	8,000	7,100	7,900	6,500	6,990	3.46	3.08	3.84	3.88	3.22
1988	10,600	9,600	10,500	8,800	9,165	4.43	3.97	4.62	3.99	4.13
1989	12,900	12,200	12,800	11,900	11,776	5.20	4.86	5.36	5.14	5.13
1990	15,300	16,200	16,300	17,146	14,117	5.93	5.90	6.17	6.05	5.99
1991	15,000	14,600	14,700	14,200	13,811	5.52	5.54	5.65	5.76	5.62
1992	13,600	13,200	13,300	12,900	12,526	4.83	4.82	4.83	5.10	4.89
1993	11,200	10,400	10,900	10,600	10,148	3.85	3.68	3.84	4.12	3.84
1994	9,200	8,400	8,900	8,400	8,156	3.06	2.89	3.00	3.24	3.02
1995	8,700	7,800	8,400	8,000	7,791	n.a.	n.a.	n.a.	n.a.	n.a.
1996	8,700	7,800	8,400	8,000	7,791	n.a.	n.a.	n.a.	n.a.	n.a.
1997	9,400	9,000	9,200	9,000	n.a.	n.a.	n.a.	n.a.	n.a.	n.a.

Note:

Data derived from various newspapers and interviews with unions. In 1995, the unions changed the mode of wage demand, and percentage figures have not been published since then.

interesting question[13], that still appears to be in need of an adequate answer. Several partial explanations are as follows.

Relative importance of firm-specific human capital

Although there exist a large number of studies on human capital, there is no work that estimates, in any direct sense, the relative magnitudes of general and specific capital. Koike (1991) conjectures, without offering any hard evidence, that the magnitude of firm-specific human capital is relatively small compared to general human capital. Other studies – as discussed in chapters 2, 5 and 9 – rely indirectly on the shapes of wage–tenure profiles. They tend to convey the quantitative importance of firm-specific capital. These studies fall short, however, of being fully convincing that tenure, even when many other influences are accounted for, provides an adequate proxy for firm-specific human capital.[14]

Inherent difficulty in evaluating and agreeing on the returns to firm-specific human capital

There exist extensive open markets for general human capital. Specific human capital, by definition, is unique to a given firm and it is difficult to evaluate exact values for its returns. It is even more difficult to agree upon the relative share of the returns between employers and employees. We discussed some theoretical implications of such communication difficulties in chapter 2. As a convenient 'rule of thumb' that avoids high transaction costs of communication and negotiation, bargaining parties in many firms may simply agree to use the going wage rates of similar firms in the same industry.

Strategic behaviour among firms

Direct wage equalisation often occurs among firms of roughly equal size that are competing with one another in the same product market. If one firm gives a large wage increase and others do not, the morale of workers in the other firms may fall, with resulting adverse effects on productivity, or even labour disputes. Since this could happen to any firm over the long run, the firms concerned may find it mutually beneficial to consult among themselves over an appropriate amount of joint pay increase. This leads to equalisation of wage increases among similar firms in the same industry.[15]

3.3 Joint consultation systems

3.3.1 The system

Many Japanese firms have a joint consultation system through which management and labour routinely communicate with one another. The system is organised at an establishment or firm or, occasionally, at industry level. The management side is usually represented by senior executives whereas labour, if it is unionised, is represented by high-level union officials. Joint consultations take place according to regularly timed schedules in some firms, or whenever necessary in others.

Table 3.5. *Proportion of establishments with joint consultation systems by industry*

	%
All industries	55.7
Mining	57.0
Construction	43.0
Manufacturing	67.6
Electricity, gas & water	91.0
Transport & communication	65.0
Wholesale, retail & restaurants	49.0
Finance & insurance	58.7
Services	38.3

Source: Ministry of Labour (1995).

Japan experienced a bitter and prolonged period of industrial disputes in the 1940s and 1950s. Factory occupations by workers and lockouts were not uncommon and they culminated in the great strike in 1959–60 involving the Mitsui Coal Mining company at its Miike site. This was regarded as the most important battle between labour and employers. From this point in time, employees and employers started to be mutually conciliatory and to set up systems to ensure industrial peace and co-operation (Shimada, 1982). The joint consultation system was promoted as one of the instruments of union–management co-operation. The Japan Productivity Centre, with the support of the Ministry of International Trade and Industry, played an important role in promoting the system. The system was diffused first among large unionised firms and later to smaller non-unionised ones.

The practice of joint consultation is now in wide use: in 1993, the proportion of establishments with a joint consultation system was 55.7 per cent of sampled establishments with over fifty employees (Ministry of Labour, 1995). Perhaps more impressively, 31.6 per cent of establishments without unions had the joint consultation system. Table 3.5 shows the proportion of establishments with joint consultation systems by industrial sector. The situation is similar to that of union density: electricity/gas/water, manufacturing and finance/insurance have high proportions, while services and wholesale/retail have low ones. According to table 3.6, the larger the firm, the higher is the proportion of establishments with joint consultation systems. Over time, however, the joint consultation system has followed a declining path, similar to, but not as drastic as, that of unionisation. The density of joint consultation systems declined from 62.8 per cent in 1974 to 55.7 per cent in 1994 (Ministry of Labour, 1995).

The range of topics discussed within the joint consultation process is quite extensive, as shown in table 3.7. Depending on the type of establishment and the nature of the items under discussion, the degree of labour involvement varies from that of merely listening to management reporting to that of direct participation with an independent

Table 3.6. *Proportion of establishments with joint consultation systems by firm size*

Size of establishment	%
5,000 or more employees	72.4
1,000–4,999	68.4
300–999	62.2
100–299	47.6
50–99	49.0

Source: Ministry of Labour (1995).

voice. We can classify the functions of the joint consultation system in the following manner.

- It deals with routine items which employees are directly concerned with, but which are deemed to be unsuitable for bargaining; these would typically concern working conditions and welfare matters.
- It provides a platform on which to prepare for collective bargaining. This would include preliminary negotiations and opinion exchanges as to appropriate spring wage increases. Japanese management is often observed to inform the union on confidential business and financial information at the joint consultation meeting in order to obtain concessions in wage negotiations. The union obtains such information in the process of joint consultation, well in advance of collective bargaining (Shimada, 1983; Shirai, 1983; Nitta, 1984), and adjusts its demands.
- It provides a channel through which labour can obtain information and express views on such topics as basic management policies, investment, production and sales plans. As shown in table 3.7, compared to other items, the proportion of establishments consulting on these matters is relatively low. Even where such consultation does take place, labour involvement is often not particularly deep. Nonetheless, it is an important fact that more than half of establishments with the joint consultation system consult on such managerial matters.

3.3.2 The German works council

The German system of worker participation has some similarities to the Japanese joint consultation system.[16] It consists of two levels of participation, both of which are statutorily guaranteed. First, workers' representatives constitute half of the supervisory board membership of the firm. Secondly, employees in establishments with more than five employees set up works councils. Works councils have a wide range of participation rights: (i) the firm must inform the council of business and financial conditions of the firm; (ii) the council must be informed of and consulted over personnel planning and changes in work processes; (iii) the council has the right to veto individual staff movements; and (iv) the council has co-determination rights over workers' welfare matters. It

Table 3.7. *Proportion of establishments with particular items on agenda of joint consultation*

Item	%	Percentage breakdown for item			
		To be explained	Opinions to be collected	To be consulted	To be agreed
Management					
Basic management policies	53.7	71.6	11.1	13.1	4.2
Production and sales plans	55.4	65.8	10.0	19.9	4.3
Organisation restructuring	59.0	65.5	9.6	18.2	9.6
Introduction of new technology	55.9	45.8	18.8	28.1	7.3
Personnel matters					
Employment and staffing rules	51.9	58.3	14.7	21.3	5.6
Promotion rules	47.6	56.6	11.3	23.8	8.3
Transfers	62.9	41.2	12.3	33.4	13.1
Layoffs and dismissals	68.1	17.5	6.7	46.8	29.0
Working conditions					
Working mode	81.6	13.5	12.5	50.6	23.3
Working hours, rest time, holidays	86.8	13.0	8.4	52.7	25.9
Health and safety	83.4	12.2	19.4	59.1	9.3
Retirement	71.5	15.0	6.9	47.1	31.0
Wages and bonuses	75.3	17.9	4.6	45.2	32.3
Overtime wage rate	71.8	20.1	6.5	41.8	31.7
Retirement allowance and pension	69.2	18.6	4.9	44.8	31.7
Others					
Education and training	61.8	44.7	18.9	30.6	5.8
Employee welfare	80.4	18.2	22.3	50.7	8.9
Cultural and athletic activities	67.2	20.5	22.3	48.5	8.7
Childcare system	68.2	17.7	9.4	44.9	28.0

Source: Ministry of Labour (1995).

is estimated that about 70 per cent of the eligible workforce is covered by works councils. Many small establishments with fewer than 100 employees do not have works councils although statutorily required so to do (Mueller-Jentsch, 1995, p. 56). German works councils are similar to Japanese enterprise unions and the joint consultation system in that both blue-collar and white-collar workers are covered. On the other hand, the Japanese joint consultation system is a voluntary and private institution, in contrast to the statutory nature of the German works council. From a policy point of view, the advantage of the Japanese system is that, arguably, it avoids imposing unnecessary restrictions and inflexibilities on the labour market. The advantage of the German system is that it serves to enhance worker–management communication and encourages consultation more widely in the economy.

3.3.3 Effects of information-sharing

What are the consequences of the joint consultation system? Some studies (e.g. Morishima, 1991a, 1991b) have examined the effects of information-sharing, as practised in the joint consultation system, on firms' profitability, productivity, labour costs and wage negotiation processes. The basic hypothesis in these studies is that 'if information provided by management can convince the union and the employees that it is to their benefit to have a well-performing firm, the union and employees will be less likely to demand a share of the firms' profits that may hurt firm performance' (Morishima, 1991a, p. 472).[17] If this kind of goal alignment between labour and management occurs, workers not only restrain their wage demands, but they also are more motivated to work hard and less likely to shirk, so that productivity and profitability of the firm are enhanced.

The studies of Morishima utilise a Japanese survey on the joint consultation during the 1981 spring offensive. The data consist of ninety-seven union–firm pairs, and include an indicator showing how much information management gave the union. Using regression methods, Morishima tried to explain firms' profitability, productivity, wage levels, negotiation duration and numbers of negotiation rounds by means of several explanatory variables, such as the degree of information-sharing, as well as by firm and industry characteristics. According to the estimated results, the more the firm was engaged in information-sharing, the shorter and easier was the negotiation process. Moreover, unions tended to demand and accept lower wages, and the firm obtained higher productivity and profitability. The results are apparently in line with the hypothesis stated above.

In the United States, there exists no widely used equivalent to the Japanese joint consultation system or the German works councils. However, the National Labor Relations Act requires management to disclose certain types of financial information to the union in the process of collective bargaining. Furthermore, some recent surveys show that large US corporations share more business information with employees than is legally required (Lewin, 1984). Kleiner and Bouillon (1988) investigated the effects of a company providing production workers with information on its financial condition based on a survey of 106 US firms conducted in 1984. According to their results, information-sharing was positively related to the wage level and unrelated to productivity in both union and non-union firms, while it was negatively related to profits in non-union firms. It is difficult to account for these results. Why should management give confidential information only to be rewarded by higher wages or lower profits? Although the data coverage is somewhat thin, the results at least seem to suggest that there is a substantial difference in the role and significance of information-sharing between Japan and the United States, and also in the underlying employee–employer relationships.

Table 3.8. *Proportion of firms with small-group activities by industry and firm size*

	%
All industries	*47.9*
Mining	38.1
Construction	31.0
Manufacturing	57.9
Electricity, gas & water	87.9
Transport & communication	44.9
Wholesale, retail & restaurants	44.9
Finance & insurance	43.8
Services	40.5
	%
5,000 or more employees	69.6
1,000–4,999	60.8
300–999	51.4
100–299	41.3
50–99	39.3

Source: Ministry of Labour (1995).

3.4 Quality control circles

3.4.1 The system

Quality control circles (QCCs) represent another Japanese industrial relations institution where labour and management share information, and where labour's voice is heard. However, there is an important difference between QCCs and the more traditional institutions such as enterprise unions and joint consultation systems. The latter are indirectly related to the firm's production or business processes, whereas QCCs are a direct business tool designed to enhance the firm's productivity and profitability at the level of the workplace. Within small groups, workers routinely discuss ways to improve the quality of their work performances. Management provides information on business operations and shares some decision-making with workers while retaining managerial prerogatives.

Small-group activities, of which QCCs form the major part, are widely spread throughout different industries and various sizes of firms.[18] Table 3.8 reveals that electricity/gas/water industries have the highest densities of such activities, with manufacturing industries in second place; mining and construction have the lowest density. The distribution with respect to size follows a pattern similar to that for the density of unions and of joint consultation systems: the larger the establishment, the higher is the

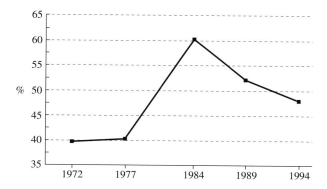

Fig. 3.11. Proportion of establishments with quality control circles, 1972–94. (*Source: Ministry of Labour, 1995*)

small-group density. This may well reflect the fact that the scale of larger firms produces a more cost-effective use of group participation. According to the survey, small-group activities existed in 54.5 per cent of unionised establishments and 41.5 per cent of non-union establishments. Their importance in both sectors is in line with the view that they are more related to direct business operations than to workers' demands on working conditions. Unions are not involved in small-group activities.

As shown in figure 3.11, the overall small-group density peaked at 60.2 per cent in 1984, and has since declined. The system probably reached maturity in the 1980s, and may have encountered some degree of apathy among workers. Again, this corresponds to the general pattern of union membership.

3.4.2 History[19]

The origin of QCCs can be traced to the occupation of Japan by the Allied forces after the Second World War. The Occupation authorities found that the low quality of Japanese products, especially in telephone communications, was a serious hindrance to the implementation of reconstruction policies in Japan.[20] For Japanese firms, it was vital to absorb techniques that would help improve their product standards. At first, this helped them to supply acceptable products to the Occupation military forces. Soon after, it became important for the Japanese economy to export its products overseas. This meant that it was necessary to dispel the low reputation of Japanese product quality in overseas markets. Japanese managers were trained in the theories and practices of American statistical quality control. More generally, industries embarked on a nationwide campaign to improve quality, inviting many American specialists to Japan and sending Japanese managers to the United States. A non-profit organisation set up in 1945, the Japanese Union of Scientists and Engineers (JUSE), played a key role in promoting and co-ordinating the quality control movement. In the course of diffusing American quality control, the Japanese grew to appreciate three important points:

(i) quality control is greatly enhanced if techniques and specific examples are discussed by small groups of employees;

(ii) quality problems are best tackled directly on the shop floor;

(iii) blue-collar workers are not only capable of participating in quality control but also best suited for conducting basic parts of it.

These developments constituted clear departures from the original American system in which quality control initiatives were seen as being mainly the prerogative of specialists. JUSE started to simplify the control methods and to popularise QCCs by such methods as issuing a quality control journal for use by foremen, broadcasting QC programmes and organising conferences.

In the event, QCCs were initiated and developed within Japanese firms and spread rapidly throughout Japanese industries. The concepts surrounding them were then exported overseas. QCCs became the first internationally recognised management tool created by the Japanese.

3.4.3 Significance of QCCs

Little research work has been undertaken into estimating the monetary gains derived from QCC activities,[21] although the persistent popularity of QCCs indirectly testifies as to their likely effectiveness. There are case studies that appear to show dramatic results – for example, Nitta (1984). However, there seems to be no systematic estimate of QCC impacts at aggregate industry or national levels, partly because of the lack of reliable data. The industrial implications of QCCs consist not only of the short-term monetary effects, but also of the long-term organisational impacts, which may have more profound implications for future prospects and even for the very nature of the firm itself.

Aoki (1988, 1990) presents a game-theoretic model of the Japanese economic system, in which horizontal co-ordination of operations at workplaces plays one of the key roles. QCCs are regarded as one of the most important institutions supporting such co-ordination. The focus on small-group operation facilitates speedy, autonomous and flexible responses to problems emerging in workplaces. It profoundly influences the business environments through its emphasis on team activities, the utilisation of on-site information, and also on intergroup communication and co-ordination. Horizontal information-sharing enables the firm to attain high degrees of efficiency, flexibility, responsibility and informational accuracy in its industrial performance. Cole (1992) points out another structural effect of QCCs. When problem-solving in QCCs is combined with group presentation and group competition, best-practice techniques for problem-solving are quickly diffused through all the workshops.

3.4.4 International comparisons

Cole (1989, 1992) has examined small-group activities in Japan, Sweden and the United States. During the early 1970s, Sweden tried to implement self-steering small work-groups at the workshop. The original ideas can be traced to the work of the Tavistock

Institute in England on group dynamics. The purpose of the small group in Sweden was 'to develop small work groups that maintained a high level of independence and autonomy . . . As a consequence, it was expected that jobs and learning possibilities would be enriched and individual responsibility increased. All this was to be achieved without any loss in productivity compared to conventional work organization' (Cole, 1992, p. 301). Great emphasis was given to the idea of industrial democracy, such as the freedom of workers from oppressive and arbitrary management controls. This Swedish idea, in connection with the co-determination law proposed at that time, was very popular among the mass media, unionists and scholars. However, emphasis was gradually shifted from democratisation to the improvement of productivity and quality in the implementation process by management. As a result, the movement lost its initial momentum.

There are two major differences between the Japanese QCCs and the Swedish small groups. First, Sweden emphasised the political idea of industrial democracy, whereas Japanese movements were mostly devoid of explicit political ideologies. Secondly, the purpose of Japanese QCCs was to increase quality standards and productivity. Productivity improvement was not of major concern in Sweden, at least at the outset of the orientation to small groups.

Although statistical quality control was developed in the United States, it did not grow within a small-group context as with the Japanese QCCs. Small-group application of the method had to be reimported later from Japan. One of the most important reasons why the United States did not progress along similar lines was its use of well-established organisational principles of functional specialisation. The American corporate system is very much based on clearly defined distinctions among functions. The job category of quality control specialists was implemented and its function was not to be infringed by other workers. On the other hand, Japanese workers have no clearly defined job territory and so they can participate directly in quality control. A closely related factor that prevented the development of the small-group system in the United States was the existence of rigid working rules and job demarcation in the workshop. The United States has a highly developed collective bargaining system in which a multitude of job demarcations and seniority rules covering promotion and layoff are rigidly specified, leaving limited room for managerial intervention. In contrast, Japan 'benefited' from its relatively late start in industrial relations; there were fewer vested interests and there was less resistance to restructuring existing working modes. The post-war environment was also favourable to change. The Occupation reform dissolved the dominating business groups called *zaibatsu* and purged many high-level managers. Democratic ideas were popularised. The barrier between white-collar and blue-collar workers was largely removed in the wartime national mobilisation campaign (Magota, 1965). Further, Japan had strong motivation to seek out new methods of work organisation in order to catch up with American and European economies.

3.5 Summary

This chapter has examined a number of major work and pay issues embraced by the Japanese industrial relations system. At the enterprise or establishment level, the enterprise union plays the key role in employer–employee relationships, and is supplemented by the joint consultation system for more routine communications. At the industrial or national level, various federations of enterprise unions are engaged in collective bargaining in the annual spring wage offensive, which critically influences the national level of wage changes. At the workplace level, workers and management share information as well as certain operational decisions through quality control circles.

If we compare the Japanese system of industrial relations with those of the United States or European countries, we notice that its core is biased more towards enterprises and workplaces. As we discussed above, this orientation is due largely to the historical fact that Japan started late in its industrialisation process and was better placed to formulate a system of industrial relations that was geared to the needs of workers and managers in large-scale modern corporations and their associated internal labour markets. Once hired as new employees of the firm, workers are placed into introductory training schemes, and proceed through various on-the-job and off-the-job training programmes throughout their career in the firm. In this way, employees and employers are engaged in intensive joint investments in human capital. Much of such investment has firm-specific characteristics. Therefore, industrial relations under such circumstances has itself evolved to be firm-specific.

More fundamentally, the differences in Japanese, European and US industrial relations are closely related to differences in their corporate governance structure. Aoki differentiated three models of decision-making in firms with three major constituents, namely shareholders (S), employees (E) and management (M). These are:

1 the *shareholders' sovereignty-cum-collective bargaining model*, in which M, acting as a surrogate of S, determines some of decision variables jointly with the representative of E (the union), and the rest of variables unilaterally;
2 the *participative management model*, in which the representatives of S (directors) and E make decisions jointly, or in which M makes decisions under the joint supervision of S and E;
3 the *corporative managerialism model*, in which neutral M makes decisions to integrate and mediate the interests of S and E. (Aoki, 1984, p. 126)

The first model corresponds to unionised sectors in the United States and Britain, the second to the German co-determination system, and the third to large corporations in Japan. In the Japanese type of employment system, workers are more deeply involved in information-sharing, decision-making and co-ordination of managerial operations. Therefore, the institutions of Japanese industrial relations reflect all these underlying shareholder–management–employer relationships in the firm.

The state of industrial relations may be in part reflected in labour dispute figures. Figure 3.12 shows the change in days lost owing to industrial disputes in Japan. The levels in the late fifties were rather high, reflecting the confrontational climate of the time. Again, in 1974 and 1975 the level soared because of the extreme economic disturbances during the first oil crisis. Since then, the level of disputes has been continuously and rapidly declining. These chronological changes in labour disputes seem consistent

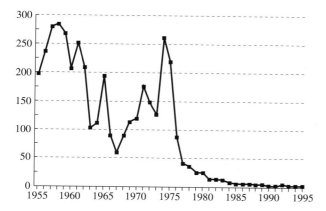

Fig. 3.12. Days lost through industrial disputes per 1,000 employees, 1955–95. (*Sources:* Number of days lost obtained from Ministry of Labour, Survey of Labour Disputes Statistics; number of employees from Ministry of Labour, Labour Force Survey.)

Table 3.9. *Days lost through industrial disputes: five-year average per 1,000 employees*

	Japan	USA	France	Germany	UK
1955–59	252.79	584.47	n.a.	65.48	210.93
1960–64	177.01	302.46	134.47	8.04	142.22
1965–69	109.47	542.52	145.31	6.83	172.32
1970–74	166.90	590.89	203.31	55.91	628.95
1975–79	81.36	429.42	194.85	49.91	508.58
1980–84	14.41	187.75	91.31	54.35	483.84
1985–89	5.22	86.31	41.49	2.05	180.10
1990–93	2.89	43.05	25.10	26.11	42.95

Notes:
USA: figures do not include disputes with fewer than 1,000 workers after 1981; France: 1960–64 figure on 1962 figure, 1965–69 figure on 1968 and 1969 figures, 1970–74 figure on 1970, 1971, 1973, 1974 figure and 1975–79 figure on 1975, 1977, 1978, 1979 figures; Germany refers to the former West Germany; All: 1990–93 figures are three year averages.
Sources: Days lost figures (apart from those for Japan) are obtained from ILO, Year Book of Labour Statistics. Number of employees figures come mainly from OECD Labour Force Statistics. US figures partly from Historical Statistics of the United States. German figures partly from German statistical Office, Lange Reihen zur Wirtschaftsentwicklung. UK figures from Office for National Statistics, Economic Trends. See the footnote of figure 3.12 for Japanese figures.

with the following story. As Japanese employers and employees searched initially for a new industrial relations framework to accompany economic reconstruction, they could not avoid communication breakdowns during the steeply rising section of the learning curve. Then the curve gradually levelled off as the parties learned to understand the benefits of compromise. They instituted a co-operative corporate system characterised by joint human capital investment and backed up by such institutions as enterprise unions, joint consultation systems and small quality control circles. Since joint investment in human capital by employers and employees takes a long time to complete, such effects will be felt in the long run, so that the low dispute levels experienced during the 1980s reflect the effects of much earlier joint investment. Table 3.9 compares the days lost internationally.[22] Up to the mid-1970s, the Japanese figures are not particularly low and on a par with French or UK levels; they are much lower than the US levels, but much higher than the German ones. Subsequently, however, days lost in Japan declined very rapidly to reach the lowest levels among all these countries by the start of the 1990s.

Notes

1   A discussion of business groups is outside the scope of our discussion. Odagiri (1992, ch. 7) provides a useful introduction to the topic.
2   Although, for political or other reasons, some enterprise unions do not belong to any industry federations.
3   Ministry of Labour, Basic Survey on Labour Unions.
4   Dore also emphasised the role of rapidly spread egalitarian ideas – backed by the authority of the Allied forces – in forming post-war Japanese employment practices.
5   We note that Blanchflower and Freeman (1992) find that the United States is an exception among industrialised countries in exhibiting clear union differentials in wages.
6   We note that Visser (1991, p. 100) warns of intercountry conceptual differences with such density statistics.
7   The UK and Japanese figures cannot be strictly compared because the smallest size class of UK data is truncated. However, the true differential should remain almost the same as shown here, because the proportion of British employees in the smallest firms is likely to be smaller than its Japanese counterpart.
8   See Freeman (1988) for methodological details.
9   This is an independent public sector institution designed to mediate over employee complaints.
10 Unions belonging to the same business group often form their own federations.
11 See the sources given for figure 3.6.
12 See Sano (1989) and Koike (1991) who comment on this similarity.
13 Koike (1962) was one of the earliest researchers to raise the question.
14 See, for example, the discussion and theoretical analysis of Felli and Harris (1996).
15 Sano *et al.* (1969) used this logic to explain steelmakers' tendencies to set the same wage increases at the same time in the spring offensive. In the spring offensive of 1997, managers of other companies were upset about a relatively high wage increase offered by Toyota, and criticised Toyota's 'selfishness'. Usually this kind of peer

pressure works very effectively in Japanese industries. Toyota's case is an exception, because Toyota is extremely strong compared with other car companies as well as with most other Japanese companies.

16 Several publications by Koike (1978, 1988, 1991) compare the German and Japanese systems.

17 It seems more likely that information-sharing is an indicator of underlying labour–management co-operation as a result of joint rent-sharing or joint firm-specific human capital investment, as discussed in chapter 2.

18 47.9 per cent of establishments with over fifty employees had small-group activities in 1994 (Ministry of Labour, 1995).

19 See Ishikawa (1981), Cole (1989) and Lillrank and Kano (1989).

20 Policy strategy from the Allies' viewpoint was not simply to aid the reconstruction of Japan, but also to use Japan as a strategic front against the spread of communism.

21 Lillrank and Kano (1989, ch. 4) provide a survey of some of the relevant literature.

22 A similar comparison was first done by Koike (1988). The figures shown here are only rough estimates, because the concepts and measurement of employees and days lost vary among countries. See the notes to table 3.9.

4 Labour costs

Much of the literature on labour compensation confines its attention almost exclusively to wages and other direct forms of remuneration. In a Japanese context, such payments consist of regular wages and bonus payments and are referred to, collectively, as cash earnings. Yet, expenditure on labour also encompasses non-wage labour costs (NWLCs). These cover a broad range of statutory and voluntary costs incurred by the firm. Not only are NWLCs quantitatively important, but their share of total cost has risen through time and their incidence is highly variable across different categories of workers.

We have four main aims in this chapter:

- to investigate the relative importance of the full range of labour cost items in Japan incorporating various breakdowns by industry;
- to examine changes in the composition of costs through time;
- to compare Japanese labour costs with comparable costs in the United States and European countries;
- to attempt a brief rationalisation of the underlying causes of NWLCs.

In general, our objective here is to assess labour costs within a broad, comparative setting. More detailed analyses and discussions of several of the cost categories are contained in later chapters.

4.1. Structure and trends in Japanese labour costs

Table 4.1 shows the structure of labour costs in Japanese manufacturing industries over the period from 1965 to 1995.

Direct remuneration is given by cash earnings, consisting of regular wages and bonus payments. Cash earnings take up the largest share of total labour costs; they accounted for 82.3 per cent in 1995. However, their share decreased over the period

Table 4.1. *Labour costs in manufacturing industries, 1965–95*

	Total labour costs (av. monthly cost per worker in yen)	As percentage of total labour costs							
		Cash earnings	Bonuses (as a percentage of cash earnings)	Severance payments	Statutory welfare costs	Non-statutory welfare costs	Training costs	Recruitment costs	Other labour costs
1965	42,022	86.30	15.32	2.56	4.73	4.50	0.35	0.32	1.24
1968	58,550	86.15	15.04	2.67	5.08	3.95	0.30	0.53	1.33
1971	91,886	86.42	18.01	2.81	5.06	4.07	0.28	0.42	0.94
1973	121,647	86.63	16.81	2.82	5.13	3.86	0.29	0.48	0.80
1976	214,837	85.68	18.39	3.58	6.12	3.42	0.23	0.18	0.79
1979	276,391	84.33	17.58	4.34	6.80	3.15	0.25	0.16	0.97
1982	329,997	84.17	18.50	3.73	7.55	3.04	0.32	0.16	1.03
1985	365,918	84.27	18.24	3.99	7.60	3.10	0.34	0.17	0.52
1988	397,398	83.68	17.82	4.31	7.89	2.84	0.38	0.22	0.68
1991	457,976	82.71	19.12	4.06	8.44	3.05	0.34	0.39	1.01
1995	488,640	82.26	22.33	4.87	8.87	3.09	0.23	0.11	0.58

Notes:

Cash earnings include bonuses, and the bonus percentage is of cash earnings. Data obtained from Ministry of Labour, General Survey of Wages and Working Hours System; Ministry of Labour, Labour Cost Survey; Ministry of Labour, Basic Survey of Wage Structure.

Table 4.2. *Changes in age, tenure and gender of employees,*
1965 and 1991

	1965	1991
	%	%
All industries		
Over 40 years of age	23.17	47.16
Over 15 years of service	13.55	30.21
Male proportion	69.55	68.74
Manufacturing		
Over 40 years of age	22.88	51.38
Over 15 years of service	11.11	36.06
Male proportion	66.66	70.92

Note:
Regular employees working in establishments with more than
ten regular employees.
Source: Ministry of Labour, Basic Survey of Wage Structure.

covered, reducing by 4 per cent. By implication, the importance of NWLCs has been
increasing over time, a trend that has been observed in most industrialised countries.
While cash earnings fell in their share of total labour costs, bonus payments increased
their share by 7 per cent. In fact, bonuses grew to an average of 22.3 per cent of total
labour costs in 1995. The payment of bonuses on this scale is a uniquely Japanese phenomenon and we devote the whole of chapter 5 to a discussion of this topic.

Why did the relative shares of regular wages and bonuses move in opposite directions
between 1965 and 1995? One clue may be provided by the data shown in table 4.2. These
reveal that the proportions of older workers and workers with longer tenure increased
significantly over these post-war years. (See also the discussion in relation to table 1.3 in
chapter 1.) As discussed in detail in chapter 5, an important argument advanced to
explain the Japanese bonus system is that bonuses represent the returns to workers'
investment in firm-specific human capital. In chapter 2, we explain how the accrual of
such investments is closely related to workers' length of tenure.

Returning to table 4.1, statutory welfare costs are the largest item of non-wage labour
costs. These costs are dominated by employers' state-enforced contributions to pensions
and health insurance. They comprised 8.9 per cent of total costs in 1995, a 4.1 per cent
increase in their overall share since 1965. A main influence on this increase is again illus-
tratred in table 4.2, that is the relative rise in the proportion of older workers. This cost
category accounts for most of the increase in total non-wage labour costs, a feature
shared in common with many other industrialised countries. Non-statutory welfare
costs, consisting of pensions and other fringe benefits privately provided by employers,
were less than half the aggregate size of statutory costs in 1995. Moreover, in stark contrast to statutory costs, non-statutory costs declined steadily from the mid-1960s; their

share decreased by 1.4 per cent over the entire period. Very tentatively, the opposing trends of statutory and non-statutory costs may suggest that the two categories act as substitutes within total welfare provision. Severance payments constitute the second largest non-wage cost. Their share rose by 2.3 per cent over the period, again almost certainly a natural consequence of an ageing working population. There were no significant changes in training costs, recruitment costs and other labour costs over the covered period. A detailed analysis of recruitment costs is presented in chapter 6, together with a little more discussion of training costs.

With minor variations, the foregoing observations for manufacturing industry with respect to cash earnings and NWLCs also apply to total industries. Breakdowns for the period 1973 to 1995 are shown in table 4.3.

Table 4.4 shows the variations in labour costs among industries for 1995. The electricity, gas and water industry appears to be the place to try to obtain a job in Japan. It incurs markedly higher average total labour costs than the other industries. It enjoys a high bonus share as well as high non-wage benefits. In this latter respect, it has the highest non-statutory welfare and training costs. This is much to do with the nature of the industry: it consists of large, tightly regulated firms that enjoy regional monopoly positions. Stable monopolistic profits are shared with workers in the form of high wages, bonuses and private fringe benefits.

It is well known that firm size significantly affects the structure of labour costs (e.g. Woodbury, 1983). Table 4.5 shows the labour cost categories broken down by five size ranges for 1995. Average labour costs of the largest firms (5,000 employees and over) were 1.8 times more than those of the small firms (30 to 99 employees). Moreover, larger firms incur higher payments in categories other than regular wages; this is especially the case for bonuses, severance payments, voluntary welfare provisions and training costs. As far as private fringe benefits are concerned, large firms are able to obtain group discounts and larger numbers of employees ensure lower per-worker costs of administration.

4.2 International cost comparisons

What are main characteristics of Japanese labour costs in comparison with those of their European and US counterparts? Strict comparison is not easy, not least because each country has its own unique employment practices and institutions. Furthermore, countries differ over definitions and classifications of labour costs; this is a particularly serious problem with respect to the United States in comparison with our other included countries. This section does not attempt to adjust official statistics to facilitate exact comparisons but, rather, tries to characterise the main differences by matching similar items in official statistics as closely as possible.[1] More specifically, table 4.6 summarises our classification of costs and its correspondence to cost definitions in the different countries.

Figure 4.1 compares the proportions of NWLCs for manufacturing industries in the United Kingdom, Germany, France, the United States and Japan between 1965 and

Table 4.3. *Labour costs in total industries, 1973–95*

	Total labour costs (av. monthly cost per worker in yen)	As percentage of total labour costs								
		Cash earnings	*Bonuses (as a percentage of cash earnings)*	Severance payments	Statutory welfare costs	Non-statutory welfare costs	Training costs	Recruitment costs	Other labour costs
1973	122,505	86.81	*16.20*	2.84	5.17	3.68	0.28	0.40	0.81
1976	218,379	85.98	*19.65*	3.32	6.23	3.18	0.27	0.18	0.83
1979	278,968	84.81	*18.24*	3.90	6.91	2.91	0.28	0.18	1.01
1982	328,476	84.38	*18.41*	3.57	7.63	2.81	0.32	0.19	1.10
1985	361,901	84.58	*18.38*	3.90	7.67	2.77	0.34	0.18	0.57
1988	398,115	83.80	*17.58*	4.15	7.87	2.78	0.38	0.29	0.72
1991	459,986	83.17	*17.82*	4.01	8.43	2.90	0.36	0.43	1.13
1995	483,009	82.95	*22.19*	4.26	8.87	2.83	0.27	0.15	0.66

Notes:
See table 4.1.

Table 4.4. *Labour costs by industries, 1995*

	Total labour costs (av. monthly cost per worker in yen)	Cash earnings	Bonuses (as a percentage of cash earnings)	Severance payments	Statutory welfare costs	Non-statutory welfare costs	Training costs	Recruitment costs	Other labour costs
						As percentage of total labour costs			
Mining	546,224	78.00	20.60	8.31	9.52	3.18	0.31	0.08	0.59
Construction	545,883	83.47	20.59	3.19	9.83	2.55	0.27	0.10	0.58
Manufacturing	488,640	82.26	22.34	4.87	8.87	3.09	0.23	0.11	0.58
Electricity, gas & water	740,781	75.61	26.95	8.66	8.64	5.35	1.06	0.05	0.62
Transport & communication	497,568	83.81	19.54	3.80	9.88	1.77	0.16	0.12	0.45
Wholesale & retail	428,200	83.98	22.35	3.72	8.43	2.50	0.34	0.22	0.79
Finance & insurance	626,025	82.11	28.53	4.82	7.77	3.57	0.31	0.18	1.25
Real estate	504,779	83.63	22.45	3.39	8.66	2.93	0.27	0.32	0.80
Services	405,811	84.49	21.87	2.95	8.64	2.70	0.27	0.29	0.65

Notes:
See table 4.1.

Table 4.5. *Labour costs by firm size: manufacturing, 1995*

Firm size (number of employees)	Total labour costs (av. monthly cost per worker in yen)	Cash earnings	Bonuses (as a percentage of cash earnings)[a]	As percentage of total labour costs					
				Severance payments	Statutory welfare costs	Non-statutory welfare costs	Training costs	Recruitment costs	Other labour costs
over 5,000	632,222	80.08	26.25	5.95	8.42	4.45	0.24	0.08	0.79
1,000–4,999	558,370	81.94	26.25	5.05	8.49	3.49	0.28	0.12	0.61
300–999	472,940	83.04	22.18	4.89	8.96	2.22	0.23	0.13	0.54
100–299	392,064	84.06	16.25	4.06	9.29	1.88	0.19	0.13	0.39
30–99	349,536	84.83	16.25	3.04	9.88	1.70	0.14	0.10	0.30

Notes:
See table 4.1.
[a] Bonus data are from Basic Survey of Wage Structure and are classified by three firm sizes: over 1,000 employees, 100–999 and 10–99.
Sources: Ministry of Labour, General Survey on Wages and Working Hours System; Ministry of Labour, Basic Survey of Wage Structure.

Table 4.6. *Matching labour cost items*

Our classification	Japan	EC	USA
Cash earnings	Cash earnings	Direct earnings	Payroll
Bonuses	Bonuses	Bonuses and premiums	n.a. (included in misc. benefit payments)
Payment for days not worked	n.a.	Payment for days not worked	Paid rest periods, etc. + payment for days not worked
Severance payment	Cost of severance pay	Severance pay	n.a.
Statutory welfare costs	Legal welfare expenses	Legal social security	Legally required payments
Non-statutory welfare costs	Non-legal welfare costs	Customary social security	Retirement and savings plan payments + life insurance and death benefit payments + medically related benefit payments
Training costs	Cost of education	Vocational training	Education expenditures
Other labour costs	Other labour costs + payments in kind + cost of recruitment	Other expenditure + taxes + payment in kind − subsidies	Miscellaneous benefit payments − education expenditures

Sources: Japan: Ministry of Labour, General Survey on Wages and Working Hours System and Basic Survey of Wage Structure; EC: Eurostat, Labour Cost Survey; USA: US Chamber Research Center, Employee Benefits.

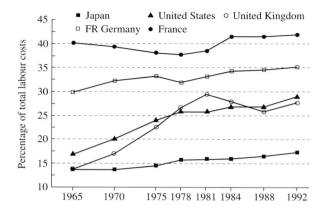

Fig. 4.1. Non-wage labour costs by country: manufacturing industry, 1965–92. (*Sources:* Japan: Ministry of Labour, General Survey on Wages and Hours System; EC: Eurostat, Labour Cost Survey; United States: US Chamber Research Center, Employee Benefits.)

1992. There are three distinct groups of countries: France and Germany have relatively very high proportions of NWLCs, Japan has the lowest, and the USA and the UK lie somewhere in the middle. These last two countries did experience relatively steep growth in NWLCs up to the beginning of the 1980s, from which time they have levelled off.[2]

Tables 4.7 and 4.8 present comparisons of labour costs in the above countries for, respectively, all industries and manufacturing industry. There are a number of important distinctions between Japan and the other countries. One of these is that the proportion of Japanese cash earnings (regular payments plus bonuses) is much larger than those of European countries and the United States for both total industries and the manufacturing industry group. In other words, as already seen in figure 4.1, Japanese NWLCs make up a lower proportion of total labour costs. Another clear distinction between Japan and elsewhere is that the share of bonuses within total costs in Japan far exceeds the corresponding European and US proportions.[3] It is also interesting to note that French and German bonuses are far larger than in the UK and the USA.

One of the most conspicuous characteristics of Japanese labour cost statistics is that they do not contain payments for days not worked. Japanese paid holiday costs were estimated by Hart *et al.* (1988), and it was found that paid holiday costs were about 2.3 per cent of the total labour costs on average over the period from 1965 to 1985. Since there has been no substantial change in the number of paid holidays in Japan, this estimate is likely to hold also for the late 1990s. In this event, the cost of paid holidays constitutes one of the most significant differences between Japanese and European/US labour costs.[4] Conservatively, payments for days not worked in Germany and France, at between 10 and 11 per cent of total labour costs, account for over four times the proportion of comparable costs in Japan.

Three other international cost distinctions are worthy of comment. First, there are

Table 4.7. *Structure of labour costs in Europe, USA and Japan: all industries (percentages)*

	UK (1992)	Germany (1992)	France (1992)	USA (1992)	Japan (1991)
Cash earnings	70.92	56.44	48.71	71.33	64.17
Bonuses	1.09	7.91	9.68	—	19.00
Payment for days not worked	7.91	10.93	10.00	9.27	—
Severance payment	2.40	1.27	0.98	—	4.01
Statutory welfare costs	7.55	14.53	21.65	6.56	8.43
Non-statutory welfare costs	3.78	3.74	6.84	12.05	2.90
Training costs	1.62	1.54	1.03	0.14	0.43
Other labour costs	4.79	3.75	2.08	0.64	1.56
Total	100	100	100	100	100

Sources: See table 4.6.

Table 4.8. *Structure of labour costs in Europe, USA and Japan: manufacturing industry (percentages)*

	UK (1992)	Germany (1992)	France (1992)	USA (1992)	Japan (1991)
Cash earnings	71.38	56.63	48.14	70.82	63.59
Bonuses	1.13	8.10	10.07	—	19.12
Payment for days not worked	8.15	11.04	8.63	9.42	—
Severance payment	2.37	1.54	1.12	—	4.06
Statutory welfare costs	7.50	14.04	21.76	6.52	8.44
Non-statutory welfare costs	3.62	3.57	7.00	12.54	3.05
Training costs	1.38	1.45	1.15	0.14	0.34
Other labour costs	4.53	3.74	1.64	0.64	1.40
Total	100	100	100	100	100

Sources: See table 4.6.

significant differences in the proportions of statutory welfare costs among the countries. This element in France and Germany dwarfs the corresponding proportions in the other countries. The Japanese proportion is larger than in the UK and the US and this serves to counteract slightly the relatively low Japanese non-statutory costs. Secondly, the Japanese proportion of severance payments within total cost is considerably larger than those of other countries. Again, this tends to offset the relatively small proportion of non-statutory costs in Japan.[5] Finally, Japanese training costs are a smaller proportion of total labour costs than in European countries. However, it does not follow that Japanese firms spend less on vocational training. Japanese firms give greater emphasis to on-the-job rather than off-the-job training, and the former type of training cost is not reflected in these statistics (see also section 6.2).

4.3 Why do firms incur non-wage labour costs?

Human capital and internal labour markets

The labour force at any given point in time is characterised by a wide range of skills, many of which have been accumulated over considerable time periods. Human capital is formed not only by schooling but also by training within firms. One of the main characteristics of the Japanese employment system is the emphasis on firm-specific human capital investment.[6] Such skill formation generates specific associated labour costs. First, recruitment cost involves the search for and selection of new workers who are deemed to be suitable for firms' training programmes. Secondly, actual training – both on and off the job – requires expenditure on training staff, physical training facilities, teaching materials and other specialist equipment. Thirdly, where training is successful, human capital investments yield positive returns. As highlighted in chapter 2, these may be shared by the firm with employees, and such shares may be realised by workers in the form of wage supplements and bonuses. This aspect will be considered empirically in chapter 5.

Scale and scope economies in welfare provision

Part of employees' non-wage compensation may arise because firms can offer special low-cost services. For example, insurance policies can be tailor-made for reasonably homogeneous groups of employees so as to take advantage of lower premiums due to group discounts. Also, where relatively large numbers of employees are involved, a wider scope of provision is possible and this in itself may generate additional demand. This is an important factor in the explanation of size differentials in NWLC provision in Japan and elsewhere. Smaller companies cannot take advantage of scale and scope economies in private welfare provision, although some small firms try to overcome this comparative disadvantage by forming wider associations.

Tax incentives

Often fringe benefits are taxed at relatively low rates, if at all. This creates strong incentives for the firm and its employees to increase the proportion of fringe benefits within total compensation. In Japan, non-statutory welfare expenditure is treated as a corporate cost for tax purposes and is supposed to be taxed as part of employees' income. However, a small amount of corporate welfare income is exempt from tax. Further, taxation coverage is rather incomplete at the employee level owing to technical difficulties in taxing individual fringe benefits and because welfare income is relatively small.

Worker and union preferences

Special company-level deals and/or tax breaks may lead workers, at the margin, to prefer fringe payments to ordinary cash payments. Unions may act to facilitate such preferences. For the United States, Mitchell (1980) found that employees of unionised establishments received over three times the level of private fringe benefits paid to those of non-unionised establishments. In general, unionisation has been found to be associated with higher proportions of fringe benefits within total compensation (Lester, 1967; Freeman, 1981;Woodbury, 1983). In particular, Freeman (1981) found that unions tended to obtain particular benefits such as pensions, insurance cover and holiday pay which favour senior workers.

How do we link unionisation, senior workers and fringe benefits? Given that pensions and holiday pay often involve elements of deferred compensation, senior workers are likely to benefit most from such payments. As their length of service with the firm increases, they are likely to place greater emphasis on fringe payments within their total compensation package. That they will be supported strongly by unions in this objective is consistent with the so-called median voter model of union behaviour. Unions are more likely to bargain harder over issues that are particularly important to recurring union voters. Senior workers with relatively long service would be a prime target constituency. These workers stand to gain more from compensation packages with a strong emphasis on pension, health insurance and holiday payments than younger workers who have higher short-term expected quit propensities.

As a related exercise, we carried out a simple regression analysis based on a set of 1991 data for nineteen Japanese industries. We hypothesise that the level of non-statutory NWLCs as a proportion of total labour costs (measured in natural logarithms) is explained by average age, average length of tenure, the proportion of employees who are university graduates, the proportion of workers in large firms (i.e. over 1,000 employees), the proportion of male workers and union density. The results are shown in table 4.9. They are consistent with the view that fringe benefits are positively related to workers' ages and lengths of tenure. In other words, senior workers do appear to obtain more voluntary welfare cover. We also find that firm size relates positively to the proportion of non-statutory NWLCs within total compensation. This finding accords with previous research (Freeman, 1981; Woodbury, 1983) and is consistent with the view that, because of scale advantages, large firms are better equipped to absorb the fixed costs of implementing and running pension and other insurance schemes. Also, large firms offer more avenues of progression for upwardly mobile employees and this would tend to reinforce the demand for fringe payments involving deferred compensation. Neither gender nor the degree of unionisation displays significant effects on the ratio of non-statutory NWLCs to total labour costs. These findings may simply reflect aggregation bias. In the case of unionisation, however, the nature of institutions that consult between employers and employees is quite diverse in Japan, and many non-unionised firms have their own institutional channels for communicating workers' preferences.

Demographic factors

Labour costs are strongly influenced by demographic factors. Figure 4.2 shows historic and forecasted demographic trends in Japan between 1960 and 2020. A relatively stable proportion of 20–64-year-olds within the total population between 1970 and 2000 is

Table 4.9. *Fringe benefits and unionisation, 1991: OLS regression results*

Variables	Coefficients	*t*-ratios
Constant	−5.608	−5.19
Average age	0.0502	1.70
Average tenure	0.0975	2.70
Proportion of university graduates among total employees	1.5348	1.99
Proportion of workers in large firms among total employees	1.1007	1.80
Proportion of male workers among total employees	−0.3603	−0.81
Union density	−0.7587	−1.36

Note:
Dependent variable: Log (non-statutory non-wage labour costs/total labour costs);
$R^2 = 0.760$; Number of Observations = 19.
Industries included: mining, construction, textile, paper, printing, chemical, rubber, steel, non-ferrous metal, metal products, general machinery, electric machinery, vehicle, sales, utilities, transport & communication, finance & insurance, real estate, services.
Sources: Ministry of Labour, General Survey on Wages and Working Hours System (for various labour costs); Union Survey (for union membership); Basic Survey of Wage Structure (for all other data).

forecast to be followed by decline over the next twenty years (from 62 per cent to 53 per cent of the total). There has been a marked decline in the birth rate in the last three decades, resulting in a fall between 1960 and 2000 from 40 per cent to 21 per cent in the proportion of persons under the age of 20. The proportion of persons over the age of 65 has risen, and is projected to rise, over the entire period, from 6 per cent in 1960 to 26 per cent in 2020. In summary, the Japanese labour market is experiencing, and will continue to experience, a particularly serious problem of a growing post-retirement cohort of individuals funded by a proportionately shrinking cohort of economically active persons.

What accounts for these demographic trends? After World War II, Japan experienced a large baby boom as people readjusted towards normal lifestyles. However, as living standards rose in line with exceptional economic growth rates, the birth rate started to decline markedly. In line with this trend, the average age of marriage also increased and the number of those who remained unmarried throughout their lives grew. The total fertility rate started to drop steadily and went below the level of population replacement. At the same time, enhanced living standards together with improved medical services greatly reduced death rates and increased life expectancy. Immediately after the war, average longevity in Japan was relatively low among the advanced industrial countries. In the intervening period, it has grown to be the highest in the world. The ageing population is exerting an inexorably rising upward pressure on the provision of pensions, severance payments and medical care. The combined demographic trends have served to increase welfare costs in relation to total labour costs and this process will continue for several decades.

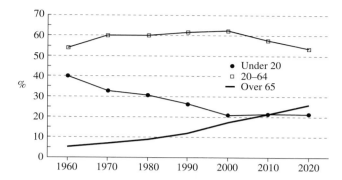

Fig. 4.2. Population structure, Japan, 1960–2020. (*Source:* Ministry of Health, 1996, p. 8.)

The government has reacted by attempting to rationalise and restructure the national pension system, integrating different pension schemes for various groups and adjusting pension payments and contributions. However, it cannot stem the tide of increasing welfare contributions by workers, enterprises and governments. Statutory and non-statutory welfare contributions as a proportion of total labour costs are bound to increase further. In fact, the effect of these adverse demographic trends has been exacerbated by recent extremely low interest rates and stagnating share prices which have led many corporate pension funds to run into financial difficulties. Some companies have had to meet fund shortfalls from their operating profits, and some pension funds have had to dissolve.[7]

The health insurance system faces similar problems. The system consists of health insurance unions organised in large firms[8] and a government-operated insurance scheme for workers in small businesses. Both have recently incurred large deficits: 77,400 million yen for the health unions and 280,000 million yen for the government-operated health insurance scheme in 1994.[9] Although the Japanese health insurance payroll tax rate (8.4 per cent on average) is still low compared with European levels (13.3 per cent for Germany and 19.4 per cent for France in 1994), a substantial increase will be inevitable in the future. This will result from the combined effect of (i) smaller than expected increases in payroll taxes in recent years due to a lack of growth in employment and pay levels, and (ii) substantially increased expenditures on medical services, due especially to the rapidly rising costs of care for the elderly.

Differences between Japanese demographic trends on the one hand and those of other major industrialised economies on the other are particularly apparent when viewed in a somewhat longer-term perspective. Figure 4.3 shows the change in importance of the over-65 year old population in Japan, the United States, the United Kingdom and France between the years 1900 and 2020. Over this period, these and other economies have experienced a series of common population transitions. They have moved from (i) a period of relatively high birth and death rates to (ii) a period of high birth rate and low death rate to (iii) a period of low birth and death rates. Japan has been no exception to

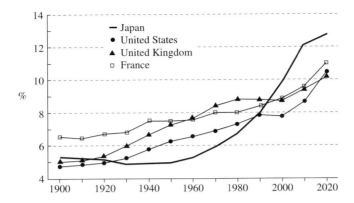

Fig. 4.3. Proportion of population over 65 by country, 1900–2020. (*Source:* Ministry of Health, 1996, p. 8.)

these progressions; its difference, however, lies in the fact that it experienced these transitions in a relatively short time span. Thus, from enjoying a relatively youthful population throughout the first two-thirds of the current century, it will have the highest proportion of retired people by the turn of the century.

Policy stances of nations

Perceived economic and social relationships among workers, employers and governments within each nation strongly influence both the mode and the incidence of welfare costs. The level and structure of NWLCs will be strongly influenced by the resulting policy stances of each nation. Generally speaking, there seem to exist three distinctive approaches to welfare provision: these are (i) the Anglo-American market-oriented principle, (ii) the mainland Western European emphasis on the role of government in mediating over national consensus between employers and employees, and (iii) the Japanese approach which is based on private level agreement between employers and employees coupled with governmental guidance. This area is discussed in relation to union structures in chapter 3.

4.4 Relative labour market implications of cost structures

On the face of it, the structure of labour costs across the five countries shown in table 4.7 is very diverse. The UK and the USA place significantly more weight on regular wages within total labour costs than the other three countries. The USA has almost twice the proportion of private fringe payments as the next highest country. France and Germany place relatively great stress on legally required welfare costs. The share of Japanese bonus payments is over twice that of France and Germany and well beyond the experience of the USA, the UK and most other industrialised nations. Severance payments in Japan are also relatively more important within total labour costs.

Do these cost differences necessarily signify contrasting private and public strategies towards labour market incentives? This is a difficult area to evaluate because it involves knowledge of the roles played by each of the major cost categories. The extent and direction of divergence between Japanese costs and those elsewhere hinges considerably on the aims and objectives that lie behind bonus payments. If bonuses represent close substitutes for regular wages – and there is a body of opinion that supports this view – then this would mean that Japan is at the top of the league in its emphasis on direct wage payments within total compensation. Essentially, this would mean that the Japanese cost structure is differentiated from elsewhere merely in the degrees of emphasis it places on wages and holiday pay as well as on statutory and non-statutory welfare provisions.

A radically different interpretation of the bonus system, however, suggests that the Japanese cost structure has a distinctive feature. This links bonus payments in Japan with labour fixity. Fixed labour costs are per-worker labour costs which only change with the number of workers employed. Recruitment and training costs are the classical examples of fixed costs. Variable costs, in contrast, are directly related to the length of per-period working time. Regular wages and overtime premium payments fall into this category. Where relatively high levels of fixed costs exist, industries are likely to adjust employment only sluggishly to changes in market conditions. As long as firms are able to meet the variable costs of marginal workers, then it may make economic sense to retain their labour service during recessionary periods, at least in the short run. Fixed costs of recruitment and training are sunk costs and will be lost to the firm, in the absence of subsequent re-hiring, if quits or layoffs occur during downturns in economic activity. As we discuss in chapters 2 and 7, this has implications for work-sharing and for labour hoarding. On the face of it, however, Japan's degree of labour fixity is no different from elsewhere. Certainly, recruitment and training costs do not appear to be on a significantly larger scale in Japan. Further, the bulk of payroll taxes in all countries represent variable costs, as do private fringe benefits. As discussed in chapter 5, bonuses in Japan may reflect workers' shares in the returns to specific human capital investments by firms. Their relative importance within total costs may reflect, in part, that per capita specific investments are higher in Japan than elsewhere. In terms of magnitude, there is nothing in Europe or the USA that matches the Japanese bonus system. If this interpretation is correct, then bonuses may reflect a unique Japanese labour market characteristic of firms and workers sharing rents derived from specific investments in order to encourage such features as long tenure, commitment and effort, and a sense of shared risk-taking and reward.

Another distinctive feature of Japanese labour costs is that statutory welfare payments are relatively small when viewed in an international perspective. In most European countries, for example, statutory social welfare contributions constitute the largest individual component of NWLCs in the typical firm. Contributions take the form of taxes on that section of the firm's payroll that lies between legislatively prescribed lower and upper wage limits. Tax rates have tended to grow systematically through time and, especially in recent times, upper limits have grown faster than average wages in several countries or have been removed completely. In part, such growth rates have occurred in order to meet the growing demand for resources to finance pay-as-you-go state pensions, health provision and unemployment benefits. As we saw in section 4.3, one historical reason for the low statutory welfare costs in Japan has been its relatively young population structure compared with Europe. This explanation has been radically undermined in recent times as the demographics of an ageing population combined with a declining birth rate have caused Japan to face steeply rising welfare costs. Due to these pressures, Japan's favourable statutory cost differentials with other countries have been declining and show strong indications of reducing further in the coming decades.

One distinctive Japanese feature remains, however. Japan has been more reluctant than most countries to adopt legislative approaches to welfare problems. This policy stance reflects a far greater than average emphasis on establishing modes of consensus between employers and employees at the level of the firm and without outside interference.

Notes

1 For other international comparative studies of labour costs, see Hart (1984), Organisation for Economic Co-operation and Development (1986), Tachibanaki (1987a), Hart *et al.* (1988) and Inoki (1995).
2 These data have considerable bearing on the European debate within the UK in recent years and support the contention that the UK enjoys a competitive cost advantage with respect to NWLCs.
3 US bonuses were between 1.2 per cent and 0.6 per cent of wages and salaries during the period from 1955 to 1992 according to US Chamber Research Center (1993, p. 33).
4 Some authors suggest that Japanese payments for days not worked cannot be compared with the US or European countries owing to the lack of Japanese paid holiday information. However, even if paid holidays were ignored this would not bias the comparison significantly since the proportion of total costs accounted for by paid holidays is almost certainly rather small.
5 Since European non-statutory welfare costs consist largely of retirement-related contributions by employers, Japanese severance payments correspond closely to these costs.
6 See, for example, Koike (1988) and Hashimoto (1990).
7 *Yomiuri Shimbun*, 20 May 1996.
8 Health insurance unions are organised and operated by firms with over 300 employees under a statutory framework. Both employers and employees are insurants. In principle, they share the costs equally. In practice, there is room for employers to pay the larger share; the average employer–employee ratio was 57:43 in 1995.
9 Nihonkeizai Shimbun, 12 July 1996.

5 **The bonus system**

It has already been established that Japanese bonus payments are significantly larger than in Europe or the United States. Tables 4.7 and 4.8 contain the key comparative international details. This is a unique and important labour market phenomenon and, accordingly, the whole of this chapter is devoted to this topic.

5.1 Hypotheses

Profit-sharing within modern Japanese industrial organisations may have deep roots in centuries of agrarian village life where communities realised the advantages of mutual support, co-operative effort and risk-sharing.[1] Over a shorter time span, there is some evidence of links between sharing practices in traditional family businesses in the late nineteenth/early twentieth centuries and the more systematic adoption of bonuses for permanent employees by capitalist enterprises of the post-war period. Initially, bonuses tended to be confined to company executives and only later extended to both blue- and white-collar workers (see Taira, 1970; Dore, 1973; Iwata, 1992). However, we are concerned here not so much with the evolution of the bonus system, but rather with attempts to understand its role within the total compensation structure of the modern firm.

5.1.1 The bonus as a disguised regular wage

As pointed out by Ito (1992), there are several reasons why we might expect, *a priori*, that Japanese bonuses are essentially disguised wages. First, like wages, many bonuses are determined annually or biannually. From a bargaining perspective, it might reasonably be assumed that annual wages and bonuses are negotiated on the basis of broadly similar performance indicators, including profitability. The parties at the bargaining table are also likely to take into account, with respect to both wages and bonuses, the current economic climate. The prospects for outside job opportunities at improved remuneration may also influence agreements over both forms of compensation. Secondly, a typical worker fully expects to receive a significant bonus at each compensation round. In the case of government officials, 'the "bonus scale" is as rigid as the wage scale' (Ito, 1992, p. 236).

This raises an obvious question. If bonuses play essentially the same role as regular wages, then why do firms and workers burden themselves with the extra complexity of bargaining over two forms of compensation? One answer may be that, while bonuses are determined in a similar fashion to regular wages, they have additional fiscal advantages (Brunello and Ohtake, 1987). In the first place, in the calculation of employers' contributions to social security, bonuses are not included as part of the payroll on which the tax is based. Secondly, bonuses serve to reduce corporate tax because companies can use the tax-saving bonus allowance system. Thirdly, for workers who have passed the official age of retirement, the tax treatment of bonuses is more favourable than wages in relation to pension payments; accordingly, older workers gain through a higher bonus-to-wage ratio.[2] Clearly, where there exist tax advantages – to either the firm or its workers – in opting for bonus-related pay then it may well be in the interest of management and workers to bargain for bonuses and to share the resulting joint tax gains. The subject of how the choice of compensation system – that is, regular wages versus profit-sharing – can be influenced by the tax structure is developed theoretically by Hart and Moutos (1995) via a firm–union bargaining model.

Explanations of the existence of bonuses that depend on tax policy – and on expectations that the policy will continue in the long term – have only a limited appeal. For example, governments in Europe and elsewhere have tried to promote the culture of profit-sharing by offering tax breaks on profit-related income. Despite their attempts, no significant movements away from wage-dominated contracts have emerged.

5.1.2 The bonus as effort compensation

Suppose that there is an unanticipated increase in the firm's product demand. How might it respond to the requirement for greater labour input? As we will see in some detail in chapter 7, it has three main modes of response: it can increase employment; it can increase average working hours per period; or it can increase hourly work intensity. Why might variations in work intensity, or effort, constitute a significant means of varying labour input? Underlying core labour market ideas are discussed in chapter 2. In the short run, meeting an unanticipated demand increase through employment adjustment alone may well not be physically feasible or economically desirable. Workers have to be hired and trained, involving time delays (Hamermesh, 1993). Moreover, once investments in search and training are undertaken they constitute sunk costs. If the demand upturn is short-lived, firms may not be able to realise adequate returns on such outlays. The alternative adjustment modes of changes in average hours or effort may be relatively more attractive, at least until sufficient time has elapsed that the firm can assess the longer-term prospects of higher demand. A particular short-term advantage is that hours and effort adjustments are more easily reversed, especially in the context of the typical Japanese firm, where, as we discussed in section 1.3, long job tenure is the norm.

While changes in average hours offer a relatively attractive response mechanism, there are limits to this means of adjustment. In the first place, the firm must take the cost of increases in hours into consideration. Increasing hours to meet increased demand may involve two forms of cost; the firm may need (i) to employ higher proportions of overtime to total hours and (ii) to remunerate longer overtime working at increased marginal premium rates (Hart and Malley, 1998). Secondly, there may be supply constraints on extra overtime working per period. Depending on work–leisure preferences, households may be reluctant to meet increases in product demand through significant reductions in their non-work time.

Therefore, the encouragement of greater hourly effort may have a significant role to play. Increased effort can generally be regarded as completing successfully more job tasks per unit of time. An obvious general example involves line production where firms have the ability to alter line speeds. But as with employment and hours of work, the firm cannot envisage more effort without also incurring higher labour cost. Ohashi (1989) views the bonus as representing compensation in this respect. By paying for past effort in the form of lump sums in two annual instalments, the firm reduces the transaction costs of frequent performance measurement and contract renegotiation. In effect, therefore, the bonus acts as an efficiency wage payment. [3] Ohashi states that

when determining the bonus size the firm will consider the level of activity; that is the labor intensity experienced since the last payment. The bonus has in effect become a compensation for past effort. In other words, a worker's current effort will be reflected in the next bonus payment.   (Ohashi, 1989, p. 455)

There is a serious problem with this hypothesis. As we show in chapter 7, it is well established that Japanese firms are particularly prone to hoard labour during the downturns of business cycles. Due to high investments in human and organisational capital, firms are reluctant in the short run to lay off workers.[4] In other words, following the human capital arguments developed in chapter 2, firms experience variations in effort due to their retention of excess labour during cyclical downturns. In the troughs of cycles, workers are not laid off even though marginal product may be less than marginal cost. Labour productivity is pro-cyclical; during cyclical upturns output rises more than proportionately to labour input (i.e. workers and average hours) because of dis-hoarding. It is not obvious under this hypothesis that workers would be compensated for increased effort during upturns in the business cycle by increased bonus payments. In effect, their compensation for variations in effort is long-run employment (and, perhaps, wage income) stability. Of course, the foregoing line of argument may serve merely to modify the quantitative importance of Ohashi's approach; effort increases may derive from both a process of dis-hoarding and incentive-compatible bonus increases.

5.1.3 The bonus as a profit share

The leading proponent of the view that the bonus is a form of profit share is Weitzman (e.g. 1984, 1985). His ideas have gained particular prominence not least because he regards profit-sharing as a contributory factor in Japan's superior economic performance in the post-war era.

In the standard neoclassical model of employment and wages, given diminishing marginal returns to labour input, the firm hires up to the point where the revenue generated by the marginal worker equals the associated cost of employment. In many countries (for example, the United Kingdom and the United States; see table 4.7), labour costs can be reasonably represented by direct wage payments.[5] Suppose, however, that instead of compensation solely in the form of wages, workers agree to receive a significant part of their total remuneration as a share of gross operating profits. In Weitzman's models, the profit-sharing contract is formulated by a so-called sequential, or recursive, bargaining framework (see Pencavel, 1991; Hart and Moutos, 1995). The relative size of profit share is determined by bargaining between management and workers. Typically in Japan, the latter would be represented by an enterprise union. Once the parties have agreed on the values of these share parameters, they are held fixed for a given period of time during which the firm has the right to vary the level of employment. On account of diminishing returns, hiring an additional worker reduces the bonus-related pay of this worker as well as all existing workers. On a macro-scale, this would tend to stimulate employment and output growth.

To illustrate the key points, we consider a simple example.[6] Suppose Firm X pays each of its workers 400,000 yen per month in direct wages. There are no other forms of payment. The firm will hire workers up to the point where the value added through the employment of an additional worker is 400,000 yen. Assume that the firm employs ten workers and that the average value added per worker (we are assuming diminishing returns) is 520,000 yen. Suppose that Firm X reaches an agreement with workers that its pure wage system is to be replaced by a profit-sharing scheme. At current employment levels, the firm agrees to pay total compensation under profit-sharing that exactly matches existing compensation under pure wages. It reserves, however, the right to vary employment for the length of the agreement. Specifically, the firm pays a per-worker monthly base wage of 370,000 yen and agrees to a monthly 'bonus' payment of 20 per cent of gross operating profit. The monthly bonus would amount to 30,000 yen per worker $[=0.2 \times (520,000 - 370,000)]$. Thus, total monthly pay per worker is the same as before. The firm has an incentive to expand its workforce and production. Suppose that the value added by an additional, eleventh, worker is also 400,000 yen. The associated marginal cost would be 370,000 yen (the base wage) plus 6,000 yen [i.e. $0.2 \times (400,000 - 370,000)$, which is the share of extra operating profits]. In other words, the firm stands to make an extra profit of 24,000 yen $(=400,000 - 376,000)$ on this worker.

Suppose we extrapolate to many other firms. Aggregate employment would be stimulated and prices would fall.[7] Such a climate would serve to eliminate unemployment –

hence, the fascination with the role of Weitzman-style profit-sharing contracts. But do such contracts reflect the Japanese bonus system as practised? Several commentators have been sceptical. There are (at least) four major objections to the contention that the Japanese bonus system plays such a role.

(1) The implication of firms expanding production and employment due to the profit-sharing incentives illustrated above is that, at least in the short run, each worker's total compensation falls. Hiring the additional worker in Firm X reduces each existing worker's total pay by 0.55 per cent.[8] It is not at all obvious that enterprise unions would willingly accept the trade-off of a larger membership for lower average wages per existing member. In a longer-term perspective, it may be that the stimulus to economic expansion heralded by profit-sharing may restore wage levels through increased demands for goods and services. Unions may be unwilling, however, to accept this possible future outcome as reason for a fall in current pay.

(2) It is doubtful whether the sequential bargaining structure in Weitzman's models captures the typical bargaining method of the Japanese enterprise system. The assumption of employers' unilateral power to determine the level of employment does not fit well with the standard model of the Japanese coalitional firm in which bargaining is carried out over a comprehensive set of variables that affect productivity and growth.

Weitzman's system does not live up to the attractive name 'share'. In his system, decisions on strategic management variables crucial to the well-being of employees, such as employment, are not shared by the employer and the union, either explicitly or implicitly, but are exclusively in the realm of managerial prerogatives. In contrast, I submit that the Japanese enterprise-based union has acquired implicit bargaining power over such strategic managerial issues as employment and relocation, which are of vital concern to its members, in exchange for its own commitment to a certain level of effort expenditure (and wage restraint, if necessary).   (Aoki, 1988, p. 153)

(3) But even if the firm retained the sole right to change the level of employment during the period for which the bonus share is fixed, are the implied timings of employment decisions feasible? According to Odagiri (1992), the answer is decidedly 'no'. The fact that bargaining over bonuses is carried out once or twice a year would mean that employment levels would need to change very rapidly. Such implied behaviour does not fit well with a system noted for its careful recruitment, high levels of specific training, and long-term employment relationships.

(4) Irrespective of union reactions and bargaining frameworks, it is not apparent that the foregoing mode of profit-sharing coincides with actual practice. As pointed out by Odagiri (1992), bonus payments are bargained over in terms of their worth to the average worker in months of salary equivalents. The calculation is not based on the percentage of total profit paid to the workforce as a whole. In this event, marginal cost will not be lower than average cost through the employment of an additional worker since the bonus rule operates for both new and existing workers.

5.1.4 The bonus as a shared return to specific investment

Hashimoto (e.g. 1979, 1990) argues that the bonus, in large part, represents workers' shares in the returns resulting from highly profitable specific human capital investments. As discussed in chapter 2, the key to Hashimoto's approach is the argument that Japanese companies enjoy relatively low transaction costs associated with the working relationship between workers and management. Cultural and institutional differences in Japan, including the enterprise union system, are conducive to limiting the costs of communicating information between the two parties and of verifying that information. Low transaction costs help to stimulate a climate of significant investments in firm-specific skills. Workers will receive a share of the returns to specific investments as part of total compensation. The bonus is regarded by Hashimoto as representing this share. Sharing serves to induce the two parties to work together efficiently in order to obtain the maximum return from the investment. For the worker, the bonus represents an increment over and above the outside, or opportunity, wage and therefore encourages work commitment and corporate loyalty.[9] The firm's profitability is also enhanced by these responses. The fact that bonuses are negotiated at frequent intervals can be interpreted as their providing a means of flexible response, in a low transaction cost environment, of meeting fluctuations in productivities. When unanticipated price movements occur, for example, it is important that the bargaining parties are in a position to recontract speedily in order to preserve joint rents.

If the bonus system in Japan has served to encourage highly profitable investments in human and organisational capital then why should it be limited to a single economy? The inference is that, typically, US and European firms do not have well-developed bonus systems because, on the average, their transaction costs are higher.[10] In other words, the suggestion is that industrial relations are more adversarial elsewhere. This explanation may have some validity but it is unlikely to account alone for the stark differences in bonus payments between the Japanese and other major industrial economies.

5.2 Empirical evidence

No empirical work has attempted to discriminate comprehensively among the four major hypotheses highlighted in the previous section. In order to encapsulate the scope of the various empirical studies that have been made, we specify three broadly defined linear estimating equations. The first two separate wage and bonus payments:

$$\text{Bonus} = a_0 + a_1(\text{Labour Market}) + a_2(\text{Profit}) + a_3(\text{Human Capital}) + a_4(\text{Effort}) + a_5(\text{Bonus})_{-1} + a_6(\text{Time}) + u \tag{5.1}$$

$$\text{Wage} = b_0 + b_1(\text{Labour Market}) + b_2(\text{Profit}) + b_3(\text{Human Capital}) + b_4(\text{Effort}) + b_5(\text{Wage})_{-1} + b_6(\text{Time}) + v \tag{5.2}$$

where $(\ )_{-1}$ indicates lagged-value variables, the as and bs are parameters, and u and v are error terms. Most variables are self-explanatory; 'Labour Market' represents variables that capture the relative tightness of the labour market. In most of the studies discussed here, researchers have either estimated restrictive versions of equations (5.1) and (5.2) or expressed their dependent variables in ratio form. The latter approach provides our third general equation:

$$(\text{Bonus/Wage}) = c_0 + c_1(\text{Labour Market}) + c_2(\text{Profit}) + c_3(\text{Human Capital})$$
$$+ c_4(\text{Effort}) + c_5(\text{Wage})_{-1} + c_6(\text{Bonus})_{-1} + c_7(\text{Time}) + w \qquad (5.3)$$

where the cs are parameters and w is an error term.

5.2.1 Profit-sharing, effort and labour market effects

We start with the work of Freeman and Weitzman (1987), if only because they estimate all three of these specifications. Based on two-digit industries between 1959 and 1983, they estimate restricted (logarithmic) versions of equations (5.1) and (5.2).[11] To represent economic conditions they use either corporate operating profits[12] or net domestic product (net output by industry of origin at market prices) or total corporate value added. They find that bonuses are more responsive than wages to these measures. Moreover, while both bonuses and wages are affected by net domestic product and value added, only bonuses are significantly associated with profit. Also, if the coefficient estimates on the lagged dependent variables can be taken to indicate adjustment speeds, then bonuses appear to be more responsive to changes in desired values than wages. Equivalent estimates for equation (5.3) reveal that bonuses are more responsive than wages to changes in economic conditions.

These results appear to lend support to the bonus-as-profit-share hypothesis. Recall from section 5.1.3 that, under this share hypothesis, the bonus would also be predicted to have a positive impact on employment. In further regressions incorporating employment as the dependent variable, Freeman and Weitzman find that basic wages have a negative effect on employment, in contrast to the bonus which has a significantly positive one.

There are a number of serious problems with the analysis, however. First, industry-level data might not be suitable for studying the mechanism of bonus agreements. As argued by Brunello and Ohtake (1987), bonus and wage payments are often closely co-ordinated *within* industries and so analysis at enterprise level is needed to study bonus determinants. Secondly, their regression analysis fails to deal with the problem that the bonus and profit are simultaneously determined. Thirdly, the analysis omits a large number of explanatory variables that have been variously argued to affect bonus payments and it is not clear that their revenue and profit variables, reflecting 'economic conditions', are not proxying other factors.

Brunello and Ohtake (1987) design their analysis to deal with the first two of these objections as well as, to a more limited extent, the third. They carry out Granger causality tests between bonuses and other relevant variables – including wages, tenure, age and profit – at individual enterprise level. They concentrate their attention on banking and finance as well as on large- and medium-sized electronics companies. Their data period is 1972–85. These researchers find that per capita value added, or profit, causes significant bonus fluctuation only in banking. The profit-sharing hypothesis receives, at best, very weak support.

More direct question-marks over the strength of the profit-sharing hypothesis come from a 1989 Japanese Ministry of Labour questionnaire survey. As reported by Odagiri (1992, p. 254), '68 per cent of firms investigated replied that they do not determine the amount of bonuses on the basis of "performance-related" or "profit sharing", and this percentage is even larger, at 84 per cent, among firms with a thousand employees or more.'

Ohashi (1989) uses a restricted version of equation (5.1) in an attempt to discriminate among profits, effort and labour market conditions as determinants of bonus payments. Naturally enough, the variable that causes most concern from a measurement viewpoint is effort. Overtime hours are chosen as a proxy since 'overtime hours are thought to reasonably indicate times when the level of business and labour intensity increase'. We will return later to this choice. Differentiating among twelve two-digit industries between 1967 and 1986, as well as between blue- and white-collar workers, Ohashi regresses (real) bonuses on (real) current and lagged profits, current and lagged overtime hours, vacancies (the ratio of job vacancies to job searchers) and a time trend. Overtime hours are found to exert positive and significant influences on the bonus for both categories of worker in most industries. However, for three industries – food and tobacco, chemicals and transport – there is no effect on either blue- or white-collar workers. Profit exhibits a similar performance; it is generally positively significant although it has no effect in machinery and transport nor in precision industries. The strongest variable by far in this study is the vacancy rate which exhibits a comprehensively significant influence on bonuses. An extension of the analysis using micro-data appears to reinforce the results with respect to labour market effects.

Ohashi's work almost certainly is more supportive of claims that the bonuses, like basic wages, reflect labour market conditions.[13] It is hard to accept that overtime primarily serves as a proxy for effort. Rather, it is much more likely to represent firms' intensive margin changes in the demand and supply of hours worked, supplementing the role of vacancies on the extensive margin (see Hart, 1973). Noticeably, overtime features current and lagged values while only current values of vacancies enter the analysis. It is well known that changes in hours *precede* changes in vacancies as an indicator of cyclical labour market change.

5.2.2 Human capital influences

None of the foregoing work casts any light on the merits of the hypothesis advanced by Hashimoto (1979) that the bonus represents workers' share of the returns to firm-specific human capital investments. In the wage-earnings growth equation (2.3), discussed in section 2.4, the log of real wages is hypothesised to be a positive function of (i) workers' years experience in the labour market (measured in Japan by age minus years of schooling minus six), (ii) years of tenure in the current job, and (iii) other variables such as years of pre-work education and firm size. The experience and tenure variables are argued to represent human capital attributes. The experience variable represents the accumulation of general human capital while tenure captures the accumulation of more specific human capital.[14] The studies discussed here are based on this Mincer formulation.

Using the (logarithm of the) ratio formulation of equation (5.3), Hashimoto (1979) estimates a Mincer-type equation for a 1970 cross-section of male workers in nine non-agricultural industries. His explanatory variables are experience, pre-work education level, firm size and age. The first three of these variables associate positively with the bonus/wage ratio, while the last is negative. Since education and firm size are argued to be positively associated with the profitability of on-the-job training, Hashimoto infers that these results lend support to his sharing hypothesis.

Nakamura and Hübler (1998) carry out an analysis similar to that of Hashimoto using pooled Ministry of Labour data on female and male Japanese workers for the years 1984, 1986 and 1988. They estimate all three equation structures set out in (5.1)–(5.3). Comparing their versions of equations (5.1) and (5.2) they find that estimated coefficients on tenure, education and firm size in the (log) bonus equation are generally larger than in the (log) regular wage equation. In other words, returns to human capital in the form of bonus payments exceed those in the form of wage payments. In their version of equation (5.3), they find that, as in Hashimoto's earlier work, the bonus-to-regular-pay ratio positively relates with tenure, education and firm size. Again, this is strongly suggestive of a particularly important role of bonus payments in workers' returns to human capital investments.

Hart and Kawasaki (1995) attempt a more stringent set of tests of Hashimoto's hypothesis. They base their investigation on specifications of equation (5.1) and (5.2) (with the dependent variables expressed in natural logarithms), incorporating measures of tenure, experience and pre-work schooling. Specifically, they attempt to tackle two problems inherent in estimating Mincer equations based on cross-sectional data, in particular, and compensation–tenure profiles, in general.

Age cohorts and cross-sectional studies

A major data source for analysing compensation growth in Japan is the Basic Survey of Wage Structure which provides detailed establishment-level information on workers' ages, lengths of job tenure and schooling characteristics (see, for example, Hashimoto and Raisian, 1985; Clark and Ogawa, 1992). The data are in the form of annual aggregate cross-sections. A particularly serious problem in estimating cross-sectionally based compensation–tenure profiles is that different age cohorts within a given cross-section may experience systematic differences in the levels of specific training. For example, suppose that per capita investments in specific human capital have grown through time owing to technological improvements and economic growth. If bonus payments represent returns to such investments, this would cause the bonus–wage profiles of successive age cohorts progressively to steepen.[15] Such outcomes would be distorted if the estimated bonus–tenure profile were based on cross-sections representing different lengths of tenure. Given strong job attachments in Japan, tenure lengths and age are highly correlated and the estimated regression would 'average out' the age-related profile slope changes. In effect, it would be expected that the cross-sectional profile would be steeper (at least over initial years of tenure) than the profiles for the longest tenure workers and less steep than those for workers with the shortest tenure.

This type of bias would not be confined to the tenure variable. Teaching methods, intensity of educational provision and the composition of the school curriculum would also be expected to change systematically through time. In turn, this would change the endowments of general human capital of successive cohorts of new entrants to the labour market with subsequent intergenerational effects on compensation–experience profiles. Moreover, to the extent that educational attainment is used as a filter when placing workers on firm-based specific training programmes, changes in the curriculum and new subject developments may alter the selection criteria and this may produce systematic shifts in compensation–tenure profiles through time.

One way of tackling these types of problem, is to create a 'pseudo-panel' consisting of variables that track given sample cohorts across successive cross-sectional data sets. Specifically, we can construct a set of data that follows given age cohorts through their years of general experience and firm-specific tenure, delineated between 1971 and 1991.[16] Three such age cohorts are shown in table 5.1.[17] Each cohort covers a five-year age band, as dictated by the aggregation of the data source. Take Cohort 1 as an example. In 1971, we can obtain compensation data (wages and bonuses) for the age group 25–29. In 1976, we can use the age group 30–34 to represent the earlier group given that they are five years older. Constructing the data in like fashion throughout the complete time period leaves us with the age group 45–49 to represent Cohort 1 in 1991.

Fixed individual and job match effects

Even if we possessed suitable panel data, or corrected cross-sectional data for the age cohort effects along the above lines, there would remain serious potential distortions in estimating operational forms of equations (5.1) and (5.2) by means of ordinary least squares regression. The error term of the equation contains unobserved individual and job characteristics as well as purely random effects. The non-random component may consist of fixed individual characteristics and so-called job match effects.

In the case of fixed individual characteristics, workers with high ability may be expected to receive higher earnings (including bonuses) and experience fewer layoffs and quits, and thereby exhibit longer tenure. If uncorrected, this effect would serve to provide a misleading interpretation of the returns to job tenure. Earnings may not be rising as a result of the accumulation of tenure, but rather because tenure is correlated positively with unobserved characteristics. As for job matches, individuals may be sorted into jobs of different durabilities and productivities (Hall, 1982; Topel and Ward, 1992). Highly paid jobs are more likely to survive for longer. Workers with good job matches will be less likely to quit. Again, if uncorrected, the associated rise in earnings would be wrongly accredited to the accumulation of tenure *per se*.[18]

A number of approaches have been adopted to correct for the influences of fixed effects. Perhaps the best known of these studies is that of Altonji and Shakotko (1987)

Table 5.1. *Age groups and cohorts*

| Time points | Age intervals | | |
	Cohort 1	Cohort 2	Cohort 3
1971	25–29	30–34	35–39
1976	30–34	35–39	40–44
1981	35–39	40–44	45–49
1986	40–44	45–49	50–54
1991	45–49	50–54	55–59

who construct a set of instruments for the tenure variables in the standard regression.[19] This procedure is adopted in the results that follow.

Estimating separate bonus and wage equations permits us to ascertain – for each of our cohorts – whether or not we can distinguish different labour market roles for bonus and regular wage payments in Japan. Following Hashimoto's hypothesis, we might suppose that bonuses mainly reflect returns to job-specific investments. Regular wages, in contrast, may be assumed to be more significantly influenced by general experience. It is therefore necessary to test for significant differences between the performances of bonuses and wages with respect to experience and tenure both within and between equations.

From the results shown in tables 5.2 and 5.3, it is clear that both experience and tenure exert significant positive influences on (logarithms of) bonuses and wages.[20] It also appears that experience acts relatively strongly on wage growth, and tenure on bonus growth. In order to examine these differences more systematically, the following procedure is adopted. Assume that a worker enters the current firm immediately after schooling and remains there until retirement. Accordingly, changing the values of experience (= tenure) in the estimated equations, we can simulate the growth profiles of log bonus and log wage. Hashimoto's maintained hypothesis is that bonus payments represent (predominantly) returns to specific investments. Accordingly, we would expect that, within the bonus equation, job-specific tenure would have a significantly greater influence than general experience on bonus growth.

The tests shown in table 5.4 reveal that tenure generally exerts a significantly stronger impact than experience on bonus growth. Moreover, in Cohorts 1 and 3, there is a tendency for the differential impact within each cohort to increase with length of tenure.

Hart and Kawasaki (1995) test for other differences in the influences of experience and tenure. They find no evidence of differential effects of tenure and experience on wage growth. However, the impact of tenure on bonus growth is significantly higher than on wage growth for all lengths of tenure. Further, for each period of tenure (five years, ten years etc.), the difference increases the younger age cohort. In the case of years of experience, there is a tendency, albeit weaker, for the direction of difference between equations to reverse. The influence of experience on wage growth exceeds that on bonus growth.

Table 5.2. *Cohort wage equations*

Variable	Cohort 1	Cohort 2	Cohort 3
Constant	4.631	4.604	4.186
	(76.450)	(49.322)	(57.488)
Experience	0.048	0.031	0.075
	(4.118)	(2.646)	(12.557)
(Experience)^2	−0.002	−0.001	−0.001
	(−2.013)	(−2.560)	(−7.172)
Tenure	0.046	0.068	0.016
	(2.746)	(4.325)	(2.401)
(Tenure)^2	−0.002	−0.002	−0.0004
	(−1.261)	(−2.783)	(1.545)
Interaction term	0.002	0.002	−0.0004
	(0.940)	(1.579)	(−1.229)
Senior high school	0.003	0.0034	0.132
	(0.101)	(0.099)	(8.350)
Junior college	0.125	0.060	0.245
	(3.335)	(1.536)	(13.533)
University	0.250	0.242	0.449
	(5.874)	(5.231)	(27.094)
$\bar{R}^2$ (N)	0.67 (526)	0.67 (524)	0.67 (526)

Notes:
The dependent variable is log (basic wage). Instrumental variable/seemingly unrelated regression estimates are shown. *t*-statistics are shown in brackets under coefficients. N is number of observations (males only).

These findings are generally supportive of Hashimoto's hypothesis that the bonus represents returns to specific investments. Further, Hart and Kawasaki produce evidence that in recent times this role of the bonus has strengthened.[21] Although not quite so strong, it is also found that, relative to bonus growth, general experience plays a more important part in the determination of wages. Within the wage growth equation, however, there is no significant difference in the explanatory contributions of tenure and experience.

Returning to the results in tables 5.2 and 5.3, the schooling variables are generally highly significant additions to both the bonus and wage equations. In both equations, higher returns are linked to higher education levels. Perhaps most interestingly, each schooling variable exerts a significantly stronger influence on bonus growth than on wage growth in each and every cohort. If, as we argue, the bonus is associated closely with specific investments then these findings support the possibility that levels of education act as a device for sorting workers into jobs with more or less skill specificity. We return to the subject of the relation between years of schooling and compensation in chapter 9.

Table 5.3. *Cohort bonus equations*

Variable	Cohort 1	Cohort 2	Cohort 3
Constant	2.901	2.858	2.658
	(26.857)	(22.739)	(12.313)
Experience	0.021	0.028	0.052
	(1.032)	(1.771)	(2.933)
(Experience)^2	0.001	0.00004	−0.0002
	(0.652)	(0.052)	(−0.433)
Tenure	0.128	0.110	0.074
	(4.227)	(5.213)	(3.650)
(Tenure)^2	0.002	0.00002	0.001
	(0.745)	(0.016)	(1.549)
Interaction term	−0.005	−0.002	−0.002
	(−1.272)	(−1.167)	(−2.480)
Senior high school	0.137	0.186	0.248
	(2.228)	(4.073)	(5.301)
Junior college	0.296	0.302	0.405
	(4.415)	(5.725)	(7.542)
University	0.569	0.603	0.699
	(7.498)	(9.666)	(11.613)
$\bar{R}^2$ (N)	0.66 (526)	0.74 (524)	0.65 (526)

Notes:
The dependent variable is log (bonus). See also notes to table 5.2.

Table 5.4. *Bonus equation (experience − tenure) impacts*

	Tenure (years)					
	5	10	15	20	25	30
Cohort 1 (25–49)	0.117	0.128	0.139	0.150	0.161	—
	(2.223)	(2.129)	(1.983)	(1.838)	(1.710)	
Cohort 2 (30–54)	0.082	0.082	0.081	0.081	0.081	0.081
	(2.379)	(2.265)	(2.097)	(1.910)	(1.727)	(1.560)
Cohort 3 (35–59)	0.034	0.046	0.059	0.071	0.083	0.095
	(1.140)	(1.643)	(2.118)	(2.501)	(2.760)	(2.905)

Notes:
The coefficients are estimates of bonus growth due to tenure minus wage growth due to tenure. Numbers in brackets in first column denote age range of each cohort. Numbers in brackets in remaining columns denote *t*-statistics.

5.2.3 Evidence from Germany and the United States

As we have seen in chapter 4, Japanese bonus payments form a significantly higher proportion of total labour costs than bonuses elsewhere. In general, in other countries compared with Japan, we find (i) bonuses are received by much smaller proportions of the
total workforce, and (ii) for those receiving bonuses, the proportion of bonus to total pay
is much lower. However, while on average bonus pay as a proportion of total pay in large
European countries like Germany is less than half of comparable Japanese figures, it is
clear from tables 4.7 and 4.8 that bonus payments are an important aspect of total compensation in some other countries. In Germany in particular and Europe in general, an
important component of bonus pay arises explicitly from profit-sharing schemes.
Elsewhere, such as in the United States, bonuses are concentrated far more towards managerial and executive workers. Whatever the motive for and targeting of bonus payments,
it is clearly of considerable interest to assess for other countries whether, like Japan,
human capital influences on bonus payments are somehow different than on regular
wages. Such an extension has been carried out in the Nakamura and Hübler (1998) study.

   Nakamura and Hübler repeated their wage and bonus regressions, reported above, for
German workers (using 1984–87 data from the German Socio-economic Panel) and for
US managers and executives (using pooled data on management/administration positions for 1976–82 from the Panel Study of Income Dynamics of the University of
Michigan). They find that, in general terms, the performance of the German and US
regressions is very similar to the Japanese ones. As before, tenure and schooling variables
display larger influences on (log) bonuses than on (log) regular wages. Further, in all
three countries, the proportion of bonus pay within total (bonus plus regular wage) pay
is positively associated with workers' qualifications.

5.3 Conclusions

In this chapter, we considered four hypotheses concerning the role of the Japanese bonus
system. These are that the bonus is (i) a disguised form of regular wage payments, (ii) a
means of compensating effort, (iii) a Weitzman type of profit share, and (iv) the workers'
share of investments in firm-specific human capital. None of the empirical work to date
has attempted to discriminate among all four possibilities.

   There is little existing support either for the effort hypothesis or for the profit-sharing
hypothesis. In the first instance, no really convincing proxy for effort has been tested
empirically. In the case of profit-sharing, even though empirical work points to a possible profit-sharing role for bonuses, there is serious doubt over whether the design and
implementation of the bonus system matches the structure of profit-sharing contracts
in Weitzman's work. There is stronger support for the view that bonus payments, as in
conventional models of regular wage determination, react to labour market pressures.
There is also support for Hashimoto's claim that Japanese bonus payments represent
returns to specific human capital investments.

   At an international level, the work of Nakamura and Hübler (1998) poses a particularly difficult puzzle. They find that human capital variables are particularly strongly

associated with bonus payments and with bonus shares within total pay in Japan, Germany and the United States. This raises the obvious question of why bonus payments in these latter economies are not as widespread across the workforce or as large per capita as in Japan. Why should the economic rationale behind shared returns to human capital investments somehow have a less powerful impact in the labour markets of other countries? This question has simply not yet been adequately addressed.

Notes

1 As discussed by Aoki (1988), the organisation of agrarian society so as to achieve collective co-operative effort was in part predicated on the need to overcome the problems associated with an expansion of rice production on land that was not ideal for rice paddy cultivation.

2 Such a tax regime in favour of older workers may have incentive-compatible effects on worker efficiency; see the discussion in Lazear (1985). This links to the discussion in section 5.1.2 which discusses the bonus as a mechanism to induce greater effort.

3 As pointed out by Ohashi, this form of incentive payment is atypical of the general efficiency wage literature in that compensation takes place after the effort has been expended.

4 The Japanese propensity to hoard labour may also be encouraged by the fact that post-war recessions have tended to be relatively mild and short-lived. As pointed out by Odagiri and Yamashita (1987) and Odagiri (1992), at the beginning of any given recession, Japanese managers would have anticipated economic downturns that were not too serious and, therefore, would have avoided worker layoffs.

5 Of course, wage schedules might be fairly complicated, perhaps involving overtime and other special payments, but this does not detract from 'the marginal cost equals marginal revenue' point at hand.

6 The example is based on Estrin and Wadhwani (1990) who provide a very useful critique of Weitzman's profit-sharing ideas (see also Nordhaus, 1988).

7 Employment and output are expanding and, in order to sell the extra production, firms reduce selling prices.

8 Gross operating profit is reduced because the profit attached to the marginal worker is below the average. Given a fixed-share parameter, this reduces each worker's bonus payment.

9 See Okuno (1984) who formally develops the idea that bonuses serve, through their actual or perceived link to corporate performance, to provide work incentives and to encourage corporate loyalty.

10 The more difficult it is for the parties to reach agreements about the values of (i) marginal products and (ii) outside opportunities arising from investments in human capital, then the greater the tendency to negotiate fixed rather than flexible wage contracts (see section 2.2). Thus, the common occurrence of three-year contracts in the United States may reflect a more adversarial environment, with higher transaction costs, in this economy.

11 They do not attempt to measure directly the degree of labour market tightness, nor do effort and human capital-related variables feature in their analysis.

12 Their measure of profit is net of bonus payments.

13 Ohashi cites other Japanese studies that purport to show that market conditions are an important determinant of bonus payments.

14 It should be emphasised that the tenure variable might not *solely* reflect specific human capital; see the discussion in Hashimoto and Raisian (1985).

15 Hashimoto and Raisian (1985) and Mincer and Higuchi (1988) discuss the relative steepness of profiles in relation to levels of specific human capital investment in their comparative studies of Japan and the United States.

16 The term pseudo-panel is used because each cell in table 5.1 represents a sample of establishments taken from a larger population. The composition of the sample will vary from year to year and, therefore, from cell to cell within a given cohort. Thus, we are not tracking a given group of establishments and workers through time. The data refer to regular workers taken from a sample of establishments in nine major industries. In 1991, the total population of regular workers represented by the sample was 29,500,000 while the sample itself covered 1,400,000, or 4.7 per cent of the population. Cells are delineated by age, schooling (defined as primary or junior high school (6–7 years of schooling), senior high school (12–13 years), junior college (14–15 years) and university (over 16 years)), industry (mining; construction; manufacturing; electricity, gas and water; transport and communication; wholesale, retail and restaurants; finance and insurance; real estate; services) and firm size (companies with more than 1,000 employees (large firms), between 100 and 999 employees (medium firms) and between 10 and 99 employees (small firms)).

17 These three cohorts constitute a subset of the seven cohorts analysed by Hart and Kawasaki (1995) in their original study.

18 Beyond these developments, Topel (1991) considers the possibility of stochastic, rather than fixed, job match effects. His two-step procedure for accommodating this problem is beyond the scope of our Japanese analysis because of data limitations.

19 The instruments consist of taking the deviations of the job tenure variables from the observed cell means.

20 In the underlying regression equations, the logarithms of real bonuses and wages are the dependent variables. They are deflated by the consumer price index (1990 = 100). The wage is defined as monthly regular wage earnings (excluding bonuses but including overtime payments). Experience is total labour market experience (calculated as age minus length of schooling minus 6). Tenure is years of service in the current firm. Conventionally, we include quadratic terms in the experience and tenure variables to capture the possibility that the respective profiles are steeper in the earlier years of experience/tenure. The interaction term is (experience) × (tenure). Conventionally, we interpret the coefficients on experience as representing the returns to general human capital and the tenure coefficients as reflecting the returns to job-specific human capital. The interaction term accommodates the possibility that the length of previous years of experience (a part of total experience) either enhances or penalises wage growth due to tenure.

21 In further simulations, they estimate profiles of accumulated regular bonus and wage growth paths over a thirty-year tenure period. The results reveal a systematic upward shift in the bonus–tenure profile from older to younger cohorts. While not so clear-cut, an upward shift is also found in the wage–tenure profile.

6 Recruitment, training, promotion and retirement

The discussion of key labour market differences between Japan and other advanced industrialised economies, such as those in the areas of wage growth, length of job tenure and employment adjustment, has stressed the role of recruitment, screening and human capital expenditures on Japanese workers. As we indicate in chapter 2 and elsewhere, the evidence that these expenditures may be important tends to be somewhat indirect, relying on comparative estimates of returns to experience and tenure in wage growth equations. In this chapter, we examine more direct estimates of recruitment and training costs.

The quality of Japanese statistics on the cost of recruitment is unrivalled and we devote considerable attention to this aspect of worker investment. We evaluate the importance of such costs in relation to the earnings of new recruits in the first year of employment as well as to the expected length of tenure with the firm. We also examine recruitment costs in relation to labour turnover. This is clearly an essential consideration: a firm with relatively high per capita expenditure on recruitment may nonetheless require a relatively small recruitment budget if its labour turnover is low. Recruitment and turnover feature prominently as variables in the theoretical labour market literature on such topics as wage contracts, job search and mobility, efficiency wages and firm–union bargaining. Yet, surprisingly little international quantitative evidence is available (Malcomson, 1997). Therefore, this topic is of interest beyond the confines of the Japanese labour market.

By contrast, our discussion of expenditure on training is much more limited. While statistics on training costs in Japan are provided on the same basis as those on recruitment costs, there are persuasive reasons for believing that published training-related data seriously underestimate the 'true' costs of training. While it may be reasonably straightforward to quantify the costs of training programmes for new recruits as well as for ongoing specific training courses and programmes, on-the-job and informal training are far from easy to measure systematically. Lack of good statistical information on training is an international phenomenon. This empirical deficiency contrasts pointedly with the vast labour market literature devoted to the theoretical importance of firms' investments in general and specific training.

Expenditures on recruitment and training are undertaken, at least in part, in order to achieve good worker–job matches. Where good matches are made, it is in the interest of both parties to establish long tenure. One aspect of this latter process, discussed in some detail in chapter 2, involves sharing returns to specific human capital investments. Sharing rents as tenure accumulates may in part be achieved through the mechanism of promotion (Carmichael, 1983) and we examine this topic in the present chapter. Our discussion of promotion points to, albeit limited, evidence that late selection during in-firm work careers in Japan contrasts with Western practices where earlier sorting and the incidence of 'high flying' seem to be more prevalent. Our discussion of late selection is linked to human capital and work incentives.

Finally, we discuss the 'official' termination of employment contracts – the date of retirement – in relation to human capital and other labour market concepts. For two reasons, Japan appears to behave differently with respect to retirement compared with other industrialised nations. First, its age of mandatory retirement is significantly lower than elsewhere. Secondly, an unusually high proportion of official retirees participate actively in the labour market.[1] As discussed below, however, the gap between Japanese retirement practices and those elsewhere appears to be narrowing rapidly.

6.1 Recruitment and turnover

Recruitment cost covers expenditures by firms on (i) advertising and other forms of search activity, (ii) screening, interviews/examinations and probationary periods of employment, and (iii) capital and labour costs that attach to recruiters. In practice, industry-wide data on recruitment generally fail to take account of all the items included under (i), (ii) and (iii). This is true even in the case of Japan which provides by far the best national data. Japanese recruitment cost statistics cover 'expenses on advertisement for recruitment and examination for employment; remuneration to recruiters; expenses paid to intermediary bodies used' (Ministry of Labour, General Survey of Wages and Hours System). Thus, for example, building facilities and equipment used in the recruitment process are not included. Nonetheless, these are uniquely detailed statistics worthy of close examination.

Firms undertake recruitment expenditure in order to obtain the best worker–job matches as vacancies occur. General elements of such expenditure include finding suitably qualified workers and attempting to discern such features as appropriate work aptitudes and the ability to integrate into work-groups. Specific expenditure may also be incurred: the firm may attempt to match the particular personality traits and abilities of job applicants to its own idiosyncratic organisation and behaviour. In much of the theoretical literature involving recruitment cost, emphasis is placed on expenditure on the marginal worker. This permits the simplest evaluation of the 'marginal cost equals marginal revenue' profit maximisation condition. Suppose training costs are zero. Then, *ceteris paribus*, employment takes place to the point where the discounted value of output of the marginal worker over the expected period of employment is sufficient to cover that worker's discounted variable costs (wages and certain types of fringe benefit) together with the initial cost of recruitment. Assessing recruitment cost in these terms naturally involves the measurement of cost in relation to new recruits. Further, it suggests that the cost of recruitment should be evaluated in relation to the expected value of the worker's lifetime earnings in the firm.[2]

The calculation of recruitment cost per worker can usefully be divided into two parts. The first concerns the direct costs of filling a given vacancy. The second involves the frequency with which vacancies need to be filled and this links to workforce turnover. As emphasised by Hamermesh (1993), the volume of turnover is determined by both gross and net changes in employment. The former reflect expansions and contractions of the firm's overall workforce while the latter stem from the quit propensities from a workforce of a given size. It is clearly of considerable interest to attempt to ascertain the relative importance of turnover within the calculation of total recruitment cost. We examine these elements of Japanese recruitment expenditure using data on twenty-five two-digit Japanese industries in 1991, including a differentiation by enterprise size.

6.1.1 The measurement of recruitment cost

We begin by distinguishing among three measures of recruitment cost in relation to other labour costs. The first two pertain to the recruitment of new workers while the last two refer to average recruitment cost with respect to all workers.

The simplest indicator of the relative importance of recruitment cost with respect to new recruits is its amount per person hired in a particular year relative to annual cash earnings received by new recruits in that year, or

$$A = \frac{\text{recruitment cost per new worker}}{\text{cash earnings per new worker in the year of recruitment}}$$

where cash earnings are wages plus bonuses.

However, in the context of human capital theory in relation to the marginal worker, measure A is inappropriate. Imagine a profit-maximising firm that incurs recruitment but not training investment in the initial period. In equilibrium, the marginal product must be such that it covers the wage plus the discounted periodic value of the initial recruitment expenditure, the discount period reflecting the worker's expected period of tenure. The relative importance of recruitment cost in relation to cash earnings in this context is given by

$$B = \frac{\text{recruitment cost per new worker}}{\text{expected lifetime earnings in the firm}}$$

where lifetime earnings refers to the sum of the discounted values of all future cash earnings in the firm.[3]

In order to gauge the quantitative significance of recruitment cost in relation to total expenditure on the entire workforce, we express

$$C = \frac{\text{recruitment cost per worker}}{\text{cash earnings per worker}}$$

Here, total recruitment cost per period is averaged over all workers and expressed as a proportion of average cash earnings with respect to all workers.

Clearly, the quantitative importance of recruitment cost is not fully understood unless it is combined with information concerning the firm's turnover. Consider two firms, 1 and 2. Suppose that per capita cost A is twice as large in Firm 1 as Firm 2. But this measure alone could give a misleading impression of the relative importance of turnover costs in the two firms. If Firm 1 has typically half the turnover of Firm 2 then total recruitment cost per period in the two firms would be the same. We are able to construct the variable TURN which is the total number of new employees during a particular year as a proportion of total regular employees at 1 January of that year.[4] We then adjust measure A to obtain

$$A' = \left(\frac{\text{recruitment cost per worker}}{\text{cash earnings per new worker in the year of recruitment}}\right) \times \left(\frac{1}{\text{TURN}}\right)$$

The equivalent adjustment for measure C is given by

$$C' = \left(\frac{\text{recruitment cost per worker}}{\text{cash earnings per worker}}\right) \times \left(\frac{1}{\text{TURN}}\right)$$

6.1.2 Recruitment cost estimates

Estimates of measures A–C are presented in table 6.1 for twenty-five Japanese one-digit and two-digit industries in 1991. Measure A reveals that recruitment cost for new workers averaged 10.5 per cent of their cash earnings in 1991. There is wide variation around the mean, however, within the range of 6 per cent (wood) to 19 per cent (textiles). Measure B then recasts recruitment costs of new workers within the context of their expected lifetime earnings. The percentages are drastically reduced, with an average of 0.41 per cent.[5] As for recruitment relative to cash earnings averaged over all workers, measure C, the average is 0.60 per cent. Again, there are wide variations around these mean values.

Do the respective figures for recruitment costs of 10.5 per cent for new recruits in relation to first year's earnings and 0.4 per cent in relation to expected lifetime earnings make sense relative to what we know from research elsewhere? Our estimates are consistent with an expected length of completed tenure of about twenty-six years (i.e. taking the ratio of 10.5 to 0.4). Hashimoto and Raisian (1985) estimate that the average tenure in Japan (all industries) in 1980 was 8.5 years in small firms, 10.2 in medium firms and 13.9 in large firms. If we assume a mean of eleven years and assume an exponential distribution, expected completed tenure is about twenty-two years. These two sets of estimates are reasonably consistent.

Table 6.1. *Recruitment costs in Japanese industry, 1991*

Industry	Proportion of male workers	Cost measures (%)			Rank order		
		A	B	C	A	B	C
Non-manufacturing							
Mining	0.87	6.71	0.22	0.29	24	23	20
Construction	0.85	7.25	0.26	0.41	19	20	14
Wholesale and retail trade	0.68	12.19	0.48	0.79	7	6	3
Finance	0.49	6.88	0.26	0.27	22	19	23
Real estate	0.72	9.92	0.51	0.87	15	4	2
Services	0.55	11.21	0.51	0.96	10	3	1
Utilities	0.89	7.15	0.22	0.08	21	24	25
Transportation	0.89	6.85	0.23	0.28	23	22	22
Manufacturing							
Food	0.57	8.07	0.31	0.41	18	17	15
Textiles	0.47	18.90	0.66	0.76	1	1	4
Apparel	0.21	11.86	0.54	0.64	8	2	6
Wood	0.72	6.05	0.21	0.29	25	25	21
Furniture	0.72	10.27	0.38	0.50	13	13	10
Paper	0.75	10.93	0.37	0.46	11	14	11
Printing	0.74	14.14	0.51	0.65	4	5	5
Chemicals	0.78	14.32	0.45	0.41	3	7	16
Rubber	0.74	7.15	0.23	0.26	20	21	24
Stone and clay	0.78	8.26	0.28	0.37	17	18	17
Steel	0.91	14.34	0.44	0.33	2	10	19
Non-ferrous metals	0.83	10.36	0.34	0.35	12	16	18
Metal products	0.77	11.33	0.41	0.56	9	11	8
Machinery	0.84	13.72	0.45	0.51	5	8	9
Electronics	0.65	10.06	0.39	0.44	14	12	12
Vehicles	0.85	13.26	0.44	0.57	6	9	7
Precision	0.67	9.70	0.35	0.42	16	15	13
Weighted average	0.72	10.46	0.41	0.60			
Standard deviation	0.16	2.60	0.11	0.25			

Definitions:
A = (recruitment cost per new worker)/(cash earnings per new worker in 1991);
B = (recruitment cost per new worker)/(expected lifetime earnings in the firm);
C = (recruitment cost per worker)/(cash earnings per worker).
Sources: General Survey on Wages and Working Hours System; Basic Survey of Wage Structure.

In order to highlight the relative quantitative effects of the different measures, table 6.1 includes the rank order of costs A, B and C; rank $= 1$ signifies the highest industrial recruitment cost percentage and rank $= 25$ the lowest. For most industries, the rank order is largely unaffected across the measures. There are a number of important exceptions, however. At one end of the spectrum, steel displays a relatively high measure of recruitment cost to cash earnings for new workers while its equivalent per worker measure is relatively low; i.e. measure A for new recruits has rank $= 2$ and per worker measure C has rank $= 19$. At the other end, real estate has the reverse ordering; measure A has rank $= 15$ while measure C has rank $= 2$. It is clear that, in particular, chemicals is comparable to steel and services to real estate.[6] Of course, the incidence of turnover may help to explain these results. If the cost of filling a new vacancy in an industry is high but turnover is low then recruitment cost relative to cash earnings for new recruits may rank significantly above recruitment cost relative to earnings of all workers. Conversely, an industry with low cost per vacancy but high turnover could experience the opposite relative rankings.

Table 6.2 contains information on cost measures A' and C' which are designed to remove the effects of turnover on recruitment cost. Turnover, TURN, displays a wide dispersion around a global mean value of 0.17; the range is from 0.09 in steel to 0.24 in real estate. In fact, it is immediately clear that the examples of significant changes in the rank order positions between measures A and C in table 6.1 coincide with industries that have either very high or very low average tenure.

Taking the example of steel, the indices that include adjustments for turnover, A' and C', have the effect of increasing the rank orders of their unadjusted equivalents, A and C. Thus, Rank $[A,C]$ is $[2,19]$ while Rank $[A',C']$ is $[1,9]$. This is a high technology industry with a relatively highly skilled workforce and it would be expected to incur significant costs in filling new vacancies but low recruitment costs in terms of expected lifetime earnings owing to relatively low turnover. Other industries that exhibit changes in the same direction include apparel, paper, rubber, chemicals, metal products, non-ferrous metals and precision. These cases also display relatively low turnover. Where there exist high rates of turnover, then we should observe opposite effects. The most notable example here is in textiles, an industry with a turnover rate more than double that of the next highest industry. We find that Rank $[A, C]$ is $[1,4]$ for textiles while Rank $[A', C']$ is $[24,23]$. Similar industries include services, sales, real estate and vehicles. Since, on average, male workers have lower turnover[7] and higher earnings,[8] we might expect the ratio of males to total workers (shown in table 6.1) to correlate negatively with the recruitment cost percentages. The simple correlations are negative: $r = -0.19$ and $r = -0.44$ between the male/total worker ratio and, respectively, measures A and C. However, we would expect these correlations to become less negative after adjusting for turnover. This is borne out by the male/total worker correlations with A' and C' which are $r = -0.17$ and $r = -0.25$, respectively.

Table 6.2. *Recruitment costs adjusted for turnover in Japanese industry, 1991*

		Recruitment cost measures					
Industry	TURN	A'	C'	Rank A'	Rank C'	Rank A	Rank C
Non-manufacturing							
Mining	0.118	0.567	0.025	15	18	24	20
Construction	0.187	0.387	0.022	22	19	19	14
Wholesale and retail trade	0.215	0.567	0.037	16	8	7	3
Finance	0.237	0.291	0.011	25	24	22	23
Real estate	0.217	0.457	0.040	19	6	15	2
Services	0.228	0.492	0.042	18	3	10	1
Utilities	0.161	0.445	0.005	20	25	21	25
Transportation	0.159	0.431	0.018	21	22	23	22
Manufacturing							
Food	0.212	0.380	0.019	23	21	18	15
Textiles	0.498	0.379	0.015	24	23	1	4
Apparel	0.118	1.009	0.054	3	1	8	6
Wood	0.117	0.518	0.025	17	17	25	21
Furniture	0.135	0.763	0.037	9	7	13	10
Paper	0.110	0.991	0.042	4	4	11	11
Printing	0.156	0.915	0.042	5	5	4	5
Chemicals	0.135	1.062	0.030	2	12	3	16
Rubber	0.119	0.599	0.022	13	20	20	24
Stone and clay	0.144	0.573	0.027	14	16	17	17
Steel	0.091	1.584	0.036	1	9	2	19
Non-ferrous metals	0.117	0.888	0.030	6	13	12	18
Metal products	0.129	0.881	0.044	7	2	9	8
Machinery	0.156	0.881	0.033	8	10	5	9
Electronics	0.153	0.658	0.029	12	15	14	12
Vehicles	0.192	0.692	0.030	11	14	6	7
Precision	0.135	0.717	0.031	10	11	16	13
Weighted average	0.169	0.573	0.031				
Standard deviation	0.078	0.214	0.011				

Definitions:
$A = $ (recruitment cost per new worker)/(cash earnings per new worker in 1991);
$A' = A \times (1/\text{TURN})$;
$C = $ (recruitment cost per worker)/(cash earnings per worker);
$C' = C \times (1/\text{TURN})$.
Sources: See sources for table 6.1; TURN is derived from Survey of Employment Trends.

6.1.3 Recruitment costs by enterprise size

A priori, recruitment costs per new worker, or averaged over all workers, are likely to be positively related to enterprise size. First, larger and more complex organisations will have to search for new recruits over a wider range of specialisms, aptitudes and abilities. This may well require the services of a dedicated personnel department with its associated labour and capital costs. Secondly, the greater visibility in the market-place of larger establishments is likely, *ceteris paribus*, to attract more applicants per vacancy. Thirdly, larger enterprises are more likely to fill job vacancies through more costly formal channels – such as advertising, interviewing and testing – while smaller organisations may rely more on recruitment through informal networks and family connections among existing workers.

Table 6.3 shows estimates of measures *A* and *C* for large, medium and small enterprises. On account of data limitations, the manufacturing sector has not been disaggregated into two-digit industrial components.[9] At the aggregate level, and in several individual cases, larger enterprises incur higher recruitment costs, both per new worker and per average worker. The pattern is by no means universal, however. In sales and finance, for example, medium-sized enterprises incur the highest recruitment costs. Further, it is clearly not the case in general that enterprises with a given ranking for one enterprise size-group exhibit similar rankings in other sizes.

6.2 Training

The economics of firm-level training – both for-the-job and on-the-job – has been particularly influential in the development of theories of labour market behaviour, especially in the field of human capital. Yet, full and comprehensive data on firms' expenditures on training are very modest in relation to the vast mountain of theoretical work which implies that training expenditures are important cost considerations. In chapter 4, we presented some evidence on aggregate Japanese training costs. The data used there refer to firms' education and training expenses, defined as 'the sum of the costs related to education and training facilities (except schools established with the aim of improving employees' cultured level), allowances and rewards given to instructors, and training consignment costs, and so on' (Ministry of Labour, Labour Cost Survey). Almost certainly, therefore, the statistics refer overwhelmingly to formal training, with little attempt to evaluate the more difficult concept of on-the-job training expenditures. In the event, therefore, the training cost breakdowns provided in tables 4.1, 4.3, 4.4 and 4.5 almost certainly grossly underestimate true training expenditures. But even this partial evidence is better than what is available elsewhere.[10]

6.3 Promotion

This section surveys some representative studies on promotion systems for Japanese workers in comparison with US/European systems. The study of promotion requires a

Table 6.3. *Recruitment costs by enterprise size in Japanese industry, 1991*

	Large enterprises				Medium enterprises				Small enterprises			
	A	C	Rank A	Rank C	A	C	Rank A	Rank C	A	C	Rank A	Rank C
Mining	16.10	0.52	1	4	7.53	0.28	4	8	1.60	0.13	9	9
Construction	8.89	0.36	5	6	6.03	0.51	7	5	3.49	0.33	6	7
Wholesale and retail trade	8.11	0.63	8	3	9.35	0.87	2	4	3.42	0.83	7	1
Finance	3.56	0.24	9	8	15.22	1.32	1	1	5.04	0.45	3	4
Real estate	8.72	1.31	6	1	6.96	0.97	6	3	3.15	0.40	8	6
Services	11.36	0.94	3	2	9.19	1.11	3	2	4.58	0.57	4	2
Utilities	11.41	0.20	2	9	4.52	0.14	8	9	3.95	0.18	5	8
Transport	8.24	0.27	7	7	4.51	0.30	9	7	5.71	0.55	2	3
Manufacturing	10.49	0.50	4	5	7.27	0.49	5	6	5.77	0.43	1	5
Weighted average	8.90	0.48			8.23	0.75			4.69	0.54		
Standard deviation	2.40	0.21			0.20	0.30			1.02	0.17		

Definitions:
Small = 30–99 employees; medium = 100–999 employees; large = 1000 or more employees;
A = (recruitment cost per new worker)/(cash earnings per new worker in 1991);
C = (recruitment cost per worker)/(cash earnings per worker).
Sources: See sources for table 6.1.

detailed examination of individual careers within firms and the fact that there is only a relatively small number of existing studies stems principally from the confidential nature of the relevant data files.

The most popular concept of Japanese promotion is that it is based on the seniority principle. Indeed, Japanese executives seem to be rather old and, in some cases, employees appear to be promoted automatically at certain ages. The seniority principle is only a part of the promotion system, however, and it has to be analysed in relation to other factors that help determine promotion.

6.3.1 Promotion of white-collar workers

In a seminal study of promotion paths, Rosenbaum (1979) found that promotion essentially followed a tournament-type scheme. This is a system in which winners gain the right to proceed further up the promotion ladder, while losers do not. Since Rosenbaum's work, there have been several career-tree studies which have followed the careers of cohorts of individual employees over a given time duration.

In analysing various career trees, we distinguish among four characterisations of the promotion process. The first refers to the *first selection* point. This is taken to be the first-time point at which the firm differentiates among employees who entered the firm at the same time. Koike (see Japan Institute of Labour, 1997) emphasises the importance of the first selection; he highlights (i) when first selection occurs, (ii) what the proportion of selected employees is, and (iii) how effective the first selection is for later promotion.

The second characterisation is the *main selection* point when less than half of employees entering the firm at the same time are first selected.[11] This enables the major branching of career paths to be pinpointed. If the firm takes a 'fast track' approach in its promotion system, the first selection and main selection should take place almost simultaneously and at a very early stage. In the contrasting, non-elitist approach, the main selection should occur at a much later stage even if the first selection occurs at an early stage. We are also interested in whether or not losers in previous contests can overtake previous winners. In other words, we might wish to examine how strictly tournament rules apply to given promotion processes.

The third characterisation seeks to deal with this aspect of promotion. This is *upper exception* which concerns whether or not the highest position attainable in the career tree was attained only by those who had won all the previous contests. In other words, did a strict tournament process hold with respect to the highest position?

The fourth characterisation is *lower exception* which concerns whether or not strict tournament rules applied to positions other than the highest one. In terms of the career-tree diagram, these two exceptions correspond to the crossings of lines representing career paths.

Hanada's study of five large Japanese corporations

Hanada (1989) studied the career paths of university graduates in five representative Japanese corporations in electrical/electronics, finance, insurance, transportation and distribution.

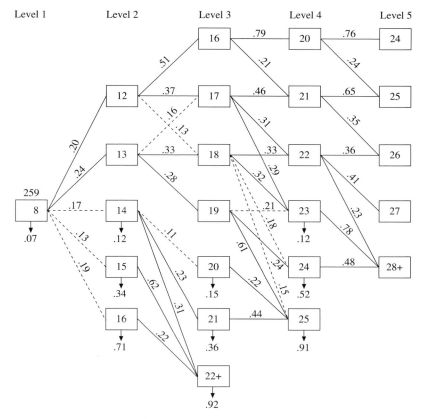

Fig. 6.1. Career tree of a Japanese manufacturer. The figure in the box indicates the number of years taken to reach the level, the figure on the line the proportion of the promotion, and the figure under the box the proportion of those who quit from the position. A broken line indicates that the transition proportion is less than 0.2. (*Source:* Hanada, 1989.)

The first case, in a large electrical/electronics firm consisted of 259 new employees entering the firm in 1955 and continuing to work for twenty-eight years. The career tree is shown in figure 6.1. The first and main selection occurred during the twelfth year, when 20 per cent of employees were differentiated by being the first group to be promoted to senior staff (Level 2). This position was eventually attained by almost all employees, although there were time lags for promotion. The highest position in this career tree, namely general manager (Level 5), was attained only by those who had won all previous contests, so that upper exception did not occur in this case. On the other hand, there were some minor disruptions with respect to other positions, as shown by some crossings of career paths between Level 2 and Level 4. Thus the lower exception held in this case.

Four other cases from Hanada's study may be summarised briefly.

(1) This case is referred to as representing a traditional firm. It contained twenty-seven employees for twenty-seven years of their careers. The first selection occurred at the fourth year when twenty-four employees were promoted to the first-level rank. All other

employees attained this position after one further year. The main selection point was the thirteenth year when ten workers attained the second level. The fourth level, which is the highest position in this career tree was attained only by those who had won in the previous contests, so that upper exception did not occur. In the second contest, there was lower exception on a very limited scale.

(2) Also referred to as traditional, this case contained forty-seven employees for twenty-four years of their careers. The first selection occurred at the tenth year when thirty-three employees attained the first promotion, and the main selection occurred at the fourteenth year when twenty-one workers attained the rank of branch deputy general manager. There was a minor upper exception and also some lower exceptions.

(3) This case consisted of 297 new entrants employed by a firm. The first and main selection occurred at the sixth year when eighty-five workers were promoted. Eventually, after some delays, every entrant attained the first rank. Some, however, could not attain the second rank. There was no upper exception, but there were some lower exceptions.

(4) This was a case where forty-eight new workers were employed by a firm. The first and main selection occurred when ten people were promoted at the fifth year. By the eighth year, everyone had been promoted to this first rank. The second rank was also attained by everyone. This firm had more upper and lower exceptions than other firms, although, on the whole, the earlier winners were more likely to attain higher positions at later stages.

Pucik's study of a Japanese trading company

Pucik (1985) studied the career path of university graduates of a leading Japanese trading company on the basis of data collected in 1983. The conclusion was that the career tree of the company, shown in figure 6.2, resembled the 'tournament career model' described by Rosenbaum in the case of an American firm. According to Pucik, there was intense competition among Japanese managers in their thirties. The competition was of two kinds: (i) among the elite competing for future promotions, and (ii) among the rest of the cohort who feared slipping too fast too soon.

The career tree of this trading firm is essentially the same as the career tree of the manufacturing firm studied by Hanada. The first and main selections occurred simultaneously when 20 per cent of the cohort were promoted at the fourteenth year. To be selected to the top rank of Grade 1, an employee had to win in all previous contests, so there was no upper exception in this firm. On the other hand, there were some crossings in the lower ranks, implying the existence of lower exceptions.

Takeuchi's study of a Japanese insurance company

Takeuchi (1995) examined the career tree, shown in figure 6.3, of a cohort of university graduates in a large insurance company over the period 1966–88. The first selection occurred when all except one of sixty-seven employees were promoted during the fifth year or when fifty-six were promoted during the eighth year. The main selection occurred when five were promoted at the twelfth year, although this rank was eventually attained by all but two of the employees in the cohort. The highest rank was attained by those

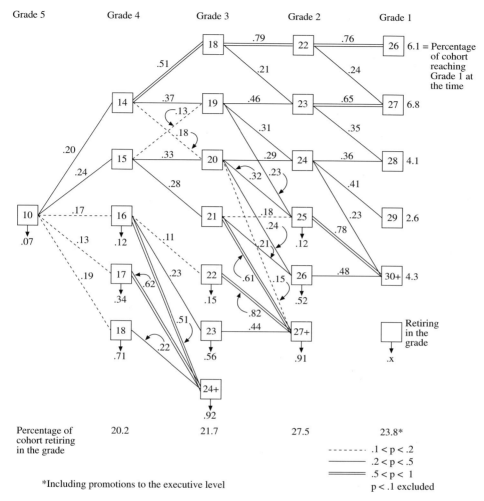

Fig. 6.2. Career tree of a Japanese trading company. (*Source:* Pucik, 1985.)

who had won in all previous contests, while there were minor crossings of careers for lower ranks.

Rosenbaum's study of a large US corporation

Rosenbaum (1979, 1984) studied the career path of about 670 employees of a large US manufacturing corporation over a thirteen-year period, 1962–75. The career tree is shown in figure 6.4. The sample included both high-school and university graduates, with no distinction made between them. This causes some difficulty in comparisons with Japanese data, which deal only with university graduates. However, since other statistical figures provided by Rosenbaum (1984) indicate that those who were promoted were mainly university graduates, comparisons may be reasonably justified.

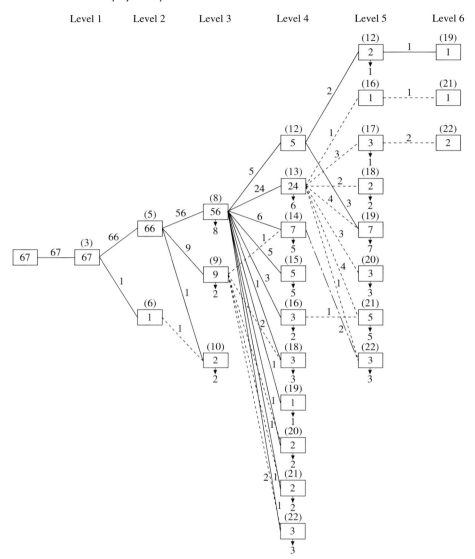

Fig. 6.3. Career tree of a Japanese insurance company. The figure in the box indicates the number of the promoted, the figure in parentheses the years taken for the promotion, and the figure under the box the proportion of those who retired from the position. A broken line indicates that the transition proportion is less than 0.2. (*Source:* Takeuchi, 1995.)

Rosenbaum's pioneering work on career trees first found that promotion competition was basically characterised as a tournament-type process. An employee's career was not a series of equal contests. Early competitions were more strongly associated with career outcomes than later competitions. By the third year of employment, an employee's eventual career chances had been fundamentally affected. Further, there existed a 'fast track'

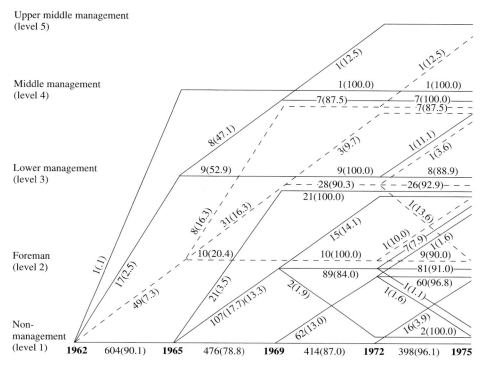

Fig. 6.4. Career tree of an American manufacturer. The figure on the line indicates the number of the promoted, with the proportion of the promoted in parentheses. (*Source:* Rosenbaum, 1984.)

system which promoted selected employees at a very early stage of employment to managerial positions. These employees attained the highest positions in the final stage. In Rosenbaum's study, observation time-points were fixed and so we do not know the exact promotion times. However, by at least the third year, one employee had been promoted to the rank of middle management and seventeen employees had been promoted to lower managers. That is, the first and main selections occurred between the third and fifth year of employment. The highest rank of upper middle management was attained by one of these eighteen people in 1975.

The company provided some limited scope for promotion for those who were not promoted in their early stages of employment. Thus, there existed some deviations from strict tournament competitions. The two positions of highest rank were attained not by the employee who was promoted to middle management in the first selection, but by one who was promoted to lower management and one who was promoted to foreman in the first selection. From figure 6.4, we notice further that, in competitions for lower positions, there were some cases in which previous losers overtook previous winners. However, there were only five cases of demotion, and the previous winners generally won in the later promotion rounds.

Other studies of US career trees

Forbes (1987) examined patterns of early upward mobility, over an eleven-year period, for a cohort of 180 employees who entered a US oil company in 1968, 1969 and 1970. The results offered only weak support for the tournament model of career mobility. Although early promotions were related to later attainment, strict tournament rules were not in force, because the losers were later able to move to promoted positions.

Shaeffer (1972) investigated fast-track programmes in large US companies. These companies had special career programmes which selected a group of prospective executive candidates when recruiting them from universities and MBA courses and trained them through cross-divisional rotation. There were no guarantees that the programme participants would automatically be promoted, and there existed intense tournament-type competition among the participants.

Comparisons between Japanese and US career trees

As shown above, career paths in the career tree diagrams in both Japan and the United States do not cross very often. This implies that promotion in both countries follows essentially tournament-type patterns. However, there are some exceptions to tournament outcomes with respect to both top- and lower-rank promotions. In the Japanese cases, in five out of seven companies considered, the top rank was attained only by those who had won all previous contests. On the other hand, this tournament rule did not hold in the US companies considered by Rosenbaum and Forbes.

Comparing some Japanese and American cases of promotion of office workers, Koike (1988) advanced the hypothesis that the Japanese promotion process could be characterised as one of late selection. According to this hypothesis, the crucial selection leading to executive positions occurs much later in Japan than in the USA. Although the evidence is very limited, the data seem to support this hypothesis. In Japan, main selection was undertaken on the average as late as the tenth year. The average first selection was at the eighth year. On the other hand, in Rosenbaum's study the first and main selections took place within three to five years.

Viewed from a slightly different perspective, only 0.3 per cent of employees attained the highest rank after thirteen years in the Rosenbaum data. Forbes's figures showed that 2 per cent reached the highest rank after eleven years. On the other hand, data from the five companies studied by Hanada indicated that, respectively, 3, 65, 74, 81 and 100 per cent of employees obtained the highest rank in fifteen years. In Pucik's data, 41 per cent attained the highest rank in twenty-five years. This contrast suggests that American firms had already selected a small number of elite employees within a fifteen-year period, while Japanese firms had yet to do so. In the Rosenbaum data, one person attained the second highest rank in three to five years. There seems to be no equivalent speedy selection in Japanese firms.

Most employees entering a Japanese firm at the same time usually attain initial promotion simultaneously. Then, the firm starts to differentiate between employees by the time of the first selection. At this stage, however, everyone will still eventually be promoted to the same rank. But the timing of promotion is decisive for later promotions.

After this stage, the seniority system does not apply strictly any longer. The firm then strengthens employee differentiation by not promoting some of its employees further.

6.3.2 Promotion of blue-collar workers

Unfortunately, there seem to be no systematic studies of career trees for production workers. Blue-collar promotion can only be inferred from more aggregated wage profiles. For example, from wage–age profiles disaggregated by different education levels and firm sizes, Koike (1988) found that the profiles of white-collar workers were relatively steep both in Japan and the West. The profiles of blue-collar workers were less steep than those of white collars within each country. However, the profile of Japanese blue-collar workers was much steeper than those of Western equivalent workers and resembled white-collar Western profiles. Koike refers to this phenomenon as 'white-collarization' of Japanese blue-collar workers. These observed patterns in blue-collar wage–age profiles indirectly suggest the following propositions for the promotion process of Japanese blue-collar workers. First, there are fewer prospects of promotion for blue-collars, which seems to hold not only in Japan but also in the West. Secondly, however, Japanese blue-collar workers seem to have a greater chance of promotion than their Western counterparts.

Koike (1994) undertook comparative case studies of blue-collar careers in a major Japanese car manufacturer and a Swedish manufacturer. The Japanese company had a job grade system ranging from P1 (Junior Worker) to P8 (Foreman) for non-managerial blue-collar positions. By the age of forty, successful production workers became sub-foremen (P6) while white collars arrived at O7, which is equivalent to P6, during the latter half of their thirties. However, only a fraction of production workers reached the level of P6, while almost all university graduates proceeded to O7. A production worker rarely attained a managerial position. As for Swedish blue-collar workers, Koike observed that: 'Whereas payment for Japanese production workers increases as their skills improve, wages hardly increased in the Swedish cases after the initial few years. Apart from the revision by collective bargaining, the basic rates for the operators on the assembly line in this Swedish car manufacturer never increased after one-and-a-half years of service, and no merit rating existed' (Koike, 1994, p. 61). This case study is consistent with the white-collarisation hypothesis.

6.3.3 The tournament system

The promotion process is often characterised as a tournament. Two different meanings of tournament are implied in the literature. The first, as used by Rosenbaum (1979), is that only the winners qualify for the next promotion contest. The second refers to rank-order tournaments, namely that promotion and compensation are determined not by individual ability, but by the relative rank of competitors.

In setting up promotion contests, why would firms consider only those employees who had won in previous competitions? The main reason stems from the notion of assessment costs. When internal labour markets develop and firm-specific human capital is accumulated, a structure of job ladders will develop inside the firm. As careers progress, workers are assigned to different jobs that require different abilities within the job rank hierarchy. It would be rather difficult and costly to compare the performances of the winners and losers, who have now quite different job ranks as a result of previous contests.

Why do firms reward employees not by individual ability but, more indirectly, by their assigned ranks? There are at least three reasons why the rank-order tournament scheme may be preferred by the firm (Ito, 1994, p. 252).

(i) Information for rank tournaments requires much coarser, less costly, information compared with that required for an individual assessment of performance.

(ii) Workers' earnings are less affected by uncontrollable noise because their performance ranking is insensitive to common random factors.

(iii) A tournament provides management with a means to commit to paying for performance. For example, the firm may decide not to raise wages upon observation of good performance by reporting that performance was not good enough. Under a tournament, the firm has nothing to gain by being dishonest, because misreporting a worker's performance leads to another worker's promotion.

However, tournament systems have their own problems. First, workers who compete for higher positions may have no incentive to co-operate. Secondly, contestants have incentives to collude in working at lower effort levels.

6.3.4 Late selection, human capital and incentives

Both Japanese and Western companies implement some kind of tournament system for promotion. Compared with Western practices, Japanese tournaments are characterised by late selection. Three conditions underlie the late selection system.

The first concerns the *labour market*. The development of internal labour markets tends to limit the degree of competition in the external labour market. The Japanese labour market in particular is noted for its long-term employment, so that mid-career job changes have been regarded somehow as deviations from normal labour practices. Those who enter a firm in mid-career typically do not fare well as far as payments and promotion prospects are concerned. Market competitiveness affects the nature of promotion systems decisively, as will be shown below.[12]

The second consideration embraces the role of *technology*. The promotion system is influenced by the nature of the technology in which the particular country specialises. Japan, as a late starter in industrialisation, has tended to specialise in industries with relatively slow, continuous technological progress. While there are notable exceptional cases, it has tended to give greater emphasis to the refinement and application of basic technology. Large Japanese firms accumulate huge stocks of technological knowledge (with an emphasis on firm-specific information) and take great care in transferring such knowledge to new generations of employees.

The third consideration is *work organisation* which, in part, is conditioned by the nature of the technological base. Japanese work organisation is designed to delegate more decision-making to lower-rank workers. Therefore, it is very important to enhance the incentives of low-rank workers in relation to high-rank workers in designing pay and promotion systems. It is also often noted that job demarcation is simpler and more fluid and that lateral interaction among workers is a significant feature. Thus, the promotion system is designed to facilitate workers' co-operation and to delay promotion in order to make reasons for job advancement more convincing to fellow workers.

The firm has to train new entrants systematically and intensively in order to transfer the accumulated knowledge stock to them. If companies institutionalise such training systems, selection should only occur after allowing for the completion of major phases of the education process. Given Japanese-type management, the qualities needed in higher-level jobs may be acquired only through long-term experience in the organisation. The managers must have a deep understanding of operating procedures, technology, other employees' skills and temperaments, and customers' and suppliers' characteristics. This type of long-term training requires selection to be late.

The question arises as to why large Japanese firms, in particular, use such intensive training. One reason is that they tend to concentrate in mature industries in which slow and steady innovation has been taking place for a considerable period of time. They have developed elaborated work organisations where interactions among workers, involving significant degrees of discretionary power, figure prominently. Seniority also plays the important role of transmitting accumulated skills and the senior–junior order is maintained in order to ensure such transmission. Not all business requires such training, however, and there are important sectors where such systems are not as relevant. For example, Japanese firms such as Nintendo, Sega and, more recently, Sony have been leading the world for a long time in the video game industry. Here, younger talented people play a leading role and do not depend on on-the-job training by older generations of workers. Notwithstanding these exceptional cases, late selection in Japan stems from a preponderance of industries with mature technologies combined with a comprehensive and systematic approach to familiarising workers with the accompanying high knowledge levels required.

Incentives also constitute important reasons for late selection in the Japanese promotion system. Japanese work organisations tend to delegate significant levels of decision-making to relatively low-rank workers. Moreover, intense lateral interaction among workers is encouraged. Arguably, fast-track approaches remove incentives for workers to develop these work modes. In other words, the potential for early promotion will discourage workers from sinking the long-term personal investments required to develop interactive skills within large work groups. In effect, late selection serves to prolong the returns from group participation and co-operation by encouraging workers to expend effort along these lines for a relatively long period. Evaluation becomes more objective because it concerns progress and adaptability over a long period and is undertaken by many superiors. It gives every employee a greater chance and has a less demoralising effect on losers. Further, all workers may feel that they are fairly treated by being given sufficient time to display their acquired capabilities. In turn, this may again help to lessen demoralisation effects for losers.

On the downside, late selection will discourage able workers. However, in an environment where innovations are steady and continuous, encouraging 'typical' workers may well be the optimal strategy. Furthermore, since the external labour market is not very competitive, job changes are rather costly.

Incentive effects of late selection also pertain to skill transfer from senior to junior workers. Senior workers can pass their acquired knowledge and skills to junior workers without the immediate fear of losing their status, because there will be no competition from junior workers during the early stages of the learning process. At later stages, some degree of competition may well take place between the two groups.

Prendergast (1992) has constructed two mathematical models with which to consider the incentive to acquire firm-specific human capital. The first model assumes that only the current employer has information on workers' abilities. The firm can either conceal the ability information and treat all workers equally (the Japanese mode), or reveal the information and promote those who are perceived to be more able (the US mode). When the labour market is not competitive, the Japanese mode provides more incentives for workers to acquire firm-specific skills, because many workers compete for future promotion. When the labour market is competitive, bids in the market tend to reveal the ability information and the current firm faces the danger of losing abler workers.

However, as Prendergast himself admits, the assumption of asymmetric ability information is rather strong. Even without a competitive labour market, abilities of workers are likely to be fairly widely known. Prendergast's second model assumes that the information on workers' ability is revealed to everyone. At the outset, based on available information, the company employs two equivalent workers. However, after a period of time has elapsed, one worker is perceived to have higher ability. The firm then provides some training to the workers. The results of his model show that workers' incentives to acquire human capital is maximised when the more able is handicapped by being given less training. This resembles Japanese practices to some extent. On the other hand, when the abler worker can renegotiate his contract, that is when the labour market is competitive, he is likely to be given more intensive training. This case is similar to a fast-track system such as practised in the USA.

Late selection provides a mechanism that promotes the accumulation of firm-specific human capital and that is compatible with the provision of work incentives. Such benefits are offset, to a greater or lesser extent, by problems associated with this approach to promotion. We list a number of potential difficulties.

(i) Delay in promotion may increase the costs associated with the misassignment of able employees to lower-level jobs.

(ii) Talented employees may quit the firm to receive higher compensation elsewhere. Under imperfect labour markets, however, this pressure is mitigated to some extent.

(iii) If education of managers requires specialised training over a long time period, then a slow selection scheme treating all workers equally in the early years of tenure may not be appropriate.

(iv) The Japanese promotion system creates strong competition among employees who enter the firm at the same time. With institutionalised training through

Table 6.4. *Distribution of retirement ages, 1967–96*

	Proportion of firms with retirement system (percentage)	Age of retirement in firms with retirement system (percentage of total)					
		55 or under	56–59	60	61–64	65	Over 65
1967	69.0	63.5	14.2	20.6	0.3	1.5	0.3
1973	66.6	52.3	12.3	32.4	0.4	2.6	0.0
1980	82.2	39.7	20.1	36.5	0.7	2.5	0.0
1985	87.3	27.1	17.4	51.0	2.1	1.8	0.5
1990	88.2	19.8	16.1	60.1	1.1	2.7	0.0
1992	92.2	11.7	11.7	71.4	1.7	3.4	0.1
1993	88.2	9.7	10.3	73.9	1.6	4.4	0.0
1994	90.5	8.1	7.8	77.1	2.0	5.0	0.0
1995	96.8	7.6	6.6	78.6	1.7	5.4	0.1
1996	93.4	5.9	5.8	80.4	1.7	6.1	0.1

Source: Ministry of Labour, Survey on Employment Management.

senior–junior relations, the direction of effort in this competition may be biased towards targets which satisfy senior workers but do not necessarily contribute to efficiency.

(v) Most seriously, fundamental new ideas from young generations of workers may never be realised or at best only slowly and sub optimally implemented. In the Japanese modernisation process in the post-war era, basic technology came from abroad. The Japanese late selection mechanism works well in such an economic catch-up stage and also copes well with continuous, relatively stable, technological progress. However, this system is not particularly suitable for creating totally new technology, systems or products.[13]

6.4 Retirement

6.4.1 The background picture

Japanese retirement practices feature high in the league table of stylised facts about the uniqueness of the Japanese post-war labour market. Japanese workers officially retire relatively early but thereafter continue to participate in the labour market in relatively large proportions. Both statements are correct. The picture with respect to mandatory retirement, however, is changing quite dramatically and shows convergence towards practices in Europe and elsewhere.

Table 6.4 shows time-series evidence on Japanese retirement over the past thirty years. More firms have been adopting retirement systems, the proportion increasing from 69 per cent in 1967 to 93.4 per cent in 1996. This trend has accompanied a clear shift towards later mandatory retirement ages. In 1967, 63.5 per cent of workers retired at 55 or earlier; by 1996, as many as 80.4 per cent of workers retired at 60. Although groups with retirement age limits of over 60 have been increasing over time, the overwhelming majority of firms are not exceeding the limit of 60. Thus, towards the end of the century, the mandatory age of Japanese retirement is much nearer to that of other countries than during the 1960s and 1970s. While mandatory retirement in Europe and elsewhere is 65 for men and 60/65 for women, the trend is downwards and, like Japan, it is 60 in countries like France, Italy and New Zealand (Organisation for Economic Co-operation and Development, 1992).

Retirement systems are more prevalent within medium-sized (300–999 employees) and larger firms (1,000–4,999 and over 5,000 employees), as illustrated for 1967 and 1996 in table 6.5. By 1996, virtually all these firms had a mandatory retirement age of 60 or over. By contrast, between only 9 and 15 per cent of them reported that their retirement age was 60 or over in 1967; in fact, the retirement ages of medium and larger firms concentrated in the age range 55 or under in 1967. Smaller firms (30–99 and 100–299 employees) also predominantly reported a retirement age of 60 or over in 1996 while, in 1967, they displayed a wider variation that was skewed towards the mid-fifties age groups. As for breakdowns by industry, it can be seen from table 6.6 that, on average in 1996, construction, finance/insurance, real estate, electricity/gas/water and manufacturing have later retirement ages while wholesale/retail/restaurant and transport/communication have earlier retirement ages.

Table 6.7 shows the proportions of economically active males in the 60–64 age group for Japan, Europe and the United States between 1960 and 1990. While decreases over this period were experienced in all cases, that of 6 per cent in Japan was extremely modest compared with the other countries. By 1990, the proportion in Japan far exceeded the proportions elsewhere. A related discussion of participation rates was presented in chapter 1.

The high propensity of older workers to remain in the economically active population should be set against demographic trends and related government economic and social policies. In 1994, 14 per cent of the Japanese population was over the age of 65, reasonably modest compared with Europe and the United States.[14] However, by 2050 this is projected to grow to 30.2 per cent, among the highest in the world (Organisation for Economic Co-operation and Development, 1997). In order to provide jobs for older people and to check the increasing demands on the pension funds, the government has been promoting the raising of retirement ages. In particular, a law was passed in 1986 with the aim of encouraging firms to raise the retirement age towards 60.[15] More recently, the law was revised to give firms with retirement systems the objective of setting the age of retirement at 60 or over from April 1998 with a longer-term aim to set the age at 65. Although the objective of a retirement age of 60 has been more or less attained, it is clear from the foregoing evidence that the vast majority of firms fall well short of the target of 65.

Table 6.5. *Retirement ages by firm size, 1967 and 1996*

Firm size	1967					1996				
	Firms with retirement system	Age of retirement in firms with retirement system (percentage of total)				Firms with retirement system	Age of retirement in firms with retirement system (percentage of total)			
(no. of employees)	(percentage)	55 or under	56–59	60 or over		(percentage)	55 or under	56–59	60 or over	
over 5,000	93.7	53.0	31.8	15.2		100.0	0.0	0.0	100.0	
1,000–4,999	95.3	60.2	30.8	9.0		99.7	0.4	1.3	98.3	
300–999[a]	96.5	68.3	20.4	11.3		99.8	1.7	2.7	95.5	
100–299[b]	76.6	66.0	8.7	25.3		98.4	3.7	3.8	92.5	
30–99	51.0	66.4	4.0	29.6		91.1	7.3	7.0	85.7	

Notes:

[a] 500–999 for 1967; [b] 100–499 for 1967.

Source: Ministry of Labour, Survey on Employment Management.

Table 6.6. *Retirement ages by industries, 1996*

Industries	Firms with retirement system (percentage)	Age of retirement in firms with retirement system (percentage of total)		
		55 or under	56–59	60 or over
Mining	89.8	5.3	11.8	82.9
Construction	83.1	3.6	1.7	94.7
Manufacturing	96.4	4.7	5.3	90.0
Electricity, gas & water	100.0	4.7	4.7	90.7
Transport & communication	98.7	8.2	8.9	82.9
Wholesale, retail & restaurants	89.5	8.7	7.6	83.7
Finance & insurance	100.0	3.8	1.6	94.6
Real estate	94.1	5.1	2.5	92.4
Services	95.2	5.5	6.0	88.5

Source: Ministry of Labour, Survey on Employment Management.

Table 6.7. *Economically active population ratio for males in age group 60–64 (active population/total population)*

	1960	1970	1980	1990
Japan	81.9	85.5	81.5	76.9
United States	77.1 (61)	73.0	57.8	55.1
France	71.1 (62)	65.7 (68)	46.7	21.1
West Germany	72.5 (61)	68.8	44.2	35.1
United Kingdom	n.a.	86.5 (71)	n.a.	54.3

Notes:
The numbers in parentheses indicate the closest year available.
Source: ILO, *Yearbook of Labour Statistics.*

6.4.2 An economic conundrum

The agency theory of Lazear (1979) offers a powerful tool that helps in understanding the age of mandatory retirement. Suppose a representative worker enjoys lifetime tenure with a firm. Lazear shows that it pays the firm and the worker to agree to a wage payments schedule in which the worker receives less than the value of her marginal product in early work years and more in later ones. This provides performance incentives to the worker who would be expected to be better off – that is, to enjoy higher lifetime wealth – under such an arrangement than, say, by receiving her marginal product each and every time period. Since the worker would be reluctant to close the contract given that pre-retirement years are highly paid relative to marginal product, mandatory retirement serves to ensure contract termination.

In fact, the theory predicts that long-tenured and more able workers are more likely to experience mandatory retirement than those with low tenure. As illustrated in chapter 1 (table 1.3), Japanese workers in large firms enjoy the longest average tenure. Yet, as shown in table 6.5, these are the very firms which appear to be at the forefront of the move to *raise* the age of retirement. Not only is this observation puzzling in terms of Lazear's theory but it is even more surprising that such firms are raising the age of retirement at the same time that the proportion of older workers is steadily increasing.

These facts do not sit comfortably with the Lazear hypothesis. Of course, the government has been vigorously campaigning to raise retirement ages. But it is still not clear what made firms adopt a policy that, if wages exceed marginal products in later years, would serve to increase their unit labour costs. Some Japanese observers, such as Ohashi (1990), have suggested that union power may have played a part in increasing the retirement age.[16] However, union power has been in decline for a long time, as clearly shown by the steady decrease in union density.

Notes

1 In large firms, it is customary for many employees aged 50 or over to be transferred to related smaller companies. They usually remain as employees of the original firms and are often compensated for any resulting wage differentials. In a recent case of a large bank, there were 880 employees in the age group 50–54. However, 660 of them were not in the bank but transferred to other firms with their formal status as the employees of the bank intact (a hearing reported in Chuma and Higuchi, 1997, p.196).

2 Strictly, the importance of recruitment costs should be measured with respect to total labour cost (including severance pay, payments in kind, obligatory and voluntary social welfare payments, vocational education as well as other smaller categories of labour costs: see chapter 4 for full cost definitions). However, we do not pursue the broader definition here since it makes a relatively small quantitative difference to the analysis in hand.

3 The denominator in measure B can be derived from a standard Mincer (1974) earnings–tenure equation (see chapter 2, equation 2.3). Lifetime earnings are derived from an estimated earnings–tenure profile in a previous study (Hart and Kawasaki, 1995). Ignoring individual, industry and time subscripts, the earnings equation is given by

$$log\ Y = a_0 + a_1E + a_2E^2 + a_3T + a_4T^2 + a_5(E \times T)$$

where log Y is the log of real cash earnings, E is total labour market experience (calculated as age minus length of schooling minus 6) and T is length of service in the current firm. Estimates are based on data from the Japanese Basic Survey of Wage Structure that are arranged to form a pseudo-panel to control for age cohorts. The cohorts covered five-year age bands and were observed between 1971 and 1991 at five-yearly intervals. The cohort used for present purposes consisted of workers aged 25–29 in 1971, 30–34 in 1976 and so on. Estimated values of the wage earnings equation are

$$\log Y = 2.995 + 0.049E - 0.009E^2 + 0.07T - 0.019T^2 + 0.024(E \times T)$$

In order to calculate expected lifetime earnings, it is assumed that a worker enters the 'representative' firm in 1991 immediately after schooling. We can then simulate wage earnings growth with respect to experience and tenure. Following standard practice, expected length of tenure in the firm is taken to be twice the length of observed tenure. The calculation of expected lifetime earnings, valued in 1991, assumes a discount rate of 0.05.

4 See table 6.2 for data sources and values of TURN by industry.

5 There is a strong positive correlation between measures A and B ($r = 0.89$).

6 Note that services and real estate incur extremely high relative values of recruitment cost per worker. Their measures of C and D lie more than one standard deviation above the mean.

7 The simple correlation between the male/total worker ratio and TURN is -0.40.

8 This negative relationship may be offset to some degree because higher male contractual earnings – and, therefore, bigger potential losses if wrong recruitment decisions are made – may lead to more careful screening Thus, *both* earnings and recruitment costs may be higher.

9 The manufacturing sector in table 6.3 contains all Japanese manufacturing industries while the separate manufacturing industries in tables 6.1 and 6.2 do not constitute an exhaustive list. For this reason, the weighted averages and standard deviations in table 6.3 cannot be compared with the earlier tables.

10 Recent evidence by Barron *et al.* (1989) provides some insight, from a 1982 US sample, into the time devoted to on-the-job training, but falls well short of providing cost estimates. See the discussion in Malcomson (1997).

11 Suppose that there are one hundred new entrants to a firm in a given year. In the fifth year, seventy people from this cohort are promoted to the lowest rank. While this is a promotion 'selection', it is a weak one because the majority of workers are selected. While somewhat arbitrary, a main selection is said to occur when less than half of the cohort are promoted. This is more likely to reflect a genuine selection procedure, rather than being greatly dominated by large elements of automatic selection.

12 Ito (1994, pp. 255–6) points out that the lack of competitiveness of the Japanese external labour market may arise endogenously from the incentive and skill formation mechanisms themselves.

13 See Aoki (1988, p. 37) and Ito (1987).

14 In 1994, Germany had 16.0 per cent of its population over the age of 65, the United Kingdom, 15.7 per cent, France 15.1 per cent and the United States, 12.7 per cent.

15 No formal penalties are imposed if firms fail to achieve new targets. Rather, bureaucrats issue administrative guidance in attempts to persuade firms to follow government policy.

16 Ohashi (1990) has attempted to model the determinants of retirement ages in the light of Lazear's theory. Using cross-sectional data for 1976 and 1980, Ohashi esti-

mated a regression in which retirement ages were explained by the slope of the wage profile, the proportion of older workers, firm size, union power and other factors. He found that the steeper the wage slope and the larger the proportion of older workers, the earlier the age of retirement. Unfortunately, significant increases in the age of mandatory retirement have occurred since these periods of study, together with increasing worries about the ageing population, and it is not at all clear whether these findings could be replicated with more up-to-date statistics.

7 Employment, productivity and costs over the business cycle

In section 1.2 attention was drawn to the cyclical features of post-war labour productivity in Japan and other countries. Labour market policy-makers devote considerable time to attempting to understand cyclical fluctuations in employment, productivity and labour costs given their close association with the problems of unemployment and labour force participation (notably the 'discouraged worker effect'). Aspects of these latter associations were reviewed in section 1.5. This chapter is devoted to labour market issues related to the cyclicality of employment and costs not only because of the importance of the topic but also because Japanese performance in several important areas appears to differ significantly from several other major economies. In broad terms, and in comparative international settings, we investigate (i) the so-called labour hoarding hypothesis in relation to Japanese business cycles and (ii) the movements of Japanese marginal cost and price over the cycle.

7.1 Pro-cyclical productivity and the labour hoarding hypothesis

Japanese labour productivity varies pro-cyclically. In other words, output per hour is observed to decrease during downturns in the business cycle and increase during upturns. This finding is by no means restricted to Japan; it is a common feature of productivity movements in all major economies, at both micro- and macro-levels of observation.[1] The dominant explanation of this phenomenon is the so-called labour hoarding hypothesis. While attention is principally confined to this hypothesis, we also comment on competing theories in section 7.6.

As discussed in chapter 2, where firm-specific human capital investments are substantial and highly profitable, firms and workers will be particularly cautious about separating in the event of an unanticipated downturn in product demand. As long as joint rents remain positive, or even if they turn negative in the short run, it may well be in the mutual interest of firms and workers to maintain long-term employment relationships. Returns to investments are uncertain and information held by the firm and its workers on productivity and outside opportunities may be asymmetric. Lower transaction costs of communication between the parties are associated with both more efficient employment contracts and higher levels of firm-specific human capital investment. High investments combined with strong mutual trust help to minimise inefficient separations. That is, fewer quits or layoffs will occur during short-term recessionary periods if expected (discounted long-term) joint rents are positive.

There has been considerable speculation in the literature that transaction costs may be relatively low in Japan. Cultural characteristics stemming from the traditional agricultural system have helped to promote and to ingrain shared decision-making in the modern industrial setting. This is exemplified, in part, by the enterprise union system and the firm being composed of a coalition of partners. Low transaction costs encourage the parties to protect firm-specific investments by emphasising price (i.e. wages) rather than quantity adjustments in the face of business cycle fluctuations. The objective is to achieve long-term returns to human capital and organisational investments. This means avoiding unplanned quits and layoffs – involving writing off sunk investment costs – and emphasising agreed short-term fluctuations in shared rents. Frequent recontracting over wages and bonuses accommodates the necessary fine-tuning. The corollary is that there is likely to be a strong tendency to retain excess stocks of employment during cyclical downturns. Given diminishing returns, labour productivity will fall in recessions and rise in expansionary periods.

7.2 The workers–hours dichotomy

If excess labour occurs on the extensive margin of the labour market due to hoarding effects, what about the intensive margin? Productivity is measured as output per hour. Its variation can be influenced by propensities to hire and fire under changing economic conditions *as well as* by changes in average hours worked and effort requirements per hour. Clearly, labour hoarding is inadequately described purely in terms of numbers of workers if average per period hours of work can also be varied.[2] For example, a given firm may try to offset a positive gap between actual and desired workforce size over some discrete time interval by reductions in average hours per employee. Is it generally the case, however, that firms with a high propensity to hoard excess labour stocks during economic downturns would be more inclined to effect speedy and large cutbacks in labour utilisation in order partially to compensate this tendency? There are two competing scenarios.

The first possibility concerns the use of hours as an internal buffer against demand fluctuations. We have already indicated that flexible wage contracts in Japan partly represent, given a relatively low transaction cost environment, an intensive margin adjustment mechanism in the event of unforecasted demand changes. Note, however, that wage costs per person are represented by the wage rate multiplied by the number of working hours per period. It may be the case that bargaining over wages during recessionary intervals may produce both wage rate *and* working time downward adjustments; in other words, average hours may also be regarded as part of the internal buffer. In this event, measuring excess labour purely by recourse to the employment stock would tend to overestimate the phenomenon of labour hoarding since an excess of actual over desired workers would be offset by reductions in labour utilisation.

An alternative role for hours derives from specific human capital considerations. The main implication of low transaction costs in Japan is that firms are more willing to risk high levels of specific human capital investments. From standard theory we know that the higher are such investments, the longer are desired investment amortisation periods. The length of amortisation per worker is related to *both* the expected length of tenure *and* the degree of work intensity. Suppose that there is an unanticipated decline in product demand and that the firm takes the short-run decision not to lay off workers. It then faces a choice between two types of cost. It can decide to maintain working hours at pre-recession levels and build up its inventories above planned or 'normal' levels. Alternatively, it can reduce working hours and, for given expected tenure lengths, incur investment costs associated with reduced amortisation time periods.[3] This links to research work (e.g. Miller, 1971; Greer and Rhoades, 1977; Topel, 1982; Rossana, 1983, 1985) that models working time within demand systems that attempt to capture the interrelatedness of hours, workers and inventories.

If the former scenario is most representative of Japanese experience – that is, hours of work, in common with wage rates, are flexibly adjusted so as to act as a buffer to demand fluctuations – then we might expect relatively speedy hours adjustment. If, by contrast, the associated human capital costs of rescheduling hours are deemed to be high relative to inventory costs – as discussed under the second scenario – then hours, like employment, should exhibit sluggish adjustment.

7.3 Fair's workers–hours model of excess labour over the cycle

With an eye to our discussion of empirical work in section 7.4, we highlight an influential approach to modelling excess labour over the cycle. This is Fair's workers–hours model (e.g. Fair, 1985).

Effective hours can be defined as per period actual working hours adjusted for variations in effort. Unfortunately, in most data sets, and especially those describing macro-level variables, measured hours differ from effective hours in two important ways. First, measured hours rarely contain adjustments for changes in productive effort. Effort may vary over the working day or week (Barzel, 1973), or seasonally, or cyclically. Secondly, measured hours typically refer to paid-for hours and these differ from actual hours worked because they contain payments for non-worked time. Examples of the latter vary among data sources and include such items as get-ready time, set-up time, refreshment breaks, holiday bonuses, paid-for vacations and public holidays.

We might reasonably assume that efficient utilisation of available hours occurs at the observed peaks of actual hourly productivity cycles. At times of cyclical peak demand, the phenomenon of excess labour is unlikely to feature prominently, if at all. Labour utilisation would be expected to be such that firms achieve maximum per period effort levels from their workers. Also, the gap between actual and paid-for hours would be minimised as firms eliminate all but essential paid-for non-work hours. Accordingly, the convention commonly adopted in the literature is to assume that peak points in time series of actual hourly productivity do in fact correspond to fully utilised, effectively worked, total hours. Joining peaks by linear segments and comparing these with actual productivity paths provides a proxy of excess labour for each time period.[4]

On the assumption that adjustment costs are incurred when changing workers and hours, Fair derives labour demand equations (e.g. Fair, 1985). The demand for workers is a function of the number of excess workers on hand and of expected future output changes. The demand-for-hours specification accommodates adjustments between actual and desired hours, adjustments of hours to excess workers as well as adjustments to expected future output changes. Proxies for excess labour depend on the above trends-through-peaks method.[5]

From the derived separate demand equations for workers and hours, three parameters are of particular interest:

- *coefficient of excess workers* which denotes the percentage of excess workers that are eliminated each period;
- *coefficient of hours adjustment* which gives the speed at which actual hours are adjusted towards desired hours;
- *coefficient of hours/excess worker adjustment* which depicts the degree to which hours each period adjust so as to accommodate the number of excess workers.

7.4 Empirical evidence from Japan, Europe and the United States

The finding that firms hold excess labour during recessions is not confined to Japan. For example, three recent studies of cyclical fluctuations in United States labour demand have reached consistent findings (Fay and Medoff, 1985; Fair, 1985; Aizcorbe, 1992).[6] In recent troughs of the business cycle, US manufacturing industry appears to hold between 4 and 8 per cent of labour in excess of that required to meet production requirements. But, might we expect a more significant tendency to react in this way in Japan? *A priori*, the answer is yes.

Arguably, Japan has both a stronger economic motive and a better industrial climate for labour hoarding. In the first respect, Hashimoto and Raisian (1985) and Mincer and Higuchi (1988) obtain results that support strongly the proposition that firm-specific human capital investments are significantly higher in Japan than the United States (see chapter 2). In the second, Hashimoto (1979) and Aoki (1988) argue that the typical Japanese firm enjoys lower transaction costs than its US equivalent.

It is more difficult to make *a priori* judgements between Japan and Europe. Differentiating between blue- and white-collar workers, Koike (1988) finds evidence of steeper wage–tenure profiles during the early years of tenure in Japan compared to the

Table 7.1. *Quarterly adjustments of workers and hours*

	Japan	Germany	UK	USA
Coefficient of excess labour	−0.06	−0.26	−0.22	−0.26
Coefficient of hours adjustment	−0.15	−0.50	−0.35	−0.39
Coefficient of hours/excess worker adjustment	0.00	−0.24	−0.08	−0.16

Note:
Estimation was made over the following periods: Japan, 1967(I)–91(IV); Germany, 1960 (II)–91(IV); UK, 1963 (II)–91(IV); USA, 1960 (II)–91(IV).
Source: Hart and Malley (1996).

United Kingdom; this supports the notion – along the lines of Hashimoto and Raisian – that specific investments are more significant in the former economy. Somewhat less direct evidence from estimated age–wage profiles by Koike point to higher investments in Japan than in the major Western European countries.[7] Other broadly based empirical evidence is provided by Odagiri (1992) who in a five-nation comparison (Japan, the United States, Federal Republic of Germany, France and the United Kingdom) of two hoarding proxies – based on employment elasticities and labour's share – shows that Japan is most prone to hoard workers during contracting demand conditions. First, for all countries, Odagiri estimates output (real GDP) elasticities of employment (measured as workers times average hours) below one; however, Japan's estimate of 0.16 is considerably smaller than the next lowest (France) at 0.56. Secondly, in a regression analysis of labour's share on real GDP, Japan like other countries displays a negative correlation. This is in line with the hoarding hypothesis, where the share would be expected to rise (fall) in a contractionary (expansionary) phase. The counter-cyclical movements are found to be most prominent in Japan and the UK and least marked in Germany and the USA.

Work on hours of work has been more mixed. Abraham and Houseman (1989) suggest that, if anything, Japanese manufacturing hours are slightly less responsive to demand fluctuations than in the United States. Hashimoto (1990) finds that the former hours adjust slightly more than the latter.

Using quarterly manufacturing data between the 1960s and the early 1990s for Japan, the Federal Republic of Germany, the United Kingdom and the United States, Hart and Malley (1996) derive excess labour estimates based on Fair's model outlined in the previous section. At the outset, it is important to emphasise an important difference between Japan and the other countries with regard to the measurement of working time. Hours of work in Japan refer to actual hours worked and not, as elsewhere, to paid-for hours. Thus, while for each and every country there will exist a gap between measured and effective hours of work due to fluctuations in effort, the German, UK and US gaps additionally include paid-for but unworked hours.

In section 7.3, we listed the three excess labour parameters that can be derived from

Table 7.2. *Excess total hours, 1970–1991 (percentages)*

	1970–91	1970–80	1981–91
Japan	4.69	6.22	3.35
Germany	2.54	2.62	2.47
UK	1.76	1.24	2.20
US	1.66	1.68	1.63

Source: Hart and Malley (1996).

Fair's methodology. Hart and Malley's estimates of these are summarised in table 7.1. The responses of workforce size to the number of excess workers are shown in row 1. Germany, the UK and the USA display remarkably similar adjustment coefficients, with between 22 and 26 per cent of excess workers being eliminated each quarter. In sharp contrast, Japan displays a 6 per cent elimination. The speed of hours adjustment to desired hours and the adjustment of hours to excess workers are shown in rows 2 and 3, respectively. Germany exhibits the fastest hours adjustment; *ceteris paribus*, actual hours per worker are adjusted 50 per cent towards desired hours per quarter. The UK and the USA provide similar estimates at, respectively, 35 and 39 per cent per quarter. Again, the Japanese estimate is a distinct outlier; a much lower degree of adjustment, at 15 per cent, is obtained. Manufacturing hours in both Germany and the USA reduce significantly in response to excess workers, with estimates of -0.24 and -0.16 respectively. The equivalent estimate for the UK is much lower at -0.08, while the coefficient for Japan is not significantly different from zero.

In relation to these estimates, what are the implications of the fact that Japanese working time statistics refer to actual hours worked while those of the other three countries measure paid-for hours? Assume that Japan and one of the other countries were able comparably to extend or reduce actual working hours within a paid-for, but classified as non-work, activity. The ability to vary vacation time provides perhaps the most obvious example.[8] In Japan, this means of changing actual hours worked would be fully reflected in the recorded data. But, elsewhere, paid-for hours would remain unchanged and so there would be no indication in the data of this mode of adjustment. Correction for this deficiency would make the estimated adjustment coefficients larger. Therefore, the hours measurement discrepancy between Japan and elsewhere serves to *narrow* the respective estimated adjustment differences. In other words, estimated values of the hours adjustment coefficients in rows 2 and 3 in table 7.1 for Germany, the UK and USA are downwardly biased to the extent that substitution possibilities exist between paid-for worked and non-worked hours.

As an additional exercise, Hart and Malley carried out dynamic simulations of the model in order to obtain estimates of excess total hours for various time periods. These were calculated over three separate periods, the first including both the 1973/4 and 1981/2 recessions and the other two including the 1970s' and 1980s' recessions separately. The main findings are reported in table 7.2. For the 1970–91 period taken as a whole, average estimated excess total hours in Japan are nearly twice those of Germany, which themselves are significantly larger than in the UK and the USA. Japan and Germany's higher rankings are retained when the period is broken down into the two decades, although the gap between the countries narrows considerably in the latter compared with the former.

Two competing hypotheses were outlined in section 7.2 concerning hours variability where there is a high propensity to hold excess labour stock. Hours may be highly variable so as to counteract the hoarding costs. Alternatively, given high levels of firm-specific investment, hours may not be reduced significantly during recessions but, instead, firms may choose to increase inventories above planned levels. Given that we observe hours rigidity in Japan then we would anticipate a higher stocks–output responsiveness over the cycle than in the other countries. For the three countries for which data exist, Hart and Malley obtained evidence that appears to confirm these latter expectations. They found, *ceteris paribus*, that a percentage point fall in output in Japan leads to a much greater increase of current stocks and that this effect persists far longer than in Germany and the UK.

Because of data availability and compatibility, comparative international studies of employment and hours adjustments, like those described above, tend to focus on data that describe aggregate (usually two-digit) industries and annual time series. There are clear dangers in this approach, however. Use of firm-level and industry-level data prevent the capture of adjustments between plants in the firm or firms in the industry. Moreover, using time periods of one year does not allow observation of very short-term adjustments. At firm level, workers may appear to be adjusting sluggishly to economic events when, in reality, unanticipated changes in employment demand may be met by continual short-term employment transfers taking place among plants within the same firm. This tendency may be expected to be especially important where a range of products, intended for different markets, are made across the plants. Hildreth and Ohtake (1998) attempt to remedy these potential aggregation problems by examining dynamic labour demand at company level. Adopting the methodology of Hamermesh (1989), they study employment, employment utilisation and hours adjustment on a monthly basis (January 1990 to October 1995) in a large manufacturing company in the Japanese motor vehicles sector. Contrary to the foregoing aggregate studies, their evidence supports the notion of swift and continual labour adjustments. In fact, they conclude that long-term employment within the firm is facilitated, in part, by the ability of employers to reach agreements with unions and workers that allow for short-term interplant mobility.

Of course, moving from high levels of aggregation to micro-based studies involves a trade-off. While disaggregation facilitates more in-depth knowledge of the true nature of the adjustment process within specific companies, it becomes difficult to argue that findings are representative of wider experience. There is no question, however, that far more company-level research projects would serve to enrich our understanding of these and related problems.

7.5 Competing theories of pro-cyclical productivity

There are three prominent alternative explanations of pro-cyclical productivity. The first involves the influence of technology shocks. In competitive real business cycle models, technology changes drive business cycle fluctuations. Labour input rises in order to achieve real wage increases resulting from the short-term technology-led stimulus to productivity. Even with assumptions of diminishing returns to labour, labour productivity varies pro-cyclically. A second explanation embraces the possibility of true increasing returns (see Hall, 1988, 1990).[9] Thirdly, pro-cyclical productivity has been argued to result from the presence of externalities (Cabellero and Lyons, 1990, 1992).

Cyclical changes in work organisation and practice have also been associated with pro-cyclical productivity. One example is studied in detail by Fay and Medoff (1985) and involves firms reallocating labour during downturns towards tasks that might influence future output; examples include maintenance, training and machinery overhaul. Another, studied by Aizcorbe (1992) in relation to US car assembly plants, centres on the correlation of labour specialisation and line speed. As line speed increases, related job tasks become more specialised and this yields productivity gains.

From chapter 2, low transaction costs of communicating between managers and workers and verifying information within the firm are likely to be positively related to relatively high per capita investments in firm-specific human capital. In turn, this should be associated with high propensities to hold excess labour during recessions as bargaining parties attempt to protect sunk investment costs as well as to safeguard expected future positive joint rents. But, of course, transaction cost considerations are not confined to within-firm information exchange. Asymmetric information among firms gives rise to potentially serious interfirm transaction costs. It may be the case that Japan has been relatively successful in reducing costs in this domain through the development of business groups consisting of independent companies that are involved in 'information exchange, the pursuit of growth through in-group joint ventures, and mutual insurance' (Odagiri, 1992). This suggests that externalities may provide an important explanation in the observation of pro-cyclical productivity in Japan. Specialised production, combined with strong interfirm networking and co-ordinated activities, may permit particularly strong and effective output responses to positive economic shocks. By contrast, higher transaction costs among firms in countries like the United States, may preclude the same degree of externality effects. Vertical integration of firms rather than co-operative association across firms is likely to be more emphasised in a high transaction cost environment. In this event, internal increasing returns rather than strong spillovers may characterise the US and similar markets.[10] Vecchi (1998) has investigated empirically these suggested distinctions between Japan and the United States.

7.6 The marginal cost of labour over the cycle in Japan and the United States

7.6.1 Setting the scene

In conventional neoclassical labour demand theory, the firm equates the ratio of the marginal productivities of labour and capital to the ratio of their respective marginal costs. In reality, even if this comparative static optimising rule constitutes an adopted goal of firms, labour market impediments may prevent its short-run realisation. One obvious impediment derives from the previous discussion. Given sunk investment costs, labour hoarding may involve the firm retaining marginal workers in the short run even if the marginal conditions are not realised. It must weigh up the costs of retaining excess labour, thereby not fulfilling short-term profit-maximising objectives, against those of laying off workers with the potential loss of longer-term positive rents.

In general, how might we expect marginal costs to change at different phases of the business cycle? In discussing this issue, we concentrate our attention on marginal labour costs. In particular, we are interested in reactions on the firm's intensive margin (i.e. variations in hours of work) to produce a marginal change in output.[11] As summarised by Blanchard and Fischer (1989), marginal cost has generally been found either to display little variation or to move counter-cyclically. Such tendencies are commonly linked to the widespread observation that labour productivity, measured as output per hour, fluctuates pro-cyclically (see Zarnowitz, 1985). During upturns, firms deal with expanding order-books by, in part, utilising workers and hours more intensively. This results in positive productivity effects. These may serve partially to offset, or more than offset, the increasing marginal costs of hiring new workers or extending the overtime schedules of existing workers. Conversely, during recessions, reduced marginal costs related to falls in the use of overtime may be counteracted by reductions in labour productivity due to hoarding.

Following Bils (1987), we can identify three major influences on short-run marginal costs on the firm's intensive margin. These are changes in the straight-time wage, the marginal wage schedule (i.e. the effect on the wage bill of a change in average hours) and total hours employed per unit of output (i.e. the inverse of hourly productivity). Hart and Malley (1998) suggest that differences in these components between Japan and the United States provide an interesting backdrop against which to study the cyclical behaviour of marginal cost between the two countries. The key comparative issues are as follows.

The measurement of hours of work

As reported in section 7.5, Japanese data record hours effectively worked while United States data report paid-for hours. The latter include hours for which there is no direct work activity. The main consequences for the measurement of marginal cost are as follows. On the upturn of the cycle, productivity increases associated with a rise in the proportion of actual worked to total hired hours would be properly recorded in Japan but exaggerated in the United States. Moreover, the Japanese observed marginal wage schedule would accurately record increases in hours worked and their associated marginal wage increments. The US schedule would underestimate the changes since part of the increased hours would constitute the (unrecorded) narrowing of the gap between actual and paid-for hours.

Hourly labour productivity

As previously discussed, the phenomenon of labour hoarding has been closely linked in the literature to the observation that hourly labour productivity is pro-cyclical. From the discussion of empirical work on this issue in section 7.5, there are reasons for believing that there are stronger industrial propensities to hoard labour in Japan than in the United States. We might expect, therefore, differential productivity effects within the total measures of marginal cost between the two countries.

Nominal and real wage flexibility

Biannual wage bargaining in Japan contrasts with the approach in the United States where three-year staggered, overlapping, wage contracts typify many bargains (see Bruno and Sachs, 1985, pp. 245–7). Cyclical variability in the manufacturing wage bill in Japan appears to stem more from nominal wage changes relative to hours of work and employment in Japan than in the United States (Gordon, 1982). Gordon's study reveals greater nominal and real wage volatility in Japan compared with the USA, findings that have been replicated in other studies (see the survey by Tachibanaki, 1987b). There has been some debate as to whether Japanese flexibility emanates primarily from bonus payments or from base wages.

The marginal wage schedule

On the firm's intensive margin, increases in marginal costs may result from a rise in the proportion of overtime in total hours, with overtime remunerated at premium rates. Increases may also stem from the fact that average overtime premium rates of pay are positively related to average hours. Individual workers may face rising overtime step functions whereby higher overtime hours per period trigger higher marginal premium rates. Given hours variations across workers, discontinuities will be smoothed out.

This latter possibility – that the mean premium will be positively related to average hours – is more likely to be a feature of the Japanese rather than the US labour market. This is because a minimum overtime premium of 25 per cent applies in Japan[12] and it is quite possible that some firms may have to pay marginal rates above this to secure overtime requirements during boom periods. In the United States, by contrast, the minimum premium rate – mandated under the 1938 Fair Labor Standards Act on weekly hours worked in excess of forty – is 50 per cent and this is exceptionally high by international standards. It is set at a level that probably precludes significant increases in rates towards peaks in the business cycle.[13]

7.6.2 Empirical findings

Following the approach of Bils (1987), Hart and Malley (1998) estimate marginal cost over the cycle in Japan and the United States. The procedure is in two stages. The first stage consists of estimating the components of the marginal wage schedule. These are (i) the change in overtime hours for a change in total hours,[14] and (ii) the change in average premium to a change in average overtime hours.[15] Estimation is based on sixteen two-digit industries in the two countries. Annual observations for each industry run from 1958 to 1990 for Japan and from 1960 to 1992 for the United States.

There are three main findings in stage one:

(i) In 1960, the base year in the United States, an increase in one hour from a base of forty regular hours, raises overtime by 0.61 hours. The response from this baseline increases to a peak in 1971 with an increase in overtime of 0.69 hours. Similar evaluation is more difficult in Japan because basic wages vary by industry and through time.[16] In the base year 1958, an increase in one hour from a base in which each industry is assumed to be working at its level of maximum regular hours (varying among industries around a mean of 41.9 hours) is associated with an increase in average overtime of 0.44 hours. This is a similar reaction to that in the United States.

(ii) While, as stated in (i), an average hours increase of one hour from a base of forty hours in the United States is associated with a 0.61 hours increase in overtime, a further one hour increase is associated with a rise in overtime of 0.66 hours. The respective changes in Japan are 0.44 and 0.54 hours.

(iii) As expected, the average overtime premium in the United States varies little from 1.5. By contrast, as Japanese average overtime hours rise from 0 to 1 the mean premium rises from 1.25 to 1.37.

The second stage of estimation involves regressing the three components of marginal cost – the straight-time wage, the estimated marginal wage schedule and total hours per unit of output (the reciprocal of hourly productivity) – separately on time trends and on a measure of the business cycle. There are four main findings:

(i) A 10 percentage point increase in real output is associated with a 6.2 percentage point decrease in total hours per unit of output in Japan and with an even larger 8.1 percentage point decrease in the United States. These results are compatible in signs, though not in relative magnitudes, with labour hoarding effects discussed in Section 7.5.[17]

(ii) There are very small cyclical changes in nominal wages in both countries; there is a pro-cyclical response in Japan and a counter-cyclical response in the United States.

(iii) The marginal wage schedule displays the expected positive association with the cycle measure, with the size of response similar in the two countries. [18]

(iv) Taking the above results together, marginal cost is markedly counter-cyclical in both countries.

7.7 The mark-up

An associated issue relates to the cyclical behaviour of marginal cost in relation to product price. In particular, does the price–cost mark-up display systematic cyclical patterns of behaviour? These questions have been of great interest to labour market and macro economists. Existing empirical work has produced very mixed findings.[19] In US studies, while Bils (1987) and Rotemberg and Woodford (1992) find that the mark-up is counter-cyclical, evidence from Domowitz *et al.* (1986) supports pro-cyclical mark-ups. In Japan, recent work by Ariga and Ohkusa (1995) supports the existence of pro-cyclical mark-ups in Japan; however, earlier work by Shinjo (1977) finds counter-cyclical mark-ups while the study of Odagiri and Yamashita (1987) produces mixed results.

Two studies are directly concerned with Japan–US comparisons. The first is by Wachtel and Adelsheim (1977). They assert, and provide empirical support with US industrial data, that where firms possess market power, as proxied by industrial concentration, they will increase price mark-ups during recessions in order to offset revenue losses due to declining sales. Odagiri and Yamashita (1987) test the Wachtel and Adelsheim hypothesis on Japanese manufacturing data. Their results are generally inconclusive although, if anything, tend to contradict the US findings.

The second study is a continuation of Hart and Malley (1998). As with marginal cost, price is also found to be counter-cyclical in both countries. A 10 percentage point increase in real output is associated with a 2.4 percentage point price fall in Japan and a 0.6 percentage point fall in the United States.[20] In Japan, the price changes over the cycle are offset to a large degree by marginal cost changes. As a result, price/marginal cost margins are mildly, though significantly, pro-cyclical. By contrast, in the United States, the price effects are smaller than the marginal cost effects with the result that price/marginal cost margins are significantly pro-cyclical. A 10 percentage point increase in real output is associated with a 6.9 percentage point increase in the margin.

7.8 Conclusions

Japanese manufacturing industry appears to be significantly more prone to hold labour in excess of production requirements during cyclical downturns than its counterparts in Europe and Japan. This is true for both the stock and utilisation dimensions of the labour input. A potentially major caveat to these aggregate findings, however, is that industry-level observations may mask a more flexible and continuous process of labour adjustment within firms themselves. The extent to which employment and average hours are maintained during the downturn in the cycle implies that Japanese firms may be more willing to hold inventory stocks above planned levels. This latter tendency is supported by evidence presented by Hart and Malley (1996).

The importance of labour hoarding also has a major bearing on the behaviour of marginal cost over the cycle. The pro-cyclical productivity effects stemming from hoarding are found to be larger than the pro-cyclical movements in marginal labour costs. The net effect is that marginal cost is found to be markedly counter-cyclical. The same is true of the United States.

As discussed by Odagiri (1992), 'the question of how much labour to hoard is inseparable from . . . the question of how much mark-up (gross of capital costs) to impose over labour and material costs'. Those firms wishing to maintain employment levels during cyclical downturns are likely to trim price margins in order to maintain as fully as possible their utilisation rates of employment stocks and contractual hours. Where significant amounts of underutilised labour inputs are held, the marginal labour cost of producing an extra unit of output is zero. In these cases, there is a clear incentive to lower margins in order to stimulate demand. Of course, at the aggregate industrial level these hoarding effects on mark-ups will not be uniform. They will be influenced by such factors as labour skill levels, degrees of competitiveness, concentrations of market power and price elasticities.

There is some evidence that US marginal costs behave in a way that is consistent with this general interpretation of events. In recessions, short-run marginal cost rises are found to derive principally from declines in hourly labour productivity. Industrial prices rise far less than proportionately with the result that the mark-up falls. Recessions also mark significant declines in hourly productivity in Japan but, here, industrial price rises are much stronger. As a result, mark-up reductions are relatively small in Japan. Two special considerations might help to explain this latter finding. First, in the post-war period, Japanese recessions have tended to be both of shorter duration and more modest than those in the United States. This is detailed in the work of Odagiri and Yamashita (1987) and Odagiri (1992) who argue that Japanese managers, expecting any given recession to be mild and short-lived, would have sought to avoid major variations in worker layoffs and price mark-ups. Second, intercompany business groups seeking to achieve risk-sharing and mutual insurance through preferential trading may play a significant role in Japan in modifying group members' pricing policies. This area is discussed by Nakatani (1984), who finds that intertemporal profit variations are smaller in firms belonging to such groups than in independent firms.

Notes

1 Fay and Medoff (1985), Bernanke and Parkinson (1991) and others indicate that a large body of international empirical work – involving both micro- and macro-levels of aggregation – finds that average labour productivity varies pro-cyclically. Detailed European evidence is provided by Christodoulakis *et al.* (1995).

2 The importance of both stock and utilisation dimensions of the labour input is emphasised by Fukao and Otaki (1993). They carry out a theoretical and empirical investigation of the impacts of technological shocks in a competitive economy that has sunk significant training costs into newly employed workers. They show that employment and working time responses to shocks can diverge considerably, in line with the empirical evidence of Gordon (1982) on Japan, the USA and the UK.

3 Decisions to cut working hours are likely to be particularly costly where specific investments relate to group, or team, production activity (see section 2.3). Hours reductions would then necessitate significant aggregate costs associated with work set-up, reorganisation and rescheduling.

4 Of the many examples of work adopting this method, see Fair (1969, 1984, 1985) for applications to workers-hours demand and Taylor (1970) for an application to the augmented Phillips Curve.

5 Two critical assumptions are made. First, the firm's labour demand decision is made

after production has been determined. Secondly, a fixed-proportions production function in workers and hours acts as a reasonable proxy for more realistic theoretical versions. As acknowledged by Fair (1985), if labour exhibits short-run decreasing returns then increases in excess labour due to falls in output will be underestimated by a trends-through-peaks model which is based on the assumption of a fixed-proportions technology. However, it is the phenomenon of short-run increasing returns that has dominated the theoretical and empirical literature.

6 Fay and Medoff (1985) surveyed 168 manufacturing firms in the United States following the 1980–81 recession, asking questions about declines in shipments and output as well as actual worker-hours used in comparison to the amount needed to produce output most efficiently. They calculated that 8 per cent more blue-collar workers were needed for regular production work. While some of these hours were used for other worthwhile work, like maintenance, 5 per cent were estimated to be purely hoarded. Fair (1985) estimated that between 4.5 and 8.5 per cent of worker-hours were hoarded at troughs in the US post-war business cycle and, in particular, that 4.5 per cent were hoarded during the 1980–81 recession.

7 Statistics on wage–tenure distributions are extremely hard to come by in Europe. However, such profiles would be expected to correlate quite closely with wage–age profiles, which are more easily obtained. (See, in particular, the discussion in Chapter 9.) Koike infers that findings 'between Japan and the UK of wages by age and length of service may be extended to other EC countries'.

8 At least for Japan, there is evidence that variations in vacation time are an important mode of employment adjustment (Hashimoto, 1993).

9 Marchetti (1994) provides a wide-ranging review of the so-called internal and externality-based increasing returns theories and empirical tests. Internal increasing returns theory has been seriously challenged empirically in a number of recent papers while externality-based theory (e.g. Cabellero and Lyons, 1992) is equally seriously challenged by Marchetti himself. He concludes that his results 'significantly enhance the traditional labour hoarding theory of pro-cyclical productivity vis-à-vis recent alternative explanations, based on (internal or external) increasing returns'.

10 As discussed by Fruin (1992), the Japanese enterprise system is typified by a large number of interdependent factories, each producing specialised components. In contrast, a higher number of employees and a greater proportion of production phases are concentrated in the same production unit in the United States. For example, Toyota buys 75 per cent of the sales value of its cars from other companies while the comparable figure for General Motors is 50 per cent.

11 Actually, as argued by Bils (1987), this approach offers more generality than is at first apparent. The firm can produce an increase in output through changes in any of a number of inputs. The latter include changes in working time or employment. The cost-minimising firm equates relative marginal costs to marginal products. A rise in marginal cost of increasing output can be inferred, *ceteris paribus*, from increasing any one of the inputs.

12 The 25 per cent minimum must be paid in the following circumstances: daily work hours exceed eight; working on a holiday which comes once every week; working on any day of the four holidays which come regularly within each four-week cycle;

working between 10 p.m. and 5 a.m. The base wage that is used as the basis for computing overtime premiums is specified by law for all types of wages and benefits; some components are excluded from the base while others are included.

13 Of workers working over forty hours per week, Trejo (1993) indicates that less than 5 per cent who are paid an overtime premium receive a rate other than time-and-a-half.

14 If all workers work the same hours per period then we would expect a small change in average hours to have no effect on overtime hours when average hours are below the level for which overtime rates apply. Similarly, an increase in average hours would be completely represented by more overtime hours if the change took place in the overtime region. However, uniform working hours are precluded by such factors as technological constraints, production scheduling and bottlenecks, and heterogeneous supply-side preferences. At any given time, we would expect variations in the number of overtime hours worked per worker and in the proportion of workers working overtime. At the level of the firm or industry, average overtime would be expected to be increasing in average total hours. As average hours rise from the trough of a cycle, the proportion of workers working overtime and average overtime hours per worker will increase relatively slightly, with much of the response arising from longer basic hours

15 How might we expect the average premium to relate to average overtime hours? First, if all workers in an industry are paid a constant overtime rate, then the mean overtime premium will also be constant. This might be expected to apply in the United States, for example. In general, the higher is the minimum imposed premium rate, the more likely are firms working overtime to adhere to a single rate at all stages of the business cycle. Secondly, all workers may face the same overtime schedule, perhaps a simple step function in which given levels of per period overtime working trigger higher marginal premiums. Given an unequal distribution of overtime across workers, however, discontinuities in the step functions would be smoothed out. The mean premium function would start at the lowest premium rate and rise to the highest rate. Note that an imposed minimum overtime premium does not preclude this scenario. In general, the lower is the mandatory rate, the more likely the occurrence of higher marginal rates as the labour market tightens.

The next two possibilities involve different categories of workers, such as skilled and unskilled, facing different overtime schedules. Thus, as the third case, each category of worker may be paid a different constant overtime rate and so the mean overtime rate would also be constant as long as the proportion of overtime workers itself remained constant as mean overtime hours change. Fourthly, if the proportion of high overtime workers increases (falls) as mean overtime increases (falls) then the mean overtime schedule will rise (fall). (See the discussion in Hart and Ruffell, 1993, for more details.)

16 Taken over all industries, average regular hours in Japan fell from a peak of 41.88 weekly hours in 1958 to 36.81 hours by 1990 with an overall mean of 39.04 hours. Overtime fluctuated pro-cyclically with an industry average maximum of 5.53 weekly hours, an average minimum of 2.15 hours and an overall mean of 3.86 hours.

17 One issue should be kept in mind here. The use of measurements of hired rather than utilised hours in the United States serves to overestimate the true pro-cyclical productivity effects.

18 The similar magnitudes of marginal wage response can be explained as follows. As the cycle turns up, a rise in the proportion of workers working overtime in the United States will have a larger impact on costs than a comparable rise in the proportion of Japanese workers because the American overtime premium is higher. This relative tendency will be offset, however, by the greater tendency in Japan for the average rate of premium pay to rise as average overtime increases.

19 Theoretical developments also offer conflicting predictions. Haskel *et al.* (1995) provide a recent review of opposing theories. They also find empirical evidence that supports pro-cyclical mark-ups for UK manufacturing.

20 Average hourly real wages are also pro-cyclical in the two economies, although exhibiting less cyclical reponsiveness in the USA. These latter results for the USA are in line with the general findings of the study of real wages and the business cycle by Abraham and Haltiwanger (1995). The Japanese real wage elasticities are considerably larger than the US comparable estimates. A 10 percentage point rise in real output is associated with a 3.5 percentage point increase in average hourly earnings in Japan and a 0.3 percentage point increase in the USA.

8 Small businesses, subcontracting and employment

The majority of Japanese workers work in small businesses. In fact, as a proportion of total employment, this group is larger than in Western countries.[1] Small businesses formed over 99.9 per cent of total establishments in 1991 according to the Establishment Census. In terms of employee numbers, they employed 88 per cent of total non-primary employees in 1991. In this chapter, we both discuss the quantitative importance of the small business sector and examine differences in pay and work conditions between small and large firms. Inevitably, a considerable part of our discussion is devoted to sub-contracting. Not only does this activity constitute a considerable part of small business activity – over 50 per cent of small firms in manufacturing industries are engaged in sub-contracting – but its *raison d'être* has also stimulated considerable interest among labour market analysts. An interesting feature in this latter respect is that the subcontracting relationship between manufacturer and part supplier closely parallels that between the firm and its workers.

8.1 Small businesses in Japan

8.1.1 The importance of the small business sector in the Japanese economy

In Japanese manufacturing industry, the employment share of small businesses was 73.8 per cent in 1991 (Management and Co-ordination Agency, the Establishment Census). Table 8.1 compares the shares of small businesses for key variables in several different countries. In terms of establishment numbers, small business constitutes an extremely high percentage share in every country. However, Japanese small businesses account for far larger shares in respect of employment, capital and value added. In general, Japanese small firms play a much larger role in the economy than those of Western countries. We note also that, within Japan itself, the share in employment is much larger than the

138

Table 8.1. *Shares of small manufacturing firms: international comparisons (percentages)*

	Firms	Employment	Capital	Value added
Japan (1989)	99.5	74.0	52.3	54.8
USA (1985)	96.0	46.2	38.2	38.4
UK (1987)	96.9	38.7	—	31.8
W. Germany (1986)	84.5	25.2	20.7	—
France (1971)	98.9	—	—	—

Note:
A small firm is defined *in this table* as having less than 250 employees (less than 200 for the USA).
Source: Small and Medium Enterprise Agency (1991).

respective shares in capital or value added. This fact indicates the existence of large size differentials in capital equipment and productivity in the Japanese economy.

Figure 8.1 shows the time trend of percentage employment shares among three different sizes of firms within total industry. Large firms' share decreased from around 40 per cent in the 1960s to 30 per cent in more recent times. On the other hand, the share of small firms has remained at around 35 per cent over the entire period, although with some fluctuations. The situation is somewhat different in manufacturing industry (figure 8.2). The share of large firms has been relatively stable, fluctuating between 30 per cent and 35 per cent. Small firms' share dropped from around 40 per cent in the 1960s and then stabilised at between 30 per cent and 35 per cent after the mid-1970s. Both in total and in manufacturing industries, medium-sized firms increased their share from around 25 per cent in the late 1950s to 35 per cent in 1996. In general, the employment share of small and medium firms did not decrease during the post-war period in Japan.

8.1.2 Why so many small businesses?

A simple answer to this question is that Japan started its industrial and commercial modernisation relatively late, so that there remain many aspects of society and economic management that date back to much earlier times. For example, an important part of small business organisation still reflects family-oriented economic activity. Japan has achieved one of the most successful economic modernisations and growth performances in the world during the post-war period, and yet the number and proportion of small businesses have persisted. So, the late development explanation is not entirely satisfactory. It is also noticeable that many developing countries have suffered from a lack of small firms supplying manufacturing parts and have had to import a significant proportion of parts from abroad.

Among several important factors contributing to the prevalence and persistence of small businesses is the existence of extensive social networks in Japanese society. In Japanese business, social connections constitute extremely important business assets;

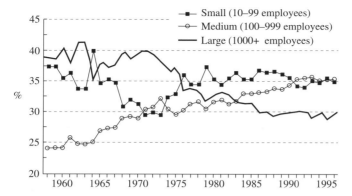

Fig. 8.1. Employment by firm size: total industries, 1958–96. (*Source:* Ministry of Labour, Basic Survey of Wage Structure.)

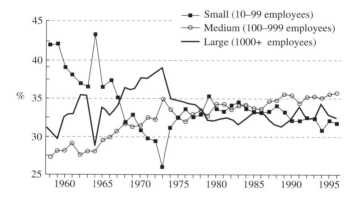

Fig. 8.2. Employment by firm size: manufacturing industry, 1958–96. (*Source:* Ministry of Labour, Basic Survey of Wage Structure.)

here we would include the roles of relatives, neighbours, friends, school contemporaries and former employers. Such networks facilitate the setting up of small firms and aid subsequent survival. Another explanation links to the workings of the labour market where there are wide variations in wages and other working conditions. Trade unions are not organised by industries but by enterprises. Many small businesses have no trade unions at all and do not face transaction costs of dealing with collectivised labour. Moreover, there are a large number of family businesses; some family members can work in the outside market, either semi-permanently or to supplement income in adversity. These structures help explain the tenacity of small businesses (Patrick and Rohlen, 1988).

Although the government provides various subsidies to small business activity, the most important governmental financial provision in this direction is lending through public financial institutions.[2] There are three governmental financial institutions specialising in such financing. The proportion of governmental funds in total lending by all financial institutions to small businesses was about 10 per cent in the 1960s and 1970s, and about 5 per cent more recently (Bank of Japan). Government funds play a very important role because obtaining such finance facilitates borrowing from private banks. In tandem, many laws and governmental regulations are designed to protect small businesses. One of the most conspicuous of these is the Large Scale Retailing Establishment Law which has served to protect small retailers since 1974. Small businesses have enormous lobbying power because of the sheer number of members as well as strong fund-raising ability. Such assets help to protect vested interests. Some businesses, such as rice and alcohol retailing, need licences to operate and this form of governmental control helps to protect small retailers from competition. Small businesses are also treated rather leniently in tax collection. Patrick and Rohlen (1987, pp. 336–8) present evidence and evaluation of tax exemptions among small businesses.

One of the most important reasons for the prevalence of small businesses, especially in manufacturing, is the practice of subcontracting. Small and large firms combine to play a significant joint role in the modern social division of labour. In Japan, subcontracting practices are widely spread and the system has evolved to become highly elaborate. About 56 per cent of small firms in manufacturing industries were engaged in subcontracting in 1986 according to a Ministry of International Trade and Industry (MITI) survey. In earlier times, the figures were 58.7 per cent in 1971, 60.7 per cent in 1976, and 65.5 per cent in 1981.[3] Subcontractors are highly concentrated in assembly-type industries such as automobiles, electrical/electronic machinery, and other machinery.

Vehicle productivity statistics, defined as cars and trucks produced per employee per year, reveal the significant difference in parts procurement modes of Japanese and US firms. General Motors (worldwide), Ford (USA) and Chrysler (worldwide) produced between 8 and 16 units in the period from 1970 to 1982. On the other hand, Nissan and Toyota produced between 30 and 61 units (Cusumano, 1985, pp. 186–7). This contrast does not (necessarily) mean that Japanese firms had higher productivity; rather, that the Japanese firms used far more subcontracted-in parts within total production.

8.1.3 Firm-size differentials in wages

Statistical overview

Figure 8.3 shows the time profile of wage differentials due to firm size in manufacturing industry from 1958 to 1996. First, we note that hourly wages of small firms have recently been about 60 to 65 per cent of those of large firms. Secondly, the differentials narrowed substantially during the economic boom of the 1960s and then widened again during the low growth period after the oil crises.[4]

Table 8.2 compares Japanese and UK gross wage differentials. Although we should be careful because of differences in definitions and size classifications, we note the following:

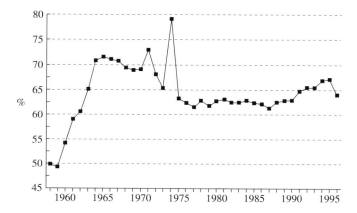

Fig. 8.3. Wage level of small firms relative to large firms' level, 1958–96. Average monthly regular wages including overtime pay but excluding annual bonus payment. Small firms are those with 10 to 99 employees; large firms those with over 1,000 employees. (*Source:* Ministry of Labour, Basic Survey of Wage Structure.)

(i) there is a larger wage differential in Japan, with workers in small firms obtaining about 70 per cent of those in large firms in Japan and about 80 per cent in the UK;

(ii) in Japan, female differentials are smaller than male differentials, whereas they are almost equal in the UK.

Statistical analysis

Using the Basic Survey of Wage Structure (Ministry of Labour), Blumenthal (1966, 1968), Stoikov (1973a, 1973b), Ono (1973), Tachibanaki (1975, 1982) and others have analysed various determinants of wage differentials. Wages are typically related to age, sex, firm size, occupation, education, work experience and industry within the framework of analysis of variance. Table 8.3 shows the relative importance of each factor, as evaluated by Tachibanaki (1982). We note first that hourly wages including bonuses were explained mostly by sex, age and work experience; these factors together explain almost 80 per cent of wages. Secondly, firm size explains between 5 and 17 per cent of the differentials. That is, there exist some pure effects of firm size after controlling for the effects of other factors. Thirdly, the effects of firm size reduced during the rapid growth period that preceded the 1970s' oil crises and expanded again thereafter. As we have seen in figure 8.3, this latter cyclical movement was observed in relation to gross wage differentials.

Using individual-level data from the Basic Survey of Wage Structure (for 1978 and 1988), Tachibanaki (1996) estimated multiple regression models explaining the log of hourly wages by size dummy variables and many of the control variables used in the foregoing studies. In order to assess whether there are relative wage advantages due to firm size, Tachibanaki computed the differences between the estimated wages for each size class after taking account of controls and the overall mean before imposing controls

Table 8.2. *Wage differentials by firm size in Japan and the UK, 1996/7 (Wages in large firms = 100)*

	Japan			UK	
	Male	Female		Male	Female
Firm size			*Firm size*		
10–99	66.61	73.54	1–9	82.06	82.23
100–999	78.29	84.83	10–24	78.44	79.88
1000–	100	100	25–99	78.96	79.11
			100–499	89.89	87.00
			500–999	89.16	90.39
			1000–	100	100

Notes:
Japan: Average gross monthly pay plus annual bonuses converted to monthly figure. Total private and public sectors; UK: Average gross weekly pay (company agreement). Total private sectors.
Sources: Japan: Ministry of Labour, Basic Survey of Wage Structure (1996); UK: Office of National Statistics, New Earnings Survey (1997).

Table 8.3. *Effect of six factors on wage differentials (partitions of the sum of squares in percentages)*

	Sex	Occupation	Size	Education	Experience	Age	Total
1958	36.0	10.6	10.1	1.1	24.3	18.1	100.0
1960	31.7	7.9	13.2	0.9	26.2	20.0	100.0
1962	32.7	8.6	11.8	1.1	26.6	19.2	100.0
1964	37.1	8.5	7.2	1.3	25.5	20.5	100.0
1966	41.6	6.8	5.1	1.4	26.4	18.8	100.0
1968	43.5	5.1	7.6	0.9	26.9	16.2	100.0
1970	41.6	4.7	11.3	1.0	23.0	18.5	100.0
1976	41.1	4.9	17.0	2.0	21.1	13.9	100.0
1978	44.7	5.0	15.6	1.4	20.1	13.3	100.0

Source: Tachibanaki (1982)

divided by the overall mean before controls; this is expressed as $(\hat{W_i} - \overline{W})\overline{W}$. The results, presented in table 8.4, show that there exist substantial wage differentials both before and after controlling for various quality variables. Tachibanaki repeated the same exercises for industrial wage differentials using the same model and the same control variables. The estimation produced a drastic reduction in industrial wage differentials after imposing the controls; the advantages of the electricity, gas and water supply industry (the highest wage-earnings industry) reduced from 42.3 to 4.7 per cent, and the advantages

Table 8.4. *Advantages and disadvantages of wage payments by firm size, 1988 (percentages)*

Number of employees	Before controls	After controls
5000–	32.1	27.16
1000–4999	21.86	15.96
500–999	9.24	2.68
300–499	−1.55	−5.60
100–299	−11.93	−15.37
30–99	−20.29	−23.36
10–29	−25.34	−28.78

Source: Tachibanaki (1996).

of the finance and insurance industry from 37.1 to 12.8 per cent for 1988 (Tachibanaki, 1996, pp. 90–1). These contrasting findings clearly indicate the significance of firm-size differentials.

Explanations

Worker quality

Why do there exist large firm-size differentials in wages? We discuss some of the most important explanations that have been advanced in relation to the Japanese scene.

One of the most fundamental reasons underpinning size differentials concerns the quality of labour. In Japan, large firms train their employees systematically and intensively over their whole career. The resulting firm-specific skills accumulated by workers are likely to form the base of higher wages in large firms. The studies highlighted above, however, show that there remain substantial wage differentials after controlling for various quality variables, such as education and work experience. Tachibanaki's (1996) study appears to show that such controls do not reduce wage differentials at all. However, these outcomes do not necessarily mean that wage differentials cannot be explained by labour quality. Workers' abilities and the quality of skills accumulated in the firm cannot be measured simply by observable years of work, educational levels and other similar general indicators (Odaka, 1984). In a mass education society like Japan, being classified as a university graduate does not in itself indicate a great deal about educational quality. Job tenure and work experience can capture only a part of the quality of firm-specific skills. Unfortunately, there is no research into the possible magnitude of unmeasured ability in Japan.

Another popular explanation of wage differentials in Japan is that large firms can afford to pay higher wages because they tend to have higher productivity resulting from better equipment and higher capital–labour ratios. However, ability-to-pay does not in itself mean higher wages in large firms. Why should firms pay higher wages when the same labour services could be obtained for lower wages? If the answer is that the quality of labour is not the same, then we again return to the quality explanation given above.

Market power

A second explanation of observed wage differentials is that wages are maintained above competitive market 'norms' by groups of workers, especially in large firms, who enjoy some degree of market power. For example, workers may have strong bargaining power. Union density is indeed much higher in larger firms in Japan (see figure 3.2). However, union density has been declining over a long period of time (see figure 3.3). If union power were the major reason for wage differentials, the differential should have been narrowing in recent years, contrary to the evidence presented.

Rent-sharing

As discussed in chapter 2, a key objective of the firm may be to maximise the joint rent for shareholders and employees. This is likely to generate firm-size wage differentials if the larger firms have the ability to obtain larger rents. In this case, both quality of labour and pure rent-sharing are relevant.

Segmented labour markets

The fourth hypothesis emphasises the importance of segmented labour markets (Ishikawa,1989). Japanese labour markets indeed seem to be divided into segments that broadly correspond to firm size. But, to admit the fact that segmentation takes place begs the question of why it takes place. The segmentation hypothesis may simply reduce to the fact that such divisions of labour link, again, to questions of labour quality and/or rent-sharing.

Compensating differentials

As for the hypothesis of compensating differentials, the theory seems to run counter to the Japanese reality. Most Japanese feel that large firms provide far better working conditions than small firms. Therefore, wages should be higher in small firms according to the theory.[5]

8.1.4 Cyclical changes in wage differentials

As we have seen above, wage differentials tend to move counter-cyclically. This phenomenon is observed not only in Japan but also in many other industrialised countries. Reder (1955) offered an explanation of this phenomenon with respect to wages for skilled and unskilled labour. In a recession the firm's labour demand decreases more for unskilled workers. Higher training investments ensure more employment stability for skilled workers. Further, hoarding costs can be mitigated if the firm can assign jobs to such workers that normally would be undertaken by lower skilled groups. Thus, the wages of unskilled workers will be relatively depressed. The opposite occurs in a recovery phase and a counter-cyclical movement in wage differentials is established.

8.2 The system of subcontracting

A manufacturer has three alternative methods of procuring parts:

   (i) buying parts in existing markets;
   (ii) making parts within the firm;
   (iii) ordering parts from subcontractors.

The advantage of the market solution is that prices may be relatively low owing to competition. On the other hand, specialised parts may be difficult to obtain and, at critical times, delivery lags may prove to be extremely costly if competition is fierce. Moreover, problems may be exacerbated if replacements for defective parts are also subject to delays. By making parts within the firm, it is possible to match parts requirements and production. However, especially in the case of larger firms, parts manufacture may mean significant additions to already complex production and management control systems, as well as increasing the variety of worker skill requirements. This could lead to organisational inefficiency. Furthermore, if required quantities of parts are relatively small, scale economies may be sacrificed.

Subcontracting has the potential of avoiding the inefficiencies of the market and internal production solutions. Subcontractors can make non-standard parts in close co-operation with assemblers. As separate companies, they can avoid organisational inefficiency. As a specialist in specific parts, the subcontractor is more likely to be geared to achieving scale economies. On the other hand, it requires a substantial investment and ongoing expense to organise and to operate a subcontracting network.

8.2.1 Main features of Japanese subcontracting

This subsection describes the main features of subcontracting in Japan, focusing on the automobile industry where the subcontracting system is the most developed. The following characterisation relies heavily on a body of work by Asanuma (1985, 1997) which is based on intensive interviews with individual companies and the study of the Massachusetts Institute of Technology's International Motor Vehicle Program (published partly by Womack *et al.*, 1990, and Nishiguchi, 1987, 1994).

Long-term transactions

A car maker guarantees subcontractors the purchase of parts for as long as the car model for which the parts are used is in mass production. The usual period is three or four years. Transactions are often renewed for many generations of models (Nishiguchi, 1994; Asanuma, 1997). Suppliers are not selected on the basis of bids, but rather on a proven record of performance. According to MITI's survey of subcontractors in 1987, 68.2 per cent of sample firms never changed buyers, 15.2 per cent have changed only once, 10.0 per cent have changed twice, and the remaining 6.6 per cent have changed more than twice (see figure 8.4).

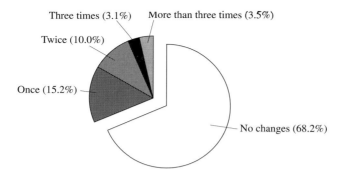

Fig. 8.4. How many times have subcontractors changed partners? (*Source: Small and Medium Enterprise Agency, 1988, p. 61.*)

Multi-tier systems

Subcontractors are hierarchically organised. One important feature of the structure is that relatively few subcontractors deal with the car maker directly. For example, a General Motors plant managed on average 1,500 suppliers, while a Toyota plant dealt directly with only 180 suppliers in 1986 (Nishiguchi, 1987). A carefully selected small number of first-tier subcontractors help to secure long-term relationships in which intense communication and detailed planning are accommodated.

A benefit of the multi-tier system is that the buyer does not need to have a detailed knowledge of low-level production. For example, General Motors, producing 6 million cars annually, employed 6,000 buyers to procure parts. In sharp contrast, 340 people are employed in purchasing by Toyota in relation to a 3.6 million car production (Nishiguchi, 1987).

Another important feature of the hierarchical system is that the lower the tier of sub-contracting, the lower the degree of necessary technological sophistication. So the skill levels of workers of each tier of subcontractors are also hierarchical.

Co-operation

Risk-sharing arrangements

Contracts between car makers and subcontractors contain carefully designed arrange-ments for risk-sharing. Subcontracting transactions are usually guaranteed at least for one model period, although the quantity of transactions may vary with the actual demand for the model. Car makers will bear the costs of dies for press, if the subcontrac-tor cannot recover the depreciation costs due to unpopularity of a specific model (Asanuma, 1997).

Joint price determination

The determination of part prices has gradually evolved from unilateral price-setting by assemblers, to bargaining between buyers and suppliers, and finally to joint problem-solving (Nishiguchi, 1994, pp. 123–5). The assembler requests detailed cost data from suppliers, and both parties discuss how to reduce costs jointly, based on value analysis techniques. Value analysis enables complex cost structures to be decomposed into smaller segments, and provides objective measurements for rational price determination.

Quality assurance and just-in-time (JIT) delivery
Assemblers have extended internal management methods, such as quality control and JIT systems, across firm boundaries. JIT systems drastically reduce inventory levels by delegating production decisions to shop floors and suppliers. The systems also enforce a high quality standard of parts, because defects cause serious potential disruption to JIT scheduling. In order to avoid costly inspection, suppliers give quality assurance to buyers through implementation of jointly agreed quality control systems.

Joint research and development
Assemblers and subcontractors co-operate closely in developing new technology. Subcontracting firms often send their engineers to the car maker to participate in parts design for coming car models. This serves to shorten significantly the development period. By 1987, approximately 60 per cent of subcontractors in the Japanese machinery industries were involved in the joint design of components (Nishiguchi, 1994, p. 128).

Supplier associations
Organised associations of subcontractors provide a formal mechanism for bringing together suppliers and purchasers, for sharing purchaser policies and goals with suppliers, and for encouraging suppliers to adopt and improve their use of management tools and new technologies (Womack *et al.*, 1990, pp. 153–6).

Competitive pressure
Multiple sourcing
Efficiency among subcontractors can be compared and checked by buyers using more than one subcontractor for the same parts. In the case of Toyota, 28 per cent of parts were single-sourced, 39 per cent had two suppliers, 19 per cent three, and 15 per cent four or five (Itami and Senbongi, 1988). In the Japanese electronics industry, the firm seeks at least two suppliers for every component it subcontracts. Another merit of multiple sourcing is that supply will not be interrupted in the event of an accident.

Concomitantly, 17 per cent of subcontractors had only one customer, 20 per cent two customers, 26 per cent three to five, 14 per cent between six and nine customers, and 22 per cent over nine customers according to the Survey on Manufacturing Systems (Ministry of International Trade and Industry, 1987). This implies that subcontractors usually supply to more than one customer, so that they too can exert competitive pressure.

Grading systems

Assemblers continually assess their suppliers' performance with respect to quality, delivery and other factors, and notify them of their grades. Good grades naturally correlate with probabilities of receiving future orders and obtaining higher-order tasks. On the other hand, if suppliers obtain unsatisfactory scores, they are requested to improve and may be given some help in doing so. If suppliers continue to perform poorly, they may be penalised by reduced orders or, in the worst scenario, being discharged (Nishiguchi, 1994, pp. 133–6).

Continuous improvement

One of the most conspicuous features of Japanese subcontracting practices is the adoption of institutionalised mechanisms that serve to promote perpetual quality improvement and cost reduction. The assembler usually assumes automatic cost reductions or quality improvements from suppliers every six to twelve months. If the subcontractors do not achieve targets, customer firms often try to discover the reasons for the problems by exhaustive data collection from subcontractors, on-site inspection and data analysis. With the assistance of recommendations from, and retraining by, the assembler, subcontractors are urged to solve impediments to attaining cost and quality goals.

Value engineering techniques are important in this dynamic process. First, the price of a new model is determined by considering market conditions. Then the cost of each part is determined by evaluating jointly the various possibilities of design, materials and the like. The costs of parts are continuously reduced through this process. It is a widespread practice that suppliers receive half of the benefits from a cost improvement proposal supplied by them. However, the benefits will be guaranteed only for half a year or so, and they will be absorbed in price reductions. This device encourages suppliers to attempt continuously to improve parts production (Nishiguchi, 1994; Asanuma, 1997).

8.3 Theories of subcontracting

There are several alternative theories to explain subcontracting relationships. Here, we summarise the two most important paradigms, namely the theory of asset specificity and the game-theoretic approach. We also discuss critically the buffer theory of subcontracting which has been very popular in Japan.

8.3.1 Asset specificity

Under the theoretical framework of Williamson (1975, 1979, 1985), efforts to economise on costs under various types of transaction lead to choice of particular modes of transaction. The costs consist of production costs and transaction costs. The latter are particularly important in the choice of transaction modes. The three critical features of transactions are (i) uncertainty, (ii) the frequency of transactions, and (iii) the degree to which transaction-specific investments are incurred. The key determinant of the transaction mode is the third factor, referred to as asset specificity. Manufacturing certain parts requires specialised equipment or specialised skills which are specific to the current transaction and cannot be easily applied in the production of other parts.

Where asset specificity exists, there arise certain difficulties with respect to transactions. Suppose that a buyer and a supplier have reached a mutually agreeable price. The supplier incurs the cost of specific investment, such as learning and tooling for the specific item. Having incurred these costs, the supplier is in a vulnerable position. The buyer knows that the supplier's investment is useless except for making this part. Thus the buyer can now demand that the price be renegotiated downwards and, having made the investment, the supplier is trapped into accepting the buyer's demand. The supplier can forecast this chain of events from the outset and may accordingly refuse a contractual offer. In this event, no transaction takes place even though both buyer and supplier would have been jointly better off. Therefore, the assurance of a continuing relationship is needed to encourage investments. However, a long-term contract is bound to be incomplete and it may be very costly to resolve all contractual problems. A high degree of asset specificity would, therefore, be expected to lead to internalised production or vertical integration. At the other end of the spectrum, the existing spot market may well prove to be an adequate vehicle for transacting over goods with a low degree of asset specificity. Subcontracting can be viewed as representing an intermediate degree of specificity.

There is some empirical evidence that asset specificity affects the degree of integration. Monteverde and Teece (1982) found that assemblers tended to own the specialised tools, jigs and patterns utilised by suppliers in fabricating parts for the vehicle companies, and that a part component was more integrated when it was more specialised. Nishiguchi (1994) conducted a comparative study of British and Japanese subcontracting in the electronics industry between 1983 and 1986. Data collected from seventy-five establishments showed that the Japanese firms had a much higher degree of asset specificity than the British firms. As the theory predicts, this matches the observation that Japanese suppliers are more closely integrated with their customers than their British counterparts.

We note that the logic of asset specificity is exactly the same as the logic of firm-specific human capital. In both theories, the specificity of skills or other assets helps to determine the type of transaction and investment.

8.3.2 Games with uncertainty and asymmetric information

Game theory is concerned with strategic interactions of economic agents. In the game-theoretic framework each agent will make rational decisions, taking into account the fact that others will react to chosen actions. The subcontracting relationship has proved to be successfully analysed under this framework. Game theory coupled with assumptions of uncertainty and informational asymmetry is called principal–agent theory, and can be used to explain the mechanism of subcontracting.

The framework of the principal–agent model is as follows. One person, the principal, wants to induce another person, the agent, to take some action for the principal. The principal may be unable directly to observe the action of the agent, but instead observes some output that is determined partly by the action of the agent. The principal's problem is to design an incentive payment scheme that induces the agent to take the best action from the viewpoint of the principal.

The supplier as the agent, being a specialist in her/his work, is likely to be better informed about the details of production conditions than the assembler. The assembler as the principal mainly observes only the outcome of production. So the assembler cannot judge whether an unfavourable outcome is the result of shirking by the supplier or of some circumstance beyond the control of the supplier. Once the activities of the supplier are no longer fully observable by the principal, the supplier's incentive to exert effort towards minimising costs may be weakened. This is a typical case of moral hazard under asymmetric information.

There may be a significant difference in the players' attitudes to risk. The assembler, being larger and possessing more diversified investments, is likely to be less risk-averse than the supplier. For convenience of argument, assume that the assembler is risk-neutral. A given contract with a supplier is likely to be only a small portion of many projects of a large firm. For the supplier, fluctuation of the contract's profit may significantly affect total profit, so that a more risk-averse approach to transactions is adopted.

When a risk-averse small firm transacts with a risk-neutral large firm, a mutually profitable exchange of risk can be made. Suppose that a simple fixed price contract is initially considered. This would leave the small firm bearing all of the risk of unforeseen production cost increases. The small firm, being risk-averse, would be willing to accept a reduction in the price received in exchange for some reduction in risk; this may take the form, for example, of guaranteeing orders for a long period. The large firm, being risk-neutral, may also find such an agreement to be beneficial. In this event, both firms are made better off by the trade-off of risk and price. In short, the transaction consists of two elements, normal purchase and insurance. The large firm acts not only as a purchaser but also as an insurer, while the small firm provides a service to the assembler as well as buying an insurance policy from the assembler. The insurance premium is paid in the form of a price discount and other concessions. [6]

If the buyer bears the risk of unpredictable production–cost increases, the agent's incentive to exert effort to hold down production costs will be weakened. The optimal contract between the assembler and the supplier must recognise this incentive problem posed by informational asymmetry and resulting moral hazard problems. This means that the degree of risk-sharing should be balanced to take account of the conflicting effects of risk-sharing and incentives.

The principal–agent model of subcontracting predicts that the principal will share more risk (i) the more risk-averse is the supplier, (ii) the more uncertain is the cost, and (iii) the smaller the degree of moral hazard experienced by the supplier. Kawasaki and McMillan (1987) estimated a model along these lines for Japanese manufacturing industries in the period from 1973 to 1982. First, they found that suppliers were indeed risk-averse. Secondly, it was found that most estimated risk-sharing parameters were larger than 0.5.[7] The contracts seemed to be geared more towards sharing risk than to giving the subcontractor appropriate incentives. In other words, assemblers absorbed a considerable portion of the risk. Thirdly, estimated results showed that the assemblers absorbed more risk, (i) the more risk-averse the suppliers were, (ii) the more the suppliers incurred fluctuations in production costs, and (iii) the less severe was the moral hazard. These results indicate that principal–agent theory is consistent with the data. Using micro-data on Japanese automobile suppliers, Asanuma and Kikutani (1992) estimated a similar model. They also obtained results in support of the principal–agent theory, and found that Japanese automobile assemblers absorbed a substantial portion of subcontracting risk (the risk-sharing parameters were around 0.9).

Principal–agent theory provides an explanation of why subcontracting is beneficial for both parties. However, this does not necessarily mean that a stable co-operation will develop between buyers and suppliers. Prisoner's Dilemma shows that there may be no co-operation even if co-operation is the best policy for both parties. However, game theorists have proved that co-operation may develop if the game is played repeatedly. The parties may abstain from short-term profit-seeking in favour of co-operative gains in the future. This type of logic helps to explain why a subcontracting relationship can be stable.

8.3.3 Buffer, or exploitation, theory of subcontracting

As we have seen above, Japan has a large proportion of small businesses compared with other industrialised countries. The labour market is also characterised by a wide dispersion of wage levels and other working conditions among workers. These facts are summarised by some commentators in terms of a dual economic structure. In this context, it is sometimes asserted that large firms exploit small businesses by utilising them as a protection against unanticipated economic downturns. That is, large firms subcontract to small firms as their business expands, only to break off some of these associations during periods of falling demand. In this way, small firms provide a buffer to larger firms by bearing the main risks of business fluctuations.

Empirical evidence does not support the buffer hypothesis, however. Available statistical evidence shows that the business risk of small subcontractors is borne by large assemblers (with some offsetting costs as explained above) contrary to the assertion of exploitation theory. In the first place, it is well documented that many subcontractors have a very long continuous trading relationship with assemblers. Subcontractors would be expected to have far shorter trading records if they were used as a business-cycle buffer. Secondly, the empirical work of Kawasaki and McMillan (1987) and Asanuma and Kikutani (1992), as summarised above, directly measured the relative degree of risk sharing in subcontracting and showed that the major portion of risk was borne by assemblers.

Historical studies show that subcontracting was not well established before World War II in Japan, and that the system has gradually evolved through intense interaction between assemblers and suppliers since the war. There is a popular view that the Japanese subcontracting system was at first exploitative but later evolved into a mutually beneficial means of transaction: 'the distinctive Japanese producer strategy of dele-gating a substantial portion of manufacturing functions to subcontractors . . . resulted in transforming the logic of subcontracting relations from exploitation to collaborative manufacturing' (Nishiguchi, 1994, p. 139). Arguably, however, there is no evidence of large firms systematically passing most of the risk to subcontractors during the earlier stages of Japanese economic growth. In a competitive market, each firm bears its own business risk. Thus, it is far more natural to interpret the history in the following manner. Relationships between large manufacturers and suppliers were at first more competitive and less co-operative and later developed to a more collaborative system in which large firms absorbed most of the business risks of small subcontractors in return for cost reductions and/or quality improvements.

8.4 Subcontracting and employment

There are two distinctive features common to long-term employment and subcontract-ing relationships. The first concerns specific investments. In employment relationships, as we detail in chapter 2, the firm and employees invest jointly in firm-specific human capital. In subcontracting, a large firm and parts suppliers are engaged in extensive joint investment projects designed to produce model-specific parts. The second common element is the mechanism of risk-sharing and incentives. Long-term employment, wage profiles and promotion systems are designed to give employees appropriate incentives and to reduce the risk of unemployment. Subcontracting contracts are also designed to balance risk and incentives for parts suppliers, as represented by the principal–agent theory.

More generally, such common features can be summarised under the framework of strategic alliances among trading partners under conditions of uncertainty, asymmetric information and firm-specificity of investment. Aoki (1988) provides one such game-theoretic framework. His theory views the firm as a coalition of shareholders with employees and other agents, such as subcontractors. Market behaviour of the firm and internal distribution within the firm are viewed as a bargaining solution among partners. The employees and subcontractors are considered to embody skills and knowledge more or less specific to the firm as a result of a long-term employment association. These parties, in co-operation with physical assets supplied by the shareholders, can produce economic gains which would not be possible through mere casual combination of mar-keted factors of production. Gains accrue to the firm from the unique and lasting inter-action of organisational resources, both human and physical, which may be termed the organisational rent. Through the acquisition of firm-specific skills and knowledge, employees and subcontractors may be able to exert implicit or explicit bargaining power over the disposition of the rent. If either the employees (subcontractors) or the share-holders do not want to co-operate with each other, the organisational rent will disappear owing to unresolved conflicts. However, if the shareholders and the employees (sub-contractors) can co-operate with a binding commitment through the mediation of the manager, organisational rent will be derived. The location of the equilibrium point among efficient points depends on the relative bargaining power of the shareholders and the employees (subcontractors). The bargaining power of each party is determined by its alternative opportunity outside the firm and its attitude to risk.

The Japanese subcontracting system has played the key role in the post-war economic growth, fully participating in the front lines of production, distribution and product development. The resulting employment effects have been significant. As we discussed above, the subcontracting systems have some systematic advantages to enhance productivity: the system provides the framework for assemblers and their suppliers to co-operate to their mutual benefit, avoids the underproduction of specific parts, and encourages the flow of information and technology among involved firms. On the other hand, the subcontracting relationships may lack the pressure of the unfettered open market owing to the stable, long-term attachments among the participants; some inefficient suppliers may be kept in existence, and innovative new suppliers may have difficulties in starting transactions. Which of these positive and negative effects dominates depends on many factors such as the socio-economic environment, industries, the stage of industrial development, and the management of the subcontracting system. In the relatively stable economic and technological environment of the 1960s, the subcontracting system worked well. The subcontracting system, by generating flexible production systems, has also provided many firms the key tool for rationalisation to overcome the problems in the low growth period after the oil crises.

8.5 Prevalence of relational contracting in Japan

Long-term relational contracting or strategic alliance is observed in almost all spheres of the Japanese economy and society. We briefly describe four such examples.

(1) Commercial transactions in Japan are strongly characterised by long-term, stable relationships among trading partners. According to a survey of ninety-four representative non-financial companies by the Fair Trade Commission (1987), 98 per cent of companies indicated that they bought a substantial proportion of materials and energy from firms with whom they had had a partnership lasting over five years. The equivalent figure with respect to the purchase of equipment and machinery was 80 per cent.

(2) Business groups provide another example of long-term relationships. Such groups contain many large firms and are extensively diversified; the six largest groups represented 17 per cent of total capital, 16 per cent of total sales and 4 per cent of total employment in Japan (Fair Trade Commission, 1992). Nakatani (1984) found that profit rate is significantly lower for group members than for independent firms, and that the variance of profit rates is significantly smaller for group-member firms than for independent firms. The results support the hypothesis that the formation of groups serves the purpose of stabilising corporate performance over time at the cost of sacrificing some corporate profits.[8]

(3) Most large Japanese firms have close financial, shareholding and managerial ties with a particular bank, known as the 'main bank'. The main bank enjoys the largest single share among financial institutions of the borrowings of the firm concerned. It is

also usually a major shareholder in the firm, although Japanese banks are not allowed to hold more than 5 per cent of the shares of a firm. The main-bank system usually performs two major functions: it facilitates risk-sharing among firms and it also performs the function of monitoring and intervention for the capital market (Sheard, 1989; Aoki and Patrick, 1994).

(4) Japan is characterised by extensive, intimate interactions among business, political parties and bureaucracy. Formal and informal networks between government officials and the private sector facilitate the effectiveness of governmental policies, but at the same time generate corruption and excessive economic intervention by the government (Johnson, 1982; Okimoto, 1989).

8.6 Uniqueness of Japanese subcontracting

As we have discussed above, subcontracting is based on rational economic behaviour under asymmetric information with diversified risk attitudes and asset specificity. Naturally, long-term relationships and subcontracting are also observable in the Western countries. For example, Macaulay (1963) found that American businessmen often avoided written contracts in transactions, relying instead on personal trust, even when considerable risks were involved. In the UK, Marks & Spencer and Sainsbury are well known for their relational contracting (Dore, 1983). However, the basic question is why subcontracting relationships are especially prevalent in Japan.

Dore (1983) criticised Williamson's asset-specificity explanation of the subcontracting relationship by pointing out that there is no difference between the United States and Japan in asset specificity. Dore instead emphasised the importance of national cultural differences, in particular the sense of benevolence and trust. By this is meant 'the sentiments of friendship and the sense of diffuse personal obligation which accrue between individuals engaged in recurring contractual economic exchange' (Dore, 1983, p. 460). Dore's basic point is that relational contracting should be explained directly by benevolence, one of the basic Confucian virtues on which Japanese society has historically been based. If a subcontractor lags behind in adopting new technology, the common practice is not to stop buying from the subcontractor but to encourage her/him to learn the technology with the possibility of financial, managerial and technical help. [9]

Can the prevalence of subcontracting in Japan be linked in large part to cultural differences as suggested by Dore? There is a major question-mark over the degree of explanation offered by this approach. As Dore himself admits, Japan in the 1920s, and again in the immediate post-war period, was a far more 'cut and thrust' competitive society than in more recent times. That subcontracting emerged against the economic background of this earlier era is hard to reconcile convincingly with the sort of cultural idealism portrayed.

In order to explain national differences in subcontracting, we require a comprehensive, dynamic socio-economic theory. In the absence of a unifying theory, we can only expand existing economic or social theories by endogenising more environmental factors. For example, Hashimoto (1990) tried to enrich the concept of transaction costs in the context of Japanese employment relationships. Ito (1994) pointed out the possible existence of multiple equilibrium points for Japanese and US employment systems depending on the different economic environments. A deeper understanding of subcontracting systems may perhaps proceed along similar paths.

Notes

1 Small businesses, more accurately described as medium- and small-sized enterprises (MSEs), are defined as establishments with less than 300 employees.
2 In the fiscal year 1980, finance to the value of 3,400,000 million yen was provided for small business through governmental institutions, while 61,000 million yen were used as subsidies for small business in the national budget (Yokokura, 1984).
3 See Small and Medium Enterprise Agency, *White Paper on Small and Medium Enterprises*, 1984 edn, p. 391; 1996 edn, p. 144.
4 There is an unusually large jump in the figure in 1974. The oil crisis suddenly generated substantial inflation and working hours dropped significantly in small firms at the same time. The same reaction occurred in large firms but to a much milder extent.
5 See Tachibanaki (1996, ch. 4) for a detailed discussion of this and other hypotheses.
6 Insurance may be 'purchased' in the form of better quality assurance or improved just-in-time delivery or greater R&D co-operation.
7 A value of 1 indicates that the principal absorbs the entire risk of the transaction, while a value of 0 means that the supplier incurs all the risk.
8 See Odagiri (1992, ch. 7) for re-examination of Nakatani's study.
9 Dore's idea that trust is the core of the subcontracting relationships has been further developed by Smitka (1991) and Sako (1992).

9 Schooling and earnings

9.1 Schooling and earnings profiles

In this chapter, we discuss the influence of pre-work education on subsequent earnings patterns within the Japanese enterprise. As discussed in section 2.4, the standard way of examining this is to study the relative positions and shapes of so-called earnings–experience profiles. These plot the log of earnings against years of experience of individual workers in given jobs. Much of our empirical discussion will centre on workers who graduated from each of the four main levels in the Japanese school system: these are (i) primary or junior high school (6–7 years of schooling), (ii) senior high school (12–13 years), (iii) junior college (14–15 years), and (iv) university (over 16 years).

Two relationships between schooling in Japan and subsequent labour market experience are relatively well established. First, the *level* of pre-work educational attainment is positively related to the level of wage-earnings (Hashimoto and Raisian, 1985). Recall that wage-earnings in a Japanese context refer to regular monthly earnings plus a (typically) biannual bonus payment. Secondly, and particularly in the context of the lifetime employment system, higher-level educational qualifications appear to signal suitable career paths within the firm rather than to provide directly usable vocational skills (see Organisation for Economic Co-operation and Development, 1993). As stated by Dore and Sako (1989):

Recruitment is for a career, not for a job. Selection criteria concentrate, consequently . . . on demonstrated ability to learn rather than on particular job competencies already acquired . . . Employers are, consequently, more likely than employers in other countries with greater job mobility, to be content, even when recruiting science, engineering, economics, business studies graduates, if they have a good general grounding in their subject as a solid basis for on-the-job training. The complaint that universities do not provide the sort of practical vocational training that makes graduates immediately useful in specific jobs is not often heard.

This view of the role of schooling combines the so-called screening hypothesis (Arrow, 1973; Spence, 1973) with a human capital interpretation. Schooling is seen to act as a

157

device for sorting recruits into different levels of on-the-job training. The Japanese enterprise appears less interested in the productivity gain derived from schooling *per se* but more with the potential ability and quality signalled by a given education qualification. In this context, schooling is not regarded in itself, as in the classical human capital theory, as a direct investment in for-the-job training.

In what way might schooling attainment affect the relative shapes of the earnings–experience profiles for individuals with different educational backgrounds? Suppose educational attainment does influence the level of per capita investments in human capital. [1] Senior-level management as well as other occupational classifications involving high degrees of individual decision-making and responsibility is likely to require relatively large investments in on-the-job and off-the-job training. It may be less risky to offer such jobs to persons with degrees who have displayed abilities to learn and understand wide-ranging and complex issues over a considerable period of time. In other words, educational attainment may contribute to efficient sorting of new recruits by signalling the appropriate level of training investment. In this event, schooling would link to the productivity of training. To the extent that employees share the rents that derive from the returns to training, it follows that compensation–tenure growth paths of different educational groups would tend to diverge with increasing years of experience.

There are three potential gains to the overall profitability and welfare of the coalitional firm from such a payments structure. First, if workers in the most productive jobs experience the steepest earnings trajectories, then they will have relatively greater incentives to remain with the firm. Secondly, and concomitantly, the amortisation of high levels of specific investment is more assured if relatively long tenure is encouraged. Thirdly, workers in lower job categories are given the maximum incentive to reach higher categories, thereby encouraging greater effort and less shirking.

In summary, under the foregoing interpretation of the role of schooling, we would expect that better educated individuals fill more senior jobs with larger associated specific investments. As experience accumulates, they are likely to receive increasingly significant returns to these investments compared to their colleagues in more narrowly defined, less responsible positions in the enterprise. *Ceteris paribus*, this will manifest itself in steeper earnings–experience profiles associated with higher education backgrounds.

However, there are also potential problems with divergent earnings growth paths between job categories. These may arise as a consequence of two particular features of work organisation in the Japanese firm (Aoki, 1988). Workers from different job categories may be (i) integrated into work teams that perform a range of interrelated job tasks, and (ii) involved in close horizontal co-operation with peers and subordinates, both within and across teams as well as with other individuals. Fluidity of job demarcation, broadly based job classifications and regular job rotation are all common features of work organisation. As summarised by Ito (1994):

The Japanese firm tends not to use detailed job classifications or to offer a clear job description to each individual worker. Jobs are assigned to groups of workers who closely collaborate to perform them, via mutual help and information-sharing. A group leader often has some discretion over job assignments within the group. Workers perform multiple tasks via intra-group job rotation.

Payment schemes may be designed, in important respects, to reinforce the effectiveness of team-oriented work. A major consequence of a team approach is the need to engender reciprocity, that is for individual workers to expend effort on enhancing the performance of other members of the team as well as on behalf of their own productive performance (Drago and Turnbull, 1988, 1991). Integrated work groups, incorporating a mix of levels of seniority, provide knowledge transfer and shared experience over a broad range of jobs. Such an organisation is particularly well geared to solving non-routine production problems (Koike, 1988).

Earnings profiles designed to stimulate and to reinforce team participation and effort may not correspond to those that seek to reward specific human capital investment in the individual. In the first place, monitoring, evaluating and rewarding relative performances would be particularly costly in such an integrated structure. Secondly, problems for intra- and inter-team co-operation and morale caused by some workers shirking may be particularly acute if these involved workers in job categories that enjoyed relatively steep earnings profiles. Thirdly, a climate of increasing differences in earnings across job categories with length of tenure is possibly not one that is best suited to stimulate workers to help one another so as to maximise general co-operative productive strength.

What relative shapes of earnings–experience profiles among different educational groups might serve to reinforce this team-orientated structure? As we have already seen, a key aspect of remuneration within the Japanese firm is that of sharing returns to (relatively large) investments in firm-specific human capital. In an important sense, as indicated by Doeringer and Piore (1971, p. 16),[2] specificity itself arises from interrelated group activities:

. . . performance in some production or managerial jobs involves a team element, and a critical skill is the ability to operate effectively with the given members of the team. The ability is dependent on the interaction skills of the personalities of the members, and the individual's work 'skills' are specific in the sense that skills necessary to work on one team are never quite the same as those required on another.

Given the costs of monitoring within groups and the need to establish team morale and co-operation, simple and transparent sharing rules among employees with differing education backgrounds may be deemed to be generally attractive. A particularly simple rule of distribution among n education groups in the firm can be expressed as $\sum_{j=1}^{n} \alpha_j B_t$, where B_t denotes workers' share of the 'base' wage at t years of tenure, α_j is a share parameter, j is education level and $\sum_{j=1}^{n} \alpha_j = 1$. For example, a university graduate may receive 110 per cent of the base wage, senior high school graduates 100 per cent and junior high school graduates 80 per cent. If these sharing parameters are approximately constant,[3] we should observe parallel log earnings profiles. That is $\log (\alpha_j B_t) = \log \alpha_j + \log B_t$, where $\log \alpha_j$ is a constant reflecting an educational difference, and $\log B_t$ is common to all educational groups with a given tenure.[4]

What are the potential advantages of parallel, or non-divergent, earnings–experience profiles for different educational groups? First, a structure in which growth rates do not diverge among groups may help to instil, at least in one dimension, a climate of egalitarianism and perceived fairness that might serve to engender reciprocal actions and thereby reinforce general team effort and productivity.[5] Secondly, parallel growth paths may reduce the need to monitor closely individual performance. In other words, such paths would lay a greater emphasis on rules establishing compensation growth rates differentials among broadly defined groups rather than on rewarding individual productive performance. Thirdly, parallel paths may help establish long-term career job ladders, with well-defined compensation progression between different job categories.[6] As surmised by Drago and Turnbull (1991), 'career job ladders, provided by internal labor markets, might both serve to motivate employees and enhance the probability of establishing workgroup effort norms, and thereby lead to efficient provision of helping efforts'.

Under the simple human capital theory of individual-based investment in specific capital, we would expect earnings profiles, grouped according to differing educational attainments, to diverge as experience in the enterprise lengthens. If emphasis is more on payment structures that reinforce team commitment and co-operation, then parallel rather than divergent profiles may be more typically observed. Can the profiles help us to differentiate between the individual-based human capital and the team-related scenarios in other ways? If it is the case that the human capital theory predominates then we might anticipate downturns in the growth paths as individuals with long experience approach the age of retirement. This would reflect the fact that reductions in per capita investments in new skills coupled with depreciation of old skills take place as the expected length of remaining job tenure shortens. By contrast, no such reductions are likely under team-orientated profiles. It would not be conducive to team effort and co-operation if it were announced in advance that the sharing conditions would lapse at some arbitrary length of work experience.

9.2 Cross-sectional earnings profiles by schooling attainment

Most of the existing literature investigates earnings profiles of different educational groups by examining simple cross-sectional plots of log earnings against either

    (i) the average age of individuals within each group, or
    (ii) the average length of experience in the current job of individuals in each group.

The most important source is Mincer (1974) who studies – in part using data derived by Fuchs (1967) – age and experience profiles of US white non-farm males categorised by years of pre-work schooling. Kuratani (1973) derives these profiles from Japanese cross-sectional data for 1970. Interestingly, Kuratani delineates his profiles both by years of schooling and by size of firm. Koike (1988) compares earnings–age profiles for male workers in Japan and the United States for 1960.

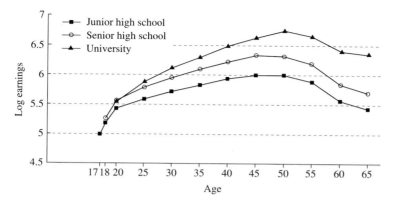

Fig. 9.1. Earnings–age profiles by schooling, 1991.

Earnings–age profiles are shown in figure 9.1 for Japanese male workers in 1991 who have graduated from either junior high school or senior high school or university.[7] The relative shapes of the graphs are typical of those found by earlier observers. Up to the age of about 50, both the absolute and relative rates of growth of earnings at given ages increase with the level of schooling. The downturn in the growth rates at later ages almost certainly represents, in large part, lower earnings of individuals after the 'official' age of retirement.

In a similar fashion to that shown in figure 9.1, Koike (1988) compares Japanese and US male earnings–age profiles by educational background for 1959. For each education level, the US profiles appear to be steeper than their Japanese counterparts among the younger age groups although, generally, the profile shapes are reasonably similar. Both sets of profiles display, as in figure 9.1, widening earnings differentials by level of education with increasing age. The US educational differentials for all age groups appear to be significantly greater than in Japan.

From this evidence, pre-work schooling appears to be associated with divergent earnings profiles. Based on the age of individuals, this conclusion is misleading, however. The problem is that different education groups from a given age cohort enter the workplace at different ages. Replacing age by length of work experience corrects for this. Figure 9.2 presents the same data as figure 9.1 but 'adjusting' the horizontal axis according to average lengths of work experience. The graphs now display considerably less divergence among the education groups. One interpretation of this difference is advanced by Mincer (1974), thus:

at given ages, the amount of 'time' people invest in human capital increases with the years of their schooling. The longer-schooled, however, do not spend more 'time' than the less-schooled at *comparable years of experience.*

In fact Mincer's data reveal parallel, or even slightly convergent, earnings–experience profiles, which might suggest that more educated workers devote less time to post-school training and education than their less educated counterparts.

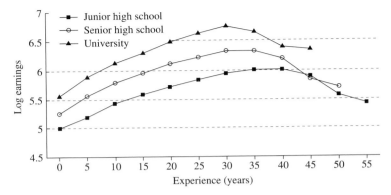

Fig. 9.2. Earnings–experience profiles by schooling, males, 1991.

Kuratani's 1970 cross-sections together with the comparable 1991 profiles shown here reveal:

(i) an upward shift in the profile related positively to the length of pre-work schooling;
(ii) divergent earnings growth paths by years of schooling through time, although much more marked in Kuratani's earlier period;
(iii) downturns in the profiles occurring at around thirty years of experience for workers with senior high school and university equivalent backgrounds.

Additionally, Kuratani's graphs display:

(iv) upward shifts in the profiles by firm size at all levels of education.

9.3 Measurement problems

The discussion so far has concentrated on simple plots of the log of earnings against age or experience. Essentially, these profiles represent gross effects; they do not involve controls for other influences on earnings growth rates. Would the schooling-related profiles be affected, for example, if we were to control for the separate influences of tenure and experience as well as for gender or industry of occupation and firm size? Schooling effects on the profiles as well as other human capital questions are better studied via regression specifications[8] which take the form

$$\log y_i = f(s_i, x_i, z_i) = u_i \qquad (9.1)$$

where $\log y_i$ is the natural log of earnings (wages plus bonuses in a Japanese context) for the ith individual, s_i represents measures of schooling characteristics, x_i measures of human capital related variables, z_i other factors influencing individual earnings (for example, size of enterprise in which the individual is currently employed, gender and geographical location), and u_i is an error term. Typically, as discussed in section 2.4, the x_i measures differentiate between job experience (taken to be the age of the individual minus years of schooling minus number of pre-school years) and the length of tenure in the current job. Experience is taken to proxy returns to general human capital while tenure proxies returns to specific human capital.[9]

Before re-examining the influence of pre-work schooling on the profiles, we return to two measurement problems that relate to the estimation of equation (9.1). These were highlighted in relation to wage–tenure profiles in chapter 5 and concern the use of cross-section data and the influence of fixed effects.

A simple cross-section provides information on individuals from differing age cohorts. For example, in the 1991 cross-sections shown in figures 9.1 and 9.2, a fifty-year-old educated up to the age of eighteen would have left school in 1959, compared to 1989 for a twenty-year-old with the same length of education. Estimating profiles based on such wide age discrepancies can lead to serious distortions. (See section 5.2.2 under the subheading 'Age cohorts and cross-sectional studies' for a discussion of the same problem in a slightly different context.) Suppose that remuneration reflects in part workers' share of the returns to investments in firm-specific human capital. If levels of per capita investments rise systematically through time, for example because of technological improvement and economic growth, then, *ceteris paribus*, this may serve to shift the earnings–experience profiles upwards for successive age cohorts. One consequence of this relates to the apparent declines in the cross-sectional profiles observed during the later years of experience. These may represent the fact that older age groups in 1991 belong to age cohorts with systematically lower earnings profiles. In this event, the downward slopes in the profiles among the older age groups might not reflect reductions in human capital investments. It may merely stem from the statistical artefact that older workers, with systematically lower profiles, dominate the end-points of the profiles.

This deficiency would ideally be counteracted by using panel data sets that track earnings, tenure, occupations and other relevant statistics for given individuals through time. Unfortunately, the richest data source in Japan – the Basic Survey of Wage Structure – is composed of annual cross-sections. Nonetheless, as highlighted in section 5.2.2, it is possible to tackle the problem of systematic age-cohort effects by rearranging these data – consisting of wages, bonuses and workers' ages, lengths of job tenure and schooling characteristics – so that specific cohorts are tracked through time (Hart and Kawasaki, 1995). An actual cohort construction – results for which will be reported in the following section – is shown in table 9.1.

Cohort A in table 9.1 covers the period 1966 to 1991, and incorporates five-year age bands. In 1966, it consists of observations on the relevant schooling and economic variables with respect to the 30–34-year-old age group. Then, in 1971, it refers to comparable data for the 35–39 age group given the earlier group are now five years older. Similar construction throughout the sample time period ends, in 1991, with observations on the 55–59 age group. This last age band straddles, in large part, the main ages of retirement. Cohort B consists of workers who are on average ten years younger than those in Cohort A, and Cohort C those who are twenty years younger. Comparing earnings–tenure profiles for the different cohorts allows us to determine whether the profiles have shown signs of systematic shifts between different age groups.

Table 9.1. *Age groups and cohorts*

	Age intervals		
	Cohort A	Cohort B	Cohort C
1966	30–34	—	—
1971	35–39	25–29	–19
1976	40–44	30–34	20–24
1981	45–49	35–39	25–29
1986	50–54	40–44	30–34
1991	55–59	45–49	35–39

Note:
There are two age groups under 19: these are 18–19 and under 18. We combined these to form a single under-19 age group.

Appropriate adjustments of age–cohort effects still leave the second type of measurement problem. Thus, estimation of equation (9.1) by ordinary least squares may be distorted because of unobserved individual and job characteristics. The problem is discussed in section 5.2.2 (under the subheading 'Fixed individual and job match effects'). Suffice it to report that in the estimation that follows, we again adopt the Altonji and Shakotko (1987) methodology as a means of tackling these potential biases.

9.4 Profiles based on regression analysis

Constructing data from the Basic Survey of Wage Structure so as to conform with the cohorts shown in table 9.1, we estimated a specific form of equation (9.1) for Japanese male workers. Dummy variables discriminate among the three levels of education shown in figures 9.1 and 9.2. Interaction terms between education levels on the one hand and experience and tenure on the other are also included. The regressions differentiate among small, medium and large establishments. Finally, the potential problem of fixed individual and job match effects is accommodated by means of an instrumental variable technique.

The pre-work education implications of these results are investigated by assuming that a worker leaves school after attaining a given level of education and then enters a firm and stays until retirement. This permits simulation of growth profiles of log earnings.

Figure 9.3 shows the results of this exercise. There are four main findings.

(i) As expected, longer years of schooling are associated with a higher-level profile. This latter shift is particularly noticeable between senior high school and university graduates on the one hand and junior high school graduates on the other. Recall that the length of schooling of senior high school and university graduates is twelve to fifteen years and over sixteen years, respectively, while it is six to seven years for junior high school leavers.

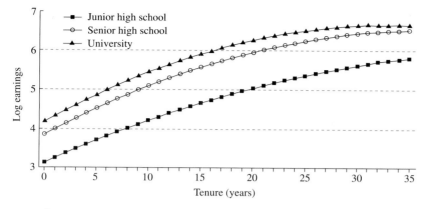

Fig. 9.3. Estimated earnings–tenure profiles by schooling, Cohort A.

   (ii) In all cases, schooling exerts a positive influence on the profiles as experience increases.
   (iii) The profiles display more or less parallel paths. There are certainly no major signs of significant divergence or convergence between the profiles through time.
   (iv) While earnings growth rates dampen towards the end points of the profiles – especially with respect to university and senior high school graduates – the levelling-off in the profiles at around thirty years of experience contrasts with the downturns displayed by the simple cross-sections in figure 9.2.

As indicated in table 9.1, two further cohorts were constructed, each representing successively younger age groups than the cohort that formed the analysis leading to figure 9.3. With these we could test the possibility that the earnings–experience profiles had shifted systematically through time. This involved undertaking separate simulations, along the lines described above, for Cohorts B and C as well as A, and allowed for a ten-year gap between successive cohorts. Note from table 9.1 that individuals in Cohort B were aged 45–49 in 1991 and for Cohort C they were aged 35–39. Accordingly, we allowed a maximum period of twenty-five years of tenure for Cohort B and fifteen years for Cohort C. This exercise was carried out only for university graduates.

Results are shown in figure 9.4. While the shapes of the profiles are quite similar, there is a clear tendency for the profiles to shift upwards among the younger cohorts. These findings provide a clue to the discrepancies between the 30–35 years' experience segments in the simple cross-sectional graphs in figure 9.2 and those of the age-adjusted graphs in figure 9.3. The older age groups within the cross-section in figure 9.2 belong to lower earnings profiles than their younger counterparts. Therefore, the simple cross-sections would tend to exaggerate reductions in growth rates towards the age of retirement.

9.5 What do we know?

The level of schooling in Japan is associated with a positive shift in the earnings–experience profile. As we might expect, given the respective average lengths of schooling, the

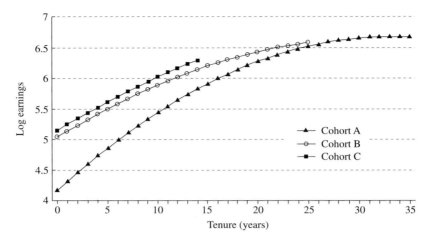

Fig. 9.4. Estimated earnings–tenure profiles by cohort, university graduates.

gap is most noticeable between university and senior high school graduates on the one hand and junior high school graduates on the other. After controlling for age and other economic/structural influences, three additional results with respect to the relative earnings–tenure are obtained. First, the earnings–tenure profiles by level of pre-work schooling are virtually parallel. Secondly, there is a slackening in the growth rates towards the age of retirement. Thirdly, the younger age cohorts of wage-earners, at least with respect to university graduates, are associated with upward shifts in the profiles.

Other factors need to be explored. In particular, the implications for the estimated profiles of job mobility and turnover among the educational groups require investigation (Topel, 1991). It may be the case that, on average, individuals who change jobs at given stages in their careers gain from their moves. Failure to account for this effect would serve to understate the returns to tenure. Furthermore, the size of the gain may be positively related to the level of schooling, in which case the relative shapes of the profiles may be affected.

Notes

1 In fact, it is common practice for employers to provide both general and specific training to new young recruits. See Sako (1994), who also compares multinational firms' company training in relation to schooling in Japan, Germany and the United Kingdom.

2 See also the discussion in Hart and Moutos (1995).

3 Updating of share parameters may be linked, for example, to major long-term changes in the demand and supply conditions in the market for new graduates. For example, this might involve age-cohort effects in the population altering the available supply of new graduates.

4 In his cross-sectional data, Mincer (1974) observes parallel, or even slightly convergent, earnings–experience growth paths.

5 Are relative 'high-fliers' disadvantaged under this sort of arrangement? They do not necessarily stand to lose *vis-à-vis* other market opportunities. They have to weigh up the potentially increased personal returns from seeking compensation systems geared to individual performance and productivity against (their share of) the increased rents stemming from team harmony and co-operation.

6 Ito (1994) reviews the relevant theoretical literature on promotion paths in the Japanese firm.

7 Senior high school and junior college data are merged in the analyses that follow. First, and most importantly, there are far fewer junior college male graduates in the data set than in each of the other three groups. Secondly, the years of schooling for the two merged groups are not significantly differentiated (i.e. 12–13 years and 14–15 years).

8 Berndt (1991, ch. 5) provides a useful and accessible survey of the applied econometrics and background theory related to this model.

9 It is also common practice to include an interaction term, i.e. (experience) × (tenure), into the regression. If, for example, the estimated coefficient on this term turns out to be negative then this indicates that earnings growth due to tenure is hindered by previous years of experience.

10 **Work and pay in Japan and elsewhere**

Fascination with Japanese employment and remuneration systems arises from the fact that both the structure and the performance of the labour market have been regarded as exhibiting significant features that differ radically from those of other advanced industrial economies. Not only have perceived differences been of interest in their own right but they have also provided distinctive labour market contrasts against which international comparative studies have been more effectively focused. This has been apparent in the growth of comparative empirical work on Japan, Europe, the United States and elsewhere. Asking why such-and-such a country's employment and pay experiences contrast with comparable Japanese practices and outcomes, given known institutional and organisational differences, has provided added insight into and understanding of labour market behaviour. Certainly, such approaches can achieve significant added value compared with (the preponderance of) single-country studies. Concomitantly, as particularly exemplified in the work of Aoki (1984, 1988), major theoretical gains in the understanding of human capital investment, principal–agent relationships, strategic bargaining, firms' optimising behaviour and industrial organisation have stemmed from international comparative settings that include and highlight Japanese practices.

But are work and pay differences more apparent than real? There is a persistent view that, in fundamental respects, Japanese industrial relations, employment and work incentive systems have the appearance of uniqueness at first levels of analysis, whereas, when examined in greater depth, they amount essentially to common experience, albeit 'packaged' in a somewhat different way. A particularly interesting example in this respect was reported in chapter 1. Recorded unemployment rates in Japan have been unequivocally below those of other OECD countries throughout the post-war period. Yet, when measures of excess labour supply are extended to embrace labour hoarding and 'hidden' unemployment, Japanese experience appears not to be so much on a limb. Japanese employment and hours responses to unanticipated downturns in business activity are more sluggish than elsewhere, especially among male workers. Moreover, 'discouraged

168

worker' effects or enforced non-participation in the labour market does appear to be a relatively important phenomenon in Japan, especially among older female workers. Adding hoarded labour and hidden unemployment to conventional unemployment measures certainly helps to redress the balance of the total measure of excess labour supply between Japan and elsewhere. However, the key point is that important unemployment-related insights can be gained through attempting to explain why Japan differs in its relative weighting of the constituent parts of excess supply. Why incur hoarding rather than layoff costs? Chapters 2 and 7 attempted to cast some light on this latter type of question. Joint rents are created by human capital and other organisational investments. Low costs of communicating and verifying information between bargaining parties in Japan help better to protect these rents in times of downturns in the cycle. The employment partnership is more strongly guaranteed, and therefore joint rents are better protected, by a stronger propensity to accommodate downturns in economic activity through reductions in marginal labour costs and/or increases of inventories.

Other labour market differences between Japan and elsewhere represent different degrees of emphasis in approach rather than wide intercountry disparities. Average male job tenure is somewhat longer in Japan than elsewhere but arguably this is merely a matter of degree and not indicative of a distinctive attitude to the desirability of a lifetime employment. There are more than faint echoes of the Japanese enterprise union structure in, for example, the German co-determination system. Japanese workers do not retire earlier than elsewhere; they merely organise ultimate withdrawal from the labour force in a different way. As with unemployment, however, contrasting tendencies rather than unique traits have been sufficient to stimulate analytical work that moves us significantly forward. At the very least, attempting to understand work and pay in Japan in relation to other economies gives added dimensions beyond those achieved by examining industrial, geographical and other cross-sectional breakdowns within a single country.

For some aspects of work and pay, it is reasonable to conclude that Japanese, European and US labour markets are showing signs of convergence. Union density is one such area, as we explored in chapter 3. These are not necessarily indicative, however, of convergence among labour market systems. A good example in this respect is the recent rise in Japanese official retirement ages from a relatively low age level, as discussed in chapter 6. Rising average retirement ages in Japan are approaching European averages; in fact, the latter have been moving in the opposite direction from far higher 'starting values'. From a Japanese perspective, the stimulus behind this change derives from the long-term supply-side pressure of declining economically active cohorts relative to total population rather than a coming together of views over the economic function of retirement within the context of working lifetimes. The fact remains that Japanese participation rates among workers aged sixty and above have remained relatively high despite the change in the official ages of retirement. The system of re-employment after official retirement still remains an important facet of the Japanese employment system.

At current levels of knowledge, however, it remains reasonably convincing that, in some important respects, work and pay practices in Japan do contrast markedly with other economies. Some of the major differences are quite transparent while others, commonly 'accepted' as stylised facts in a wide-ranging literature, are still less than fully confirmed by measurement and observation.

One measurably important difference between Japan and elsewhere is the former's emphasis on bonus payments within total compensation. This topic was reviewed in chapter 5. While the bonus system may act as a disguised form of regular pay, its link with human capital-related variables, such as job tenure and education, is reasonably well established in a growing number of studies. In important respects, bonus payments do appear to represent a means of compensating workers for their share of the returns accruing to human capital investments. It is particularly intriguing that bonuses may well play much the same role in the United States and Germany (Nakamura and Hübler, 1998) and yet bonus experience is not nearly so prevalent or quantitatively significant in these and other economies.

Of the other relatively well established differences between Japan and elsewhere, two are particularly noteworthy. First, as discussed in chapter 3, while other economies enjoy aspects of industrial relations systems that are similar to typical Japanese experience, the size of coverage, the organisational structure and the bargaining framework of enterprise unionism are not matched elsewhere. Secondly, small business activity in general and subcontracting in particular are also familiar aspects of the economic life of many countries but, as shown in chapter 8, they do not match the scale, information networking and organisational structure experienced in Japan.

Other distinctive features of the Japanese labour market have become widely accepted but have arisen more through implicit reasoning than explicit verification. Good communications and information flow between management and workers and between assemblers and subcontractors are broadly argued to reflect a relatively low transaction cost environment in the Japanese labour market. Similar arguments apply to other industrial and commercial sectors, such as in the relationship between a business group and its 'main' bank. As mentioned above, and in several earlier chapters, such reasoning helps underpin the notion that human capital investments are higher in Japan than elsewhere and this in turn leads to wider reasoning about the relative performance of the Japanese labour market. For instance, low transaction costs together with high per capita specific investments are consistent with higher employment stability and hence with a greater tendency in the Japanese economy to buffer against unforeseen changes in product demand by use of the intensive margin, such as wage variability and flexible work arrangements. But there is little hard evidence in support of these communication-related conjectures. Even more surprisingly, there is very little *direct* evidence that firm-specific investments are higher in Japan than elsewhere. Most information on such investments is derived either from very partial statistical information or by indirect methods. Included in the former are data on the firm-level availability of training programmes, although the precise nature of the training undertaken and the full cost of the training are rarely available. As for the latter, inferences about the degree of investments in human capital – as discussed in chapters 2, 5 and 9 and elsewhere – are made from the shapes of wage–experience and wage–tenure profiles.

It turns out that general modelling frameworks that attempt to integrate institutional and analytical representations of how the Japanese labour market works in relation to elsewhere invariably consists of a patchwork of factually observed detail interwoven with inferred or conjectured modes of behaviour. Of course, such a mix is not unique to analyses involving Japan. However, there is considerably more room for research that attempts to utilise detailed and matching micro-level databases that accommodate levels of analytical and descriptive detail that are on a par with the best of the single-country studies.

Finally, it is worth pointing out that, from time to time, 'natural tests' take place of the robustness of Japanese work and pay institutions and practices. These consist of observing their survivability in the face of severe economy-wide conditions and in the context of a highly competitive global economy. On the basis of recent experience, it might be questioned whether long-term employment contracts, bonuses, enterprise union bargaining and other features closely linked to Japan will withstand, in a major sense, the economic rigours of the financial crisis that began in the early 1990s. This might be regarded as the acid test of the permanency of the 'unique' aspects of the system. In other words, do the existing work and pay institutions and practices serve to provide an efficiently working labour market? If so, they will survive largely intact. Or, are they somewhat anachronistic quirks that do not match with best international practice? Then, they will greatly diminish in importance. It is worth recalling that while the Japanese economy was strongly and adversely affected by the first OPEC supply shock in 1973/4, it displayed such a resilience that, by the second shock in 1979, it outperformed virtually all other OECD economies. Certainly, the distinctive work and pay features covered in this book survived these earlier crises intact.

It may well be the case that, unlike earlier post-war economic upheavals, the Japanese economic problems of the 1990s will lead to changes in the organisation of the labour market. There are two important catalysts for change. The first relates to the extreme crisis within the financial system. Traditional methods of employment are being closely scrutinised by companies that have been particularly affected and new practices are likely to emerge. In this event, service and manufacturing sectors in a wider perspective may see the need to follow suit. Interestingly, two exceptionally well performing industries in current times – TV games and convenience stores – adopt employment methods that differ markedly from the traditional system. Secondly, an important pressure on existing businesses practices has been introduced by the digital revolution in information and communications technology. With a considerable lag behind the United States, company restructuring in the wake of this technology is now a major priority. Again, this may impact on traditional work and pay practices.

Differences in collective bargaining, employment and labour payments between Japan and elsewhere are likely to survive into the longer term. Indications are that Japanese work and pay systems are displaying tendencies towards convergence with competitor economies. It will be interesting to observe relative outcomes in the aftermath of financial and technological revolutions.

References

Abraham, K. G. and J. C. Haltiwanger (1995), 'Real wages and the business cycle', *Journal of Economic Literature*, 33: 1215–64.

Abraham, K. and S. Houseman (1989), 'Job security and work force adjustment: how different are US and Japanese practices?', *Journal of the Japanese and International Economies*, 3: 500–21.

Aizcorbe, A. (1992), 'Procyclical labour productivity, increasing returns to labour, and labour hoarding in US auto assembly plant employment', *Economic Journal*, 102: 860–73.

Altonji, J. and R. Shakotko (1987), 'Do wages rise with seniority?', *Review of Economic Studies*, 54: 437–59.

Aoki, M. (1984), *The Co-operative Game Theory of the Firm*, Oxford: Clarendon Press.
  (1988), *Information, Incentives and Bargaining in the Japanese Economy*, Cambridge: Cambridge University Press.
  (1990), 'Toward an economic model of the Japanese firm', *Journal of Economic Literature*, 28: 1–27.

Aoki, M., K. Koike and I. Nakatani (eds.) (1989), *The Globalization of the Japanese Firm*, Tokyo: PHP (in Japanese).

Aoki, M. and M. Okuno-Fujiwara (eds.) (1996), *Comparative Institutional Analysis: A New Approach to Economic Systems*, Tokyo: University of Tokyo Press (in Japanese).

Aoki, M. and H. Patrick (eds.) (1994), *The Japanese Main Bank System: Its Relevancy for Developing and Transforming Economies*, Oxford: Oxford University Press.

Argy, V. and L. Stein (1997), *The Japanese Economy*, London: Macmillan.

Ariga, K. and Y. Ohkusa (1995), 'Procyclical markups in Japan', Institutute of Economic Research, Kyoto University (mimeo).

Arrow, K. J. (1973), 'Higher education as a filter', *Journal of Public Economics*, 2: 193–216.

Asanuma, B. (1985), 'The organization of parts purchases in the Japanese automotive industry', *Japanese Economic Studies*, 13: 32–53.
  (1997), *Japanese Enterprise System – Mechanism of Innovative Adaptation*, Tokyo: Toyo-keizai-shimpo-sha (in Japanese).

172

Asanuma, B. and T. Kikutani (1992), 'Risk absorption in Japanese subcontracting: a microeconometric study of the automobile industry', *Journal of the Japanese and International Economies*, 6: 1–29.

Barron, J. M., M. C. Berger and D. A. Black (1997), 'How well do we measure training?', *Journal of Labor Economics*, 15: 507–28.

Barron, J. M., D. A. Black and M. A. Loewenstein (1989), 'Job matching and on-the-job training', *Journal of Labor Economics*, 7: 1–19.

Barzel, Y. (1973), 'The determination of daily hours and wages', *Quarterly Journal of Economics*, 87: 220–38.

Becker, G. S. (1964), *Human Capital: A Theoretical and Empirical Analysis, with Special Reference to Education*, New York: National Bureau of Economic Research.

Bernanke, B. S. and M. L. Parkinson (1991), 'Procyclical labor productivity and competing theories of the business cycle: some evidence from interwar US manufacturing industries', *Journal of Political Economy*, 99: 439–59.

Berndt, E. R. (1991), *The Practice of Econometrics*, New York: Addison-Wesley.

Bils, M. (1987), 'The cyclical behaviour of marginal cost and price', *American Economic Review*, 77: 838–55.

Blanchard, O. and S. Fischer (1989), *Lectures on Macroeconomics*, Cambridge, Mass.: MIT Press.

Blanchflower, D. G. and R. B. Freeman (1992), 'Unionism in the United States and other advanced OECD countries', *Industrial Relations*, 31: 56–79.

Blinder, A. S. (1976), 'On dogmatism in human capital theory', *Journal of Human Resources*, 11: 8–22.

Blumenthal, T. (1966), 'The effect of socio-economic factors on wage differentials in Japanese manufacturing industries', *Kikan Rironkeizai*, 17: 53–67.

(1968), 'Scarcity of labor and wage differentials in the Japanese economy, 1958–64', *Economic Development and Cultural Change*, 17: 15–32.

Brown, C. and J. Medoff (1978), 'Trade unions in the production process', *Journal of Political Economy*, 86: 355–78.

(1989), 'The employer size–wage effect', *Journal of Political Economy*, 97: 1027–59.

Brunello, G. and F. Ohtake (1987), 'The relation between bonuses, wages, profits and employment in Japan: a reconsideration based on microeconomic data', *Osaka Economic Review*, 37: 28–41 (in Japanese).

Bruno, M. and J. D. Sachs (1985), *Economics of worldwide stagflation*, Cambridge, Mass.: Harvard University Press.

Burdett, K. (1978), 'A theory of employee job search and quit rates', *American Economic Review*, 68: 212–20.

Burnside, C. R., R. Eichenbaum and J. L. Powell (1993), 'Labor hoarding and the business cycle', *Journal of Political Economy*, 101: 245–73.

Cabellero, R. J. and R. K. Lyons (1992), 'External effects in US procyclical productivity', *Journal of Monetary Economics*, 29: 209–25.

Carmichael, L. (1983), 'Firm-specific human capital and promotion ladders', *Bell Journal of Economics*, 14: 251–8.

Christodoulakis, N., S. P. Dimelis and T. Kollintzas (1995), 'Comparisons of business cycles in the EC: idiosyncrasies and regularities', *Economica*, 62: 1–27.

Chuma, H. and Y. Higuchi (1997), *Labour Economics*, Tokyo: Iwanami (in Japanese).

Clark, R. L. and N. Ogawa (1992), 'Employment, tenure and earnings profiles in Japan and the United States: comment', *American Economic Review*, 82: 336–45.

Cole, R. E. (1979), *Work, Mobility, and Participation: A Comparative Study of American and Japanese Industry*, Berkeley: University of California Press.

(1989), *Strategies for Learning: Small-Group Activities in American, Japanese, and Swedish Industry*, Berkeley: University of California Press.

(1992), 'Some cultural and social bases of Japanese innovation: small-group activities in comparative perspective', in S. Kumon and H. Rosovsky (eds.), *The Political Economy of Japan, vol. III: Cultural and Social Dynamics*, Stanford: Stanford University Press.

Cusumano, M. A. (1985), *The Japanese Automobile Industry*, Cambridge, Mass.: Harvard University Press.

Darby, J., R. A. Hart and M. Vecchi (1998), 'Labour force participation and the business cycle: a comparative analysis of France, Japan, Sweden and the United States', Discussion Paper 98/1, Department of Economics, University of Stirling.

(1999), 'Wages and unemployment: participation, hoarding and the claimant count', University of Stirling, mimeo.

Denison, E. F. and W. K. Chung (1976), 'Economic growth and its sources', in H. Patrick and H. Rosovsky (eds.), *Asia's New Giant*, Washington: Brookings Institution.

Doeringer, P. and M. Piore (1971), *Internal Labor Markets and Manpower Analysis*, Lexington, Mass.: Heath.

Domowitz, I. G., R. Hubbard and B. C. Petersen (1986), 'Business cycles and the relationships between concentration and price–cost margins', *Rand Journal of Economics*, 17: 1–17.

Dore, D. (1973), *British Factory – Japanese Factory: The Origins of National Diversity in Industrial Relations*, Berkeley, University of California Press.

(1983), 'Goodwill and the spirit of market capitalism', *British Journal of Sociology*, 34: 459–81.

(1987), *Taking Japan Seriously*, London: Athlone Press.

Dore, R. P. and M. Sako (1989), *How the Japanese Learn to Work*, New York: Routledge.

Drago, R. and G. K. Turnbull (1988), 'Individual versus group piece rates under team technologies', *Journal of the Japanese and International Economies*, 2: 1–10.

(1991), 'Competition and cooperation in the workplace', *Journal of Economic Behavior and Organization*, 15: 347–64.

Estrin, S. and S. Wadhwani (1990), 'Profit sharing', in D. Sapsford and Z. Tzannatos (eds.), *Current Issues in Labour Economics*, London: Macmillan.

Fair, R. C. (1969), *The Short-Run Demand for Workers and Hours*, Amsterdam: North Holland.

(1984), *Specification, Estimation, and Analysis of Macroeconomic Models*, Cambridge, Mass.: Harvard University Press.

(1985), 'Excess labor and the business cycle', *American Economic Review*, 75: 239–45.

Fair Trade Commission (1987), 'Survey on continuous trading relationships in Japanese firms', mimeo. (in Japanese).

(1992), *Japan's Six Largest Business Groups*, Tokyo: Toyo-keizai-shimpo-sha (in Japanese).

Fay, J. and J. Medoff (1985), 'Labor and output over the business cycle', *American Economic Review*, 75: 638–55.

Felli, L. and C. Harris (1996), 'Learning, wage dynamics, and firm-specific human capital', *Journal of Political Economy*, 104: 838–68.

Forbes, J. B. (1987), 'Early intraorganizational mobility: patterns and influences', *Academy of Management Journal,* 30: 110–25.

Freeman, R. B. (1981), 'The effect of unionism on fringe benefits', *Industrial and Labor Relations Review*, 34: 489–509.

(1988), 'Contraction and expansion: the divergence of private sector and public sector unionism in the United States', *Journal of Economic Perspectives*, 2(2): 63–88.

Freeman, R. B. and E. Lazear (1995), 'An economic analysis of works councils', in J. Rogers and W. Streeck (eds.), *Works Councils – Consultation, Representation, and Cooperation in Industrial Relations*, Chicago: University of Chicago Press.

Freeman, R. B. and J. L. Medoff (1979), 'The two faces of unionism', *The Public Interest*, 57 (Fall): 69–93.

(1984), *What Do Unions Do?*, New York: Basic Books.

Freeman, R. B. and M. E. Rebick (1989), 'Crumbling Pillar? Declining union density in Japan', *Journal of the Japanese and International Economies*, 3: 578–605.

Freeman, R. B. and M. L. Weitzman (1987), 'Bonuses and employment in Japan', *Journal of the Japanese and International Economies*, 1: 168–94.

Fruin, W. M. (1992), *The Japanese Enterprise System*, New York: Clarendon Press.

Fuchs, V. R. (1967), 'Differentials in hourly earnings by region and city size', *Occasional Papers in Economics* 101, New York: National Bureau of Economic Research.

Fukao, K. and M. Otaki (1993), 'Accumulation of human capital and the business cycle', *Journal of Political Economy*, 101: 73–99.

Gerschenkron, A. (1966), *Economic Backwardness in Historical Perspective*, Cambridge, Mass.: Harvard University Press.

Gordon, R. J. (1982), 'Why US wage and employment behaviour differs from that in Britain and Japan', *Economic Journal*, 92: 13–44.

Greer, D. F. and S. A. Rhoades (1977), 'A test of the reserve labour hypothesis', *Economic Journal*, 87: 290–9.

Hall, R. E. (1982), 'The importance of lifetime jobs in the US economy', *American Economic Review*, 72: 716–24.

(1988), 'The relation between marginal cost and price in US industry', *Journal of Political Economy*, 96: 921–47.

(1990), 'Invariance properties of Solow's productivity residual', in P. Diamond (ed.), *Growth, Productivity, Employment*, Cambridge, Mass.: MIT Press.

Hamermesh, D. S. (1989), 'Labour demand and the structure of adjustment costs', *American Economic Review*, 79: 674–89.

(1993), *Labor Demand*, Princeton: Princeton University Press.

Hanada, K. (1989), 'The principle of competition in Japan's personnel system', *Japanese Economic Studies*, 17: 32–43.

Hart, R. A. (1973), 'The role of overtime working in the recent wage inflation process', *Bulletin of Economic Research*, 25: 73–87.

(1984), *The Economics of Non-wage Labour Costs*, London: Allen & Unwin.

Hart, R. A., D. N. F. Bell, R. Frees, S. Kawasaki and S. A. Woodbury (1988), *Trends in Non-wage Labour Costs and Their Effects on Employment,* Programme for Research and Actions on the Development of the Labour Market, Brussels: Commission of the European Communities.

Hart, R. A. and S. Kawasaki (1995), 'The Japanese bonus system and human capital', *Journal of the Japanese and International Economies*, 9: 225–44.

(1996), 'Schooling and earnings growth in Japan', Department of Economics, University of Stirling (mimeo.).

Hart, R. A. and J. R. Malley (1996), 'Excess labour and the business cycle: a comparative analysis of Japan, Germany, the United Kingdom and the United States', *Economica*, 63: 325–42.

(1998), 'Marginal cost and price over the business cycle: comparative evidence from Japan and the United States', Department of Economics, University of Stirling (mimeo.).

Hart, R. A. and T. Moutos (1995), *Human Capital, Employment and Bargaining*, Cambridge: Cambridge University Press.

Hart, R. A. and R. J. Ruffell (1993), 'The cost of overtime working in British production industries', *Economica*, 60: 183–201.

Hashimoto, M. (1975), 'Wage reduction, unemployment and specific human capital', *Economic Inquiry*, 13: 485–504.

(1979), 'Bonus payments, on-the-job training and lifetime employment in Japan', *Journal of Political Economy*, 87: 1086–104.

(1990), *The Japanese Labor Market in a Comparative Perspective with the United States*, Kalamazoo, Mich.: Upjohn Institute for Employment Research.

(1993), 'Three aspects of employment and unemployment in Japan: a contrast with the United States', *Journal of Labor Economics*, 11: 136–61.

Hashimoto, M. and J. Raisian (1985), 'Employment tenure and earnings profiles in Japan and the United States', *American Economic Review*, 75: 721–35.

(1989), 'Investments in employer–employee attachments by Japanese and US workers in firms of varying size', *Journal of the Japanese and International Economies*, 3: 31–48.

(1992), 'Employment tenure and earnings profiles in Japan and the United States: reply', *American Economic Review*, 82: 346–54.

Hashimoto, M. and B. T. Yu (1980), 'Specific capital, employment contracts and wage rigidity', *Bell Journal of Economics*, 11: 536–49.

Haskel, J., C. Martin and I. Small (1995), 'Price, marginal cost and the business cycle', *Oxford Bulletin of Economics and Statistics*, 57, 25–41.

Hildreth, A. K. G. and F. Ohtake (1998), 'Labour demand and the structure of adjustment costs in Japan', *Journal of the Japanese and International Economies*, 12: 131–50.

Hirschman, A. O. (1970), *Exit, Voice, and Loyalty*, Cambridge, Mass.: Harvard University Press.

Hutchens, R. M. (1989), 'Seniority, wages and productivity: a turbulent decade', *Journal of Economic Perspectives*, 3: 49–64.

ILO (annual), *Yearbook of Labour Statistics*, Geneva.

Inoki, T. (1995), 'Toward international comparison of enterprise welfare systems', in T. Inoki and Y. Higuchi (eds.), *Japanese Employment System and Labour Market*, Tokyo: Nihon-keizai-shimbun-sha (in Japanese).

Ishihata, S. (1990), *Japanese Trade Unions*, Tokyo: Japan Institute of Labour (in Japanese).

Ishikawa, K. (1981), *Japanese Quality Control*, Tokyo: Nikka-giren (in Japanese).

Ishikawa, T. (1989), 'Theoretical examination of dual wage structures', in M. Tsuchiya and Y. Miwa (eds.), *Japanese Small Businesses*, Tokyo: Tokyo University Press (in Japanese).

Itami, H. and S. Senbongi (1988), 'Competition by invisible hand and subcontracting efficiency', Hitotsubashi University (mimeo.).

Ito, H. (1987), 'Information processing capacities of the firm', *Journal of the Japanese and International Economies*, 1: 299–326.

  (1994), 'Japanese human resource management from the viewpoint of incentive theory,' in M. Aoki and R. Dore (eds.), *The Japanese Firm*, Oxford: Oxford University Press.

Ito, T. (1992), *The Japanese Economy*, Cambridge, Mass.: MIT Press.

Iwata, R. (1992), 'The Japanese enterprise as a unified body of employees', in S. Kumon and H. Rosovsky (eds.), *The Political Economy of Japan*, vol. III: *Cultural and Social Dynamics*, Stanford: Stanford University Press.

Japan Institute of Labour (1993), 'Determinants of declining union density', Research Report no. 43 (in Japanese).

  (1997), *International Comparison of Human Resource Development and Employment System of University Graduates*, Tokyo (in Japanese).

Johnson, C. (1982), *MITI and the Japanese Miracle: The Growth of Industrial Policy, 1925–1975*, Stanford: Stanford University Press.

Jovanovic, B. (1979), 'Firm-specific capital and turnover', *Journal of Political Economy*, 87: 1246–60.

Kawasaki, S. and J. McMillan (1987), 'The design of contracts: evidence from Japanese subcontracting', *Journal of the Japanese and International Economies*, 1: 327–49.

Klein, B., R.G. Crawford and A. A. Alchian (1978), 'Vertical integration, appropriable rents, and the competitive contracting process', *Journal of Law and Economics*, 21: 297–326.

Kleiner, M. M. and M. L. Bouillon (1988), 'Providing business information to production workers: correlates of compensation and profitability', *Industrial and Labor Relations Review*, 41: 605–17.

Koike, K. (1962), *Wage Bargaining in Japan*, Tokyo: University of Tokyo Press (in Japanese).

  (1978), *Workers' Participation in Management*, Tokyo: Nihon-hyoron-sha (in Japanese).

  (1988), *Understanding Industrial Relations in Modern Japan*, London: Macmillan.

  (1991), *Economics of Work*, Tokyo: Toyo-keizai-shimpo-sha (in Japanese).

  (1994), 'Learning and incentive systems in Japanese industry', in M. Aoki and R. Dore (eds.), *The Japanese Firm*, Oxford: Oxford University Press.

Komatsu, R. (1971), *The Origin of Enterprise Unions*, Tokyo: Ocha-no-mizu-shobo (in Japanese).

Kuratani, M. (1973), 'A theory of training, earnings, and employment: an application to Japan', unpublished Ph.D. dissertation, Columbia University.

Lazear, E. P. (1979), 'Why is there mandatory retirement?', *Journal of Political Economy*, 87: 1261–84.

  (1981), 'Agency, earnings profiles, productivity, and hours restrictions', *American Economic Review*, 71: 606–20.

  (1983), 'Pensions as severance pay', in Z. Brodie and J. Shoven (eds.), *Financial Aspects of the US Pension System*, Chicago: Chicago University Press.

  (1985), 'Incentive effects of pensions', in D. Wise (ed.), *Pensions, Labor and Individual Choice*, Chicago: Chicago University Press for NBER.

(1986), 'Retirement from the labor force', in O. Ashenfelter and R. Layard (eds.), *Handbook of Labor Economics*, vol. I, Amsterdam: North Holland.

Lester, R. A. (1967), 'Benefits as a preferred form of compensation', *Southern Economic Journal*, 33: 488–95.

Lewin, D. (1984), *Opening the Books: Corporate Information Sharing with Employees*, New York: The Conference Board.

Lewis, H. G. (1963), *Union Relative Wages in the United States*, Chicago: University of Chicago Press.

(1986), 'Union Relative wage effects', in O. Ashenfelter and R. Layard (eds.), *Handbook of Labor Economics*, vol. II, Amsterdam: North Holland.

Lillrank, P. and N. Kano (1989), *Continuous Improvement: Quality Control Circles in Japanese Industry*, Ann Arbor: Center for Japanese Studies, University of Michigan.

Macaulay, S. (1963), 'Non-contractual relations in business: a preliminary study', *American Sociological Review*, 28: 55–70.

Magota, R. (1965), 'A critical comment to some arguments on labour relations during the Pacific War', *Nihon-rodo-kyokai-zasshi*, 76: 11–23 (in Japanese).

Malcomson, J. M. (1997), 'Contracts, hold-up and labor markets', *Journal of Economic Literature*, 35: 1916–57.

Marchetti, D. J. (1994), 'Procyclical productivity, externalities and labor hoarding: a reexamination of evidence from US manufacturing', Working Papers in Economics, 94/13, European University Institute, Florence.

McMillan, J. (1990), 'Managing suppliers: incentive systems in Japanese and US industry', *California Management Review*, 27: 38–55.

Milgrom, P. and J. Roberts (1992), *Economics, Organization and Management*, Eaglewood Cliffs, N.J.: Prentice Hall.

Miller, R. L. R. (1971), 'The reserve labour hypothesis: some tests of its implications', *Economic Journal*, 81: 17–35.

Mincer, J. (1974), *Schooling, Experience and Earnings*, New York: National Bureau of Economic Research.

Mincer, J. and Y. Higuchi (1988), 'Wage structure and labor turnover in the United States and Japan', *Journal of the Japanese and International Economies*, 2: 97–133.

Mincer, J. and B. Jovanovic (1981), 'Labor mobility and wages', in S. Rosen (ed.), *Studies in Labor Markets*, Chicago: University of Chicago Press.

Ministry of Health (1996), *Introduction to Social Security*, Tokyo: Chuohoki Shuppan (in Japanese).

Ministry of International Trade and Industry (1987), *Survey of Manufacturing Systems*, Tokyo.

Ministry of Labour (1975), *White Paper on Labour*, Tokyo: Japan Institute of Labour (in Japanese).

(1995), *Survey on Labour–Management Communications (1994)*, Tokyo: Romugyoseikenkyujyo (in Japanese).

Mitchell, D. J. B. (1980), *Wages, Unions and Inflation*, Washington: Brookings Institution.

Monteverde, K. and D. J. Teece (1982), 'Appropriable rents and quasi-vertical integration', *Journal of Law and Economics*, 25: 321–8.

Moore, G. H. (1983), *Business Cycles, Inflation, and Forecasting Studies in Business Cycles, no. 24*, Cambridge, Mass.: National Bureau of Economic Research.

Morishima, M. (1991a), 'Information sharing and collective bargaining in Japan: effects on wage negotiation', *Industrial and Labor Relations Review*, 44: 469–87.

(1991b), 'Information sharing and firm performance in Japan', *Industrial Relations*, 30: 37–61.

Mortensen, D. (1978), 'Specific capital and labor turnover', *Bell Journal of Economics*, 9: 572–86.

Mueller-Jentsch, W. (1995), 'Germany: from collective voice to co-management', in J. Rogers and W. Streeck (eds.), *Works Councils – Consultation, Representation, and Cooperation in Industrial Relations*, Chicago: University of Chicago Press.

Muramatsu, K., (1983), *An Analysis of Japanese Labour Markets*, Tokyo: Hakuto-shobo (in Japanese).

(1984a), 'The effect of trade unions on productivity in Japanese manufacturing industries', in M. Aoki (ed.), *The Economic Analysis of the Japanese Firm*, Amsterdam: North Holland.

(1984b), 'Quit behaviour and trade unions', in K. Koike (ed.), *Unemployment in Modern Time*, Tokyo: Dobun-kan (in Japanese).

Nakamura, M. and O. Hübler (1998), 'The bonus share of flexible pay in Germany, Japan and the US: some empirical regularities', *Japan and the World Economy*, 10: 221–32.

Nakamura, T. (1981), *Postwar Japanese Economy: Its Development and Structure*, Tokyo: University of Tokyo Press.

Nakatani, I. (1984), 'The economic role of financial corporate grouping', in M. Aoki (ed.), *The Economic Analysis of the Japanese Firm*, Amsterdam: North Holland.

Nihon-keizai-shimbun-sha (1996), *Miscalculation in Pension*, Tokyo: Nihon-keizai-shimbun-sha (in Japanese).

Nishiguchi, T. (1987), 'Competing systems of automobile components supply', IMVP Forum Paper, MIT, Cambridge, Mass.

(1994), *Strategic Industrial Sourcing: The Japanese Advantage*, Oxford: Oxford University Press.

Nitta, M. (1984), 'Conflict resolution in the steel industry – collective bargaining and workers' consultation at a steel plant', in T. Hanami and R. Blanpain (eds.), *Industrial Conflict Resolution in Market Economies*, Antwerp: Kluwer Law & Taxation Publishers.

Norbinn, S. C. (1993), 'The relation between marginal cost and price in US industry: a contradiction', *Journal of Political Economy*, 101: 1149–64.

Nordhaus, W. (1988), 'Can the share economy conquer stagflation?', *Quarterly Journal of Economics*, 103: 201–17.

Odagiri, H. (1992), *Growth Through Competition, Competition Through Growth*, Oxford: Clarendon Press.

Odagiri, H. and T. Yamashita (1987), 'Price mark-ups, market structure, and business fluctuations in Japanese manufacturing industries', *Journal of Industrial Economics*, 35: 317–31.

Odaka, K. (1984), *Analysis of Labour Markets*, Tokyo: Iwanami-shoten (in Japanese).

(1993), '"Japanese-type" industrial relations', in T. Okazaki and M. Okuno (eds.), *The Origin of Modern Japanese Economic Systems*, Tokyo: Nihon-keizai-shimbun-sha (in Japanese).

Ohashi, I. (1989), 'On the determinants of bonuses and basic wages in large Japanese firms', *Journal of the Japanese and International Economies*, 3: 451–79.

(1990), *Theory of the Labour Market*, Tokyo: Toyo-keizai-shimpo-sha (in Japanese).

Oi, W. (1962), 'Labor as a Quasi-fixed Factor', *Journal of Political Economy*, 70: 538–55.

(1983), 'The fixed employment costs of specialised labor', in J. E. Triplett (ed.), *The Measurement of Labor Cost*, Chicago: University of Chicago Press.

Okimoto, D. (1989), *Between MITI and the Market*, Stanford: Stanford University Press.

Okuno, M. (1984), 'Corporate loyalty and bonus payments: an analysis of work incentives in Japan', in M. Aoki (ed.), *The Economic Analysis of the Japanese Firm*, Amsterdam: North Holland.

Ono, A. (1973), *Wage Determination in Post-war Japan*, Tokyo: Toyo-keizai-shimpo-sha (in Japanese).

Organisation for Economic Co-operation and Development (1986), 'Non-wage labour costs and employment', in *OECD Employment Outlook*.

(1992), 'Labour market participation and retirement of older workers', in *OECD Employment Outlook*.

(1993), 'Enterprise tenure, labour turnover and skill training', in *OECD Employment Outlook*.

(1994), *The OECD Jobs Study*, Paris.

(1970), *Labour Force Statistics, 1975–1995*, Paris.

(annual), *OECD Employment Outlook*, Paris.

Parsons, D. O. (1986), 'The employment relationship: job attachment, work effort, and the nature of contracts', in O. Ashenfelter and R. Layard (eds.), *Handbook of Labor Economics*, vol. II, Amsterdam: North Holland.

Patrick, H. and T. Rohlen (1987), 'Small-scale family enterprises', in K. Yamamura *et al.* (eds.), *The Political Economy of Japan*, vol. I, Stanford: Stanford University Press.

Pencavel, J. (1986), 'The labour supply of men: a survey', in O. Ashenfelter and R. Layard (eds.), *Handbook of Labor Economics*, vol. I, Amsterdam: North Holland.

(1991), *Labor Markets under Trade Unionism*, Oxford: Blackwell.

Prendergast, C. (1992), 'Career development and specific human capital collection', *Journal of the Japanese and International Economies*, 6: 207–27.

Pucik, V. (1985), 'Promotion patterns in a Japanese trading company', *Columbia Journal of World Business*, 20: 73–9.

Reder, M. W. (1955), 'The theory of occupational wage differentials', *American Economic Review*, 45: 833–52.

Rogers, J. and W. Streeck (eds.) (1995), *Works Councils – Consultation, Representation, and Cooperation in Industrial Relations*, Chicago: University of Chicago Press.

Rosenbaum, J. E. (1979), 'Tournament mobility: career patterns in a corporation', *Administrative Science Quarterly*, 24: 220–41.

(1984), *Career Mobility in a Corporate Hierarchy*, New York: Academic Press.

Rossana, R. J. (1983), 'Some empirical estimates of the demand for hours in US manufacturing industries', *Review of Economics and Statistics*, 65: 560–9.

(1985), 'Buffer stocks and labor demand: further evidence', *Review of Economics and Statistics*, 67: 16–26.

Rotemberg, J. J. and M. Woodford (1992), 'Mark-ups and the business cycle', in D. J. Blanchard and S. Fischer (eds.), *NBER Macroeconomics Annual*, vol. VI, Cambridge, Mass.: MIT Press.

Sako, M. (1992), *Prices, Quality and Trust: Inter-firm Relations in Britain and Japan*, Cambridge: Cambridge University Press.

(1994), 'Training, productivity, and quality control in Japanese multinational companies', in M. Aoki and R. Dore (eds.), *The Japanese Firm*, Oxford: Clarendon Press.

Sakurabayashi, M. (1985), *The Organization and Functions of Sangyo-hokoku-kai*, Tokyo: Ocha-no-mizu-shobo (in Japanese).

Sano, Y. (1970), *Econometric Analysis of Wage Determination*, Tokyo: Toyo-keizai-shimpo-sha (in Japanese).

(1981), *Economics of Wages and Employment*, Tokyo: Chuo-keizai-sha (in Japanese).

(1989), *Internal Labour Markets*, Tokyo: Yuhi-kaku (in Japanese).

Sano, Y., K. Koike and H. Ishida (eds.) (1969), *Behavioural Analysis of Wage Bargaining*, Tokyo: Toyo-keizai-shimpo-sha (in Japanese).

Sato, H. (1996), 'Industrial relations', in K. Kaizuka, Y. Kosai and I. Nonaka (eds.), *Dictionary of Japanese Economy*, Tokyo: Nihon-keizai-shimbun-sha (in Japanese).

Shaeffer, R. G. (1972), *Staffing Systems: Managerial and Professional Jobs*, New York: Conference Board.

Sheard, P. (1989), 'The main bank system and corporate monitoring and control in Japan', *Journal of Economic Behavior and Organization*, 11: 399–422.

Shimada, H. (1982), 'Perception and the reality of Japanese industrial relations' role in Japan's post-war success', *Keio Economic Studies*, 19: 1–21.

(1983), 'Wage determination and information sharing: an alternative approach to incomes policy?', *Journal of Industrial Relations*, 25: 177–200.

Shinjo, K. (1977), 'Business pricing policies and inflation: the Japanese case', *Review of Economics and Statistics*, 59: 447–55.

Shinohara, M. (1986), *Lectures on Japanese Economy*, Tokyo: Toyo-keizai-shimpo-sha (in Japanese).

Shirai, T. (1979), *Enterprise Union*, Tokyo: Chuo-koron-sha (in Japanese).

(1980), *Industrial Relations,* Tokyo: Japan Institute of Labour (in Japanese).

(1982), *Labour Management in Modern Japan*, Tokyo: Toyo-keizai-shimpo-sha (in Japanese).

Shirai, T. (ed.) (1983), *Contemporary Industrial Relations in Japan*, Madison: University of Wisconsin Press.

Shirai, T., T. Hanami and K. Koshiro (1986), *A Reader in Trade Unions*, 2nd edn, Tokyo: Toyo-keizai-shimpo-sha (in Japanese).

Small and Medium Enterprise Agency (annual), *White Paper on Small and Medium Enterprises*, Tokyo: Printing Office, Ministry of Finance (in Japanese).

Smitka, M. (1991), *Competitive Ties: Subcontracting in the Japanese Automobile Industry*, New York: Columbia University Press.

Spence, M. A. (1973), 'Job market signalling', *Quarterly Journal of Economics*, 87: 355–74.

Stoikov, V. (1973a), 'Size of firm, worker earnings, and human capital: the case of Japan', *Industrial and Labor Relations Review*, 26: 1095–106.

(1973b), 'The structure of earnings in Japanese manufacturing industries: a human capital approach', *Journal of Political Economy*, 91: 340–55.

Tachibanaki, T. (1975), 'Wage determinations in Japanese manufacturing industries – structural change and wage differentials', *International Economic Review*, 16: 562–86.

(1982), 'Further results on Japanese wage differentials: nenko wages, hierarchical position, bonuses, and working hours', *International Economic Review*, 23: 447–61.

(1987a), 'Non-wage labour costs: their rationales and the economic effects', Institute of Economic Research, Kyoto University (mimeo.).

(1987b), 'Labour market flexibility in Japan in comparison with Europe and the US', *European Economic Review*, 31: 647–78.

(1996), *Wage Determination and Distribution in Japan*, Oxford: Oxford University Press.

Tachibanaki, T. and T. Noda (1993), 'Union effects on wages and working conditions', in T. Tachibanaki and Rengo-sogo-seikatsu-kaihatsu-kenkyujyo (eds.), *Economics of Trade Unions*, Tokyo: Toyo-keizai-shimpo-sha (in Japanese).

Tachibanaki, T. and K, Sakurai (1991), 'Labour Supply and Unemployment in Japan', *European Economic Review*, 35: 1575–87.

Taira, K. (1970), *Economic Development and the Labor Market in Japan*, New York: Columbia University Press.

(1977) 'In praise of the Japanese-type enterprise union', *Chuo-koron*, March (in Japanese).

Takeuchi, Y. (1995), *Japan's Meritocracy – Structure and Mentality*, Tokyo: Tokyo University Press (in Japanese).

Taylor, J. (1970), 'Hidden unemployment, hoarded labor, and the Phillips Curve', *Southern Economic Journal*, 37: 1–16.

Tomita, Y. (1993), 'Quit rate and the voice effect of trade unions', in T. Tachibanaki and Rengo-sogo-seikatsu-kaihatsu-kenkyujyo (eds.), *Economics of Trade Unions*, Tokyo: Toyo-keizai-shimpo-sha (in Japanese).

Topel, R. H. (1982), 'Inventories, layoffs and the short-run demand for labor', *American Economic Review*, 72: 769–87.

(1991), 'Specific capital, mobility, and wages: wages rise with seniority', *Journal of Political Economy*, 99: 145–76.

Topel, R. H. and M. P. Ward (1992), 'Job mobility and the careers of young men', *Quarterly Journal of Economics*, 107: 439–79.

Trejo, S. J. (1993), 'Overtime pay, overtime hours, and labor unions', *Journal of Labor Economics*, 11: 253–78.

Tsuru, T. (1995), 'Trade unions in contemporary Japan and apathy of union members', in T. Inoki and Y. Higuchi (eds.), *Employment Systems and Labour Markets in Japan*, Tokyo: Nihon-keizai-shimbun-sha (in Japanese).

US Chamber Research Center (1993), *Employee Benefits*, Washington: US Chamber of Commerce.

Vecchi, M. (1998), 'Increasing returns, labour utilisation and externalities: pro-cyclical productivity in US and Japan', Department of Economics, University of Stirling (mimeo.).

Visser, J. (1991), 'Trends in trade union membership', in *OECD Employment Outlook*, Paris.

Wachtel, H. M. and P. D. Adelsheim (1977), 'How recession feeds inflation: price markups in a concentrated economy', *Challenge*, 20(4): 6–13.

Weitzman, M. L. (1984), *The Share Economy*, Cambridge, Mass.: Harvard University Press.

(1985), 'The simple macroeconomics of profit sharing', *American Economic Review*, 75: 937–53.

Williamson, O. E. (1975), *Markets and Hierarchies*, New York: The Free Press.

(1979), 'Transaction–cost economics: the governance of contractual relations', *Journal of Law and Economics*, 22: 233–61.

(1985), *The Economic Institutions of Capitalism*, New York: The Free Press.

Womack, J., D. T. Jones and D. Roos (1990), *The Machine That Changed The World*, New York: Rawson Associates.

Woodbury, S. A. (1983), 'Substitution between wage and non-wage benefits', *American Economic Review*, 73: 166–82.

Yokokura, N. (1984), 'Small business', in R. Komiya, M. Okuno and K. Suzumura (eds.), *Japanese Industrial Policy*, Tokyo: University of Tokyo Press (in Japanese).

Zarnowitz, V. (1985), 'Recent work on business cycles in historical perspective: review of theories and evidence', *Journal of Economic Literature*, 23: 523–80.

Index